THE TASTE OF COURAGE

THE WAR, 1939-1945

VOLUME II: THE AXIS TRIUMPHANT

Edited by DESMOND FLOWER and JAMES REEVES

A BERKLEY MEDALLION BOOK
PUBLISHED BY
BERKLEY PUBLISHING CORPORATION

ACKNOWLEDGMENTS

Grateful acknowledgment is made to the following for permission to reprint selections included in this book:

Brandt & Brandt
 I Was There by Admiral William D. Leahy. Published by McGraw-Hill Book Co.
 Admiral Halsey's Story by William F. Halsey and Joseph Bryan. Published by McGraw-Hill Book Co.
 Hitler and His Admirals by Anthony Martienssen. Copyright 1949 by Anthony Martienssen.
 Defeat in the West by Milton Shulman. Copyright 1948 by Milton Shulman.
Cassel & Co. Ltd.
 Sunk by Mochitsura Hashimoto. Copyright 1954 by Henry Holt & Co., Inc.
Constable & Co. Ltd.
 Retreat, Hell! by William Camp. Copyright 1943 by William Martin Camp. Published by Appleton-Century-Crofts, Inc.
Curtis Brown, Ltd.
 Still Digging by Mortimer Wheeler. Copyright © 1955 by Eric Robert Mortimer Wheeler. Published by E.P. Dutton & Co.
 The Green Beret by Hilary St. George Saunders. Reprinted by permission of the author's estate.
 The Spirit in the Cage by Peter Churchill.
The John Day Company
 The Invisible Flag by Peter Bamm.
Dodd, Mead & Company
 Going to the Wars by John Verney. Copyright © 1955 by John Verney.

TO THE

30,000,000

DEAD

INTRODUCTION

THIS is a documentary conspectus of the worst war in history, beginning at the German invasion of Poland on 1 September 1939 and ending with the last Japanese surrenders in September and October 1945. But it is not a history of the war: that has been written—by Sir Winston Churchill and by other historians, official and unofficial. This book could not have been written by one man, for it is an attempt to put together a chronicle of how it actually felt to be alive twenty years ago; to see, to hear, to smell, to feel the war at first hand. As service men and women, politicians and diplomats, workers in the resistance movements and victims of aggression, as men and women in civil occupations, and even as children, millions were aware of the war as a world-wide cataclysm hanging over the whole of life. Some, comparatively few but still numerous, wrote down their experience of that part of the war in which they were immediately involved; this book is a mosaic of such records. The contributors are world leaders, soldiers, sailors and airmen, journalists, firemen, hospital staff, factory workers, peasants—anyone who has written down in the spirit of an eye-witness or a participant his impressions of some aspect of war experience, of greater or lesser significance.

What must impress the reader of these pages is the vastness of the war: its totality, the extent to which it penetrated like an evil contagion into every corner of the inhabited world. As Marshal Pétain, the misguided master of Vichy, remarked at one stage—"Now for the first time the whole world is at war." In these pages will be found the views and feelings of housewives in London, Berlin, Moscow and Tokyo: their problems, joys and sorrows are much the same. Here, too, we present the views of British and Germans facing one another at El Alamein, of Russians and Germans creeping forward through the frozen ruins of Stalingrad, of Americans and Japanese inching through a sodden Pacific jungle. All these, and many more, were men and women committed the world over to a problem from which none could escape once the politicians had decreed that the shooting should begin. This second World War produced heroism comparable with anything which had gone before, cowardice, inefficiency, brilliance, greatness, and a dedication to one object—on whichever side it might be—of more people that have ever before been involved in a single, terrifying catastrophe.

One of us responsible for this volume was concerned in 1937 with the production of a similar book describing the first World War: it was called *Vain Glory*. In our present task we find a difference. About the second World War there was little either vain or glorious. It was a bitter, sordid affair—for even the horrors of Passchendaele had an heroic dignity which cannot be equalled. It was not in vain, since it was begun to remove the evil men of Nuremberg, and in that at least it succeeded. But, to the surprise of those who found themselves involved in it, it developed into a display of hard-hitting brutality—sparing neither men, women, nor children—which only the mythical depredations of Genghis Khan may have challenged.

If there is ever a third world war, it will no doubt be a very clean job of destruction started at a range of thousands of miles by technicians suitably protected below ground and pressing a knob. But when the first scientific flurry is over, the destruction will be so great that it will be left to the surviving men, women and children to stick it out and somehow try to get the mess through to a conclusion.

In compiling this book we have paid our respects to military prowess—the actions of the professional soldiers who have triumphed with all the skill to which their lives have been devoted; but the victims of any war are the people: people in uniform, people out of uniform, people fighting, and people fleeing. There will be nowhere to flee next time, so this book offers a record of what may be the last of its kind: for better or for worse.

D. F. J. R.
Headley, Hants Chalfont St. Giles, Bucks

CONTENTS

MAPS

ACKNOWLEDGMENTS

WE wish to express our gratitude to the individuals, libraries, and other bodies listed below, all of whom have been of the greatest possible assistance in the preparation of this book. The authors and publishers of the extracts used are acknowledged in full between pages 393 and 398.

> The American Embassy Library
> The Guildhall Library
> The Imperial War Museum Library
> The Information Bureau, Chatham House
> The Book Information Bureau, National Book League
> The Walter Hines Page Memorial Library
> The War Office Library
> Mr. J. A. Williams

We would also like to thank the many publishers and literary agents who have lent us new books in typescript, proof, or bound copy form, a kindness which has allowed the inclusion of much recently published material. We also wish to thank Mr. T. R. Nicholson for his great editorial help in the closing stages of the preparation of the book for the printer, Mrs. Herta Ryder, who throughout has kept under her control the vast amount of material which accumulated, and Mr. Antony Brett-James for his assistance in checking proofs.

D F.   J. R.

NOTE

The contributions to this book are chosen from documentary sources. In one or two cases, where no eye-witness account is available, a reliable historian has been drawn upon for the record. Fiction has only been used when the Editors are satisfied that the writer was present at and witnessed the events which he has woven into his narrative. The war and its ramifications were so great and so many that some aspects have not been mentioned in these pages. To those on all sides whose work has not been recognized, we offer our apologies and hope that they will find some satisfaction in the overall picture of the vast struggle.

D. F.   J. R.

IDENTIFICATION
OF EXTRACTS

IN order to discover the source of any extract, the reader should note the number of the page on which it begins and its heading and first words, and then refer to the section entitled *Key to the Sources of Extracts* (pages 385 to 392). There, following the page number and brief identification of the passage, will be found a key number. Reference to this key number in the following section, entitled *Sources* (pages 393 to 398), will reveal the title, author, publisher and publication date of the work drawn upon.

The italicized passages between extracts have been interpolated by the Editors to provide a consecutive narrative.

Signatures: A very few extracts are not signed. These are the small minority of completely impersonal passages written by historians, inserted, when of a sufficiently high standard, for lack of first-hand material. Of the signed extracts, a few are anonymous; for example, "British gunner". In these cases the Editors have been unable to ascertain the writer's identity, or else the writer has wished to remain anonymous. In some cases the signatures of servicemen do not include ranks. These are omitted either because the appropriate rank could not be ascertained, or because it was thought more effective to omit them. Where a rank is given, it changes appropriately in the cases of the most famous men, and in other cases remains the same throughout, the rank likely to sound most familiar or natural to the reader being given. These are broad principles, but individual circumstances may have had to dictate some exceptions, at the expense of rules of consistency.

. . . THERE is a great danger in this war. But if we are among those that get back, we shall have nothing to tell. I have had adventures—pioneering mail lines; flying the Andes; being forced down among rebellious Arabs in the Sahara. But war is not a true adventure. It is a mere *ersatz*. Where ties are established, where problems are set, where creation is stimulated—there you have adventure. But there is no adventure in heads-or-tails, in betting that the toss will come out life or death. War is not an adventure. It is a disease. It is like typhus.

Antoine de Saint-Exupéry

If it be Life that awaits, I shall live forever unconquered: If Death, I shall die at last strong in my pride and free.

Scottish National Memorial

1

OPERATION BARBAROSSA

Having secured his lines of communication by means of his conquests in the Balkans, Hitler launched his offensive against Soviet Russia on 22 June 1941. One hundred and twenty divisions were massed on the eastern frontier for this task.

The Northern Army Group, commanded by von Loeb, was to deploy twenty-nine divisions in the direction of Leningrad; von Bock's Central Army Group consisted of fifty divisions and was to drive for Smolensk; the Southern Army Group, under von Rundstedt, contained forty-one divisions with the lower Dnieper as its objective. There were twenty-six divisions in reserve, and a considerable quantity of Finnish and Roumanian troops available for use on the northern and southern fronts respectively.

THE GRAND DESIGN

THE German armed forces must be prepared to crush Soviet Russia in a quick campaign before the end of the war against England (case "Barbarossa").

For this purpose the army will have to employ all available units with the reservation that the occupied territories will have to be safeguarded against surprise attacks.

For the Eastern campaign the air force will have to free such strong forces for the support of the army that a quick completion of the ground operations may be expected and that damage of the eastern German territories will be avoided as much as possible. This concentration of the main effort in the East is limited by the following reservation: that the entire battle against enemy air attacks and that the attacks on England and especially the supply for them must not be permitted to break down.

Concentration of the main effort of the navy remains unequivocally against England also during an Eastern campaign.

If occasion arises I will order the concentration of troops for action against Soviet Russia eight weeks before the intended beginning of operations.

Preparations requiring some time to start are—if this has not yet been done—to begin presently and are to be completed by 15 May 1941.

Great caution has to be exercised that the intention of the attack will not be recognized. . . .

                 Adolf Hitler, 18 December 1940

When "Barbarossa" commences, the world will hold its breath and make no comment.

                 Adolf Hitler, 3 February 1941

This war with Russia is a nonsensical idea, to which I can see no happy ending. But if, for political reasons, the war is unavoidable, then we must face the fact that it can't be won in a single summer campaign. Just look at the distances involved. We cannot possibly defeat the enemy and occupy the whole of western Russia, from the Baltic to the Black Sea, within a few short months. We should prepare for a long war and go for our objectives step by step.

                 Field-Marshal von Rundstedt, May 1941

Canaris was terribly worried about the approaching

campaign. He criticized in the strongest terms the Wehrmacht leaders who, despite their expert knowledge, were irresponsible and foolish enough to support the views of a man like Hitler in his assumption that we should be able to conclude the Russian campaign within three months. He would not be a party to this, and could not understand how the Generals, von Brauchitsch, Halder, Keitel and Jodl, could be so complacent, so unrealistic, and so optimistic. But any attempt at opposition was useless; he had already made himself unpopular by his repeated warnings. Only a few days earlier Keitel had said to him, "My dear Canaris, you may have some understanding of the Abwehr, but you belong to the navy, you really should not try to give us lessons in strategic and political planning." When Canaris repeated such remarks he would usually rein in his horse, look at me with wide eyes and say quite seriously, "Wouldn't you find all this quite comic—if it weren't so desperately serious?"

Walter Schellenberg

From the report of the Ambassador in Moscow: "All observations show that Stalin and Molotov, who alone are responsible for Russian foreign policy, are doing everything to avoid a conflict with Germany. The entire behaviour of the Government, as well as the attitude of the Press, which reports all events concerning Germany in a factual, indisputable manner, supports this view. The loyal fulfilment of the economic treaty with Germany proves the same thing."

German Foreign Office docket, 7 June 1941

From every source at my disposal, including some most trustworthy, it looks as if a vast German onslaught on Russia was imminent. Not only are the main German armies deployed from Finland to Roumania, but the final arrivals of air and armoured forces are being completed.

Winston Churchill to Franklin D. Roosevelt, 15 June 1941

On the evening of Friday, 20 June, I drove down to Chequers alone. I knew that the German onslaught upon Russia was a matter of days, or it might be hours. I had arranged to deliver a broadcast on Saturday night dealing with this event. It would of course have to be in guarded terms. Moreover, at this time the Soviet Government, at once haughty and purblind, regarded every warning we gave as a mere attempt of beaten men to drag others into ruin. As a result of my reflexions in the car I put off my broadcast till Sunday night, when I thought that all would be clear.

Winston Churchill

Tension rose steadily on the German side. By the evening of the 21st we assumed that the Russians must have realized what was happening, yet across the River Bug on the front of 4 Army and Second Panzer Group, that is to say between Brest-Litovsk and Lomza, all was quiet. The Russian outposts were behaving quite normally. At a little after midnight, when the entire artillery of the assault divisions and of the second wave too was already zeroed in on its targets, the international Berlin-Moscow train passed without incident through Brest-Litovsk. It was a weird moment.

General Gunther Blumentritt, Chief of Staff, 4 Army

Ribbentrop to Count Schulenburg,
German Ambassador in Moscow

Berlin, 21 June 1941

1. Upon receipt of this telegram all of the cipher material still there is to be destroyed. The radio set is to be put out of commission.

2. Please inform Herr Molotov at once that you have an urgent communication to make to him and would therefore like to call upon him immediately. Then please make the following declaration to him:

". . . . The Government of the Reich declares that

the Soviet Government, contrary to the obligations it assumed,

(1) has not only continued, but even intensified, its attempts to undermine Germany and Europe;

(2) has adopted a more and more anti-German foreign policy;

(3) has concentrated all its forces in readiness at the German border.

Thereby the Soviet Government has broken its treaties with Germany and is about to attack Germany from the rear, in its struggle for life. The Führer has therefore ordered the German armed forces to oppose this threat with all the means at their disposal."

Please do not enter into any discussion of this communication.

Ribbentrop

At six o'clock in the morning of 22 June 1941, the German Ambassador, Count von Schulenburg, handed Molotov a Note of the German Government declaring war on the Soviet Union.

Both Count von Schulenburg and Molotov were pale with emotion. The Commissar for Foreign Affairs took the Note wordlessly, spat on it and then tore it up. He rang for his secretary Poskrebichev.

"Show this gentleman out through the back door."

Ivan Krylov, Soviet staff officer

BARBAROSSA IS LAUNCHED

At dawn the next day, 22 June 1941, the Wehrmacht began the offensive on all sectors of the front, from the Black Sea to the northern regions of Finland. In General Halder's diary is the following entry:

"I have just described the plan for the Russian

Campaign to the Führer; the Russian armies will be destroyed in six weeks."

Reactions

The Russians were clearly taken entirely by surprise on our front. Almost at once our signals intercept service listened in to a Russian message: "We are being fired on. What shall we do?" They heard the reply from the senior headquarters to whom this request for orders was addressed: "You must be insane. And why is your signal not in code?"

General Blumentritt

I saw Poskrebichev at nine o'clock. He had come to Colonel Smaguine to ask for a list of the personnel of our military attaché in Berlin.

"Molotov is so calm you'd almost think he didn't realize what was at stake," he said. "Stalin isn't in Moscow at the moment, but he'll be returning to-morrow. The Politburo is meeting in special session to discuss the conduct of operations. To-day those members who are already in Moscow will hold a meeting."

"To discuss the war?"

"No, to discuss the situation at home. Beria is presenting a rather alarming report. He's afraid the reservists will honour the old Russian custom of raiding the vodka before going to the front. The townspeople are calm enough, but when the peasants come to Moscow they are bound to be a bit turbulent."

"Well, what's Beria proposing to do? Machine-gun them?"

"Not at all. I'm beginning to think that Lavrenti Pavlovitch is a highly intelligent man. He proposes to supply each reservist arriving in Moscow with two litres of alcohol and then confine them to barracks for two or three days and have them guarded by N.K.V.D. troops. After that they'll go to the front like lambs."

I went to see Muraviev. I found him very calm.

"Everything's going well, Vania. They're fighting."

"Who is?"

"Our men. I've just had a talk with Brest-Litovsk. There's been no trouble except with 2 Infantry division, and they're all *Khokli,** as you know. They made an attempt to murder their commanders and political commissars and surrender to the Germans. There is some cause for apprehension. You know the peasants get awkward when war starts; in particular the *Khokli* and the men from Northern Caucasia. They expect the Germans to proclaim the independence of their republics."

Ivan Krylov

The mood of Britain towards Russia had for a long time been far from friendly, but the Prime Minister, with characteristic statesmanship, promptly associated his country with Russia's struggle against Nazism, and assured Russia of the utmost material assistance.

At four o'clock this morning Hitler attacked and invaded Russia. All his usual formalities of perfidy were observed with scrupulous technique. A nonaggression treaty had been solemnly signed and was in force between the two countries. No complaint had been made by Germany of its non-fulfilment. Under its cloak of false confidence, the German armies drew up in immense strength along a line which stretches from the White Sea to the Black Sea; and their air fleets and armoured divisions slowly and methodically took their stations. Then, suddenly, without declaration of war, without even an ultimatum, German bombs rained down from the air upon the Russian cities, the German troops violated the frontiers; and an hour later the German Ambassador, who till the night before was lavishing his assurances of friendship, almost of alliance, upon the Russians, called upon the Russian Foreign Minister to tell him that a state of war existed between Germany and Russia. . . .

* Contemptuous expression used by Russians to describe Ukrainians.

All this was no surprise to me. In fact, I gave clear and precise warnings to Stalin of what was coming. I gave him warning as I have given warning to others before. I can only hope that this warning did not fall unheeded. All we know at present is that the Russian people are defending their native soil and that their leaders have called upon them to resist to the utmost.

Any man or State who fights on against Nazidom will have our aid. Any man or State who marches with Hitler is our foe. This applies not only to organized States but to all representatives of that vile race of quislings who make themselves the tools and agents of the Nazi régime against their fellow-countrymen and the lands of their birth. They—these quislings—like the Nazi leaders themselves, if not disposed of by their fellow-countrymen, which would save trouble, will be delivered by us on the morrow of victory to the justice of the Allied tribunals. That is our policy and that is our declaration. It follows, therefore, that we shall give whatever help we can to Russia and the Russian people. We shall appeal to all our friends and allies in every part of the world to take the same course and pursue it, as we shall, faithfully and steadfastly to the end. . . .

Winston Churchill, 22 June 1941

The entire Soviet people is rising in defence of the Fatherland at the side of the Red Army. It is a question of life and death for the Soviet State, for the people of the U.S.S.R.—a question whether the peoples of the Soviet Union shall be free or reduced to slavery.

Great Lenin, who founded our State, used to say that the basic qualities of the Soviet men should be valour and daring: they should be fearless in battle and resolved to fight against the enemies of our country. The Red Army and Navy and all the citizens of the Soviet Union must defend every inch of the Soviet soil, fight to the last drop of their blood, defend their towns and villages, and show their daring and ingenuity—qualities that are characteristic of our people.

In the event of the retreat of the Red Army all railway rolling stock must be brought away. We must not leave a single engine to the enemy, nor a single railway coach. We must not leave a single pound of grain or a single gallon of petrol to the enemy. The collective farmers must take away all their cattle and place their corn in the care of State organizations to be transported to the rear zone. All valuable materials which cannot be taken away must be resolutely destroyed.

In the areas occupied by the enemy, foot and horse guerrilla detachments must be created, as well as groups of saboteurs entrusted with fighting against the units of the enemy army, with the launching of guerrilla warfare everywhere, with blowing up bridges and roads, with wrecking telephone and telegraph communications, and with setting forests, depots and trains on fire. It is necessary to create in invaded areas conditions unbearable for the enemy and all his accomplices. . . .

In this war of liberation we shall not be alone. In this great war we shall have faithful allies in the person of the peoples of Europe and America. Our war for the freedom of our Fatherland is merged into the struggle of the peoples of Europe and America for their independent freedom. It is the united front of the peoples who stand for freedom against the threat of enslavement by Hitler's Fascist armies.

In this connection the historic utterance of the British Prime Minister, Mr. Churchill, about aid to the Soviet Union, and the declaration of the Government of the United States signifying readiness to give assistance to our country are fully comprehensible and symptomatic.

Comrades! Our forces are numberless. The overweening enemy will soon learn this to his cost. Side by side with the Red Army many thousand workers, collective farmers, and intellectuals are rising to fight the enemy aggressor. The masses of our people will rise up in their millions.

Stalin

ADVANCE

At first, like Napoleon's invasion more than a century before, everything went almost too well. All three German Army Groups advanced rapidly, and the pattern was the same, the Russians were prepared always to sacrifice their two inexhaustible assets—men and space—to gain time. For example, at the end of July when the Germans took Smolensk after four weeks' fighting, they took a hundred and eighty thousand prisoners, but they could not quite shut the trap, and the hard core of the Soviet forces drew away, just out of reach. And although it was summer, there was rain—a mere shadow of the horror to come, but one with its own problems.

The infantry had a hard time keeping up. Marches of twenty-five miles in the course of a day were by no means exceptional, and that over the most atrocious roads. A vivid picture which remains of these weeks is the great clouds of yellow dust kicked up by the Russian columns attempting to retreat and by our infantry hastening in pursuit. The heat was tremendous, though interspersed with sudden showers which quickly turned the roads to mud before the sun reappeared and as quickly baked them into crumbling clay once again.

By 2 July the first battle was for all intents and purposes won. The haul was astounding. A hundred and fifty thousand prisoners taken, some twelve hundred tanks and six hundred guns captured or destroyed. First impressions revealed that the Russian was as tough a fighter as ever. His tanks, however, were not particularly formidable and his air force, so far as we could see, non-existent.

The conduct of the Russian troops, even in this first battle, was in striking contrast to the behaviour of the Poles and of the Western allies in defeat. Even when encircled, the Russians stood their ground and fought. The vast extent of the country, with its forests and swamps, helped them in this. There were not enough German troops available completely to seal off a huge encirclement such as that of Bialystok-Slonim. Our motorized forces fought on or near to the roads: in the great trackless spaces between them the Russians were left largely unmolested. This was why the Russians were able not infrequently to break out of our encirclements, whole columns moving by night through the forests that stretched away eastwards. They always attempted to break out to the east, so that the eastern side of each encirclement had to be held by our strongest troops, usually Panzer troops. Nevertheless, our encirclements were seldom entirely successful.

General Blumentritt

By late afternoon we had pressed the retreating Russians right to the edge of the marshlands, across which the only passage was the bridge of logs. They fled across it, but our heavy machine-guns raked the bridge and picked them off at will. As we saw them being mown down, unable to jump either to right or left to escape the cross-fire, we thought uneasily of our own fate when we reached the other end of the crossing, which was likely to be under equally murderous fire from the Reds. But there was no alternative. We had to take our chance on the log bridge.

At dusk our assault troops and pioneers set off across the logs and the rest of the battalion followed them after a short interval. If we could only make the crossing safely during the darkness, we would be in an excellent position the following morning to press home our advantage against the fleeing Red Army. The bridge was only six yards wide. On the more solid ground, the poles lay directly on the earth: in the swampier places, they were supported by wooden piles. Our marching column stretched like eerie shadows into the fast-falling night. The logs slowly sank under our weight and marsh gases gurgled on either side of us. Random and apparently aimless bursts of tracer bullets arced playfully and fantastically over our heads. Farther and farther we marched. Monotonously we heard the tramp of our own marching feet. Nobody spoke a word. Our ears strained to catch any sound coming across the treacherous marshes.

Then to the right of the causeway I heard a voice calling pitifully. It became more and more distinct as we got nearer. The ghostly cries were in a foreign tongue—the pleading cries for help of a Russian soldier, only a few yards from the bridge. He was being sucked into the swamp, deeper and deeper. Silently, the German troops marched by.

"Surely we can help him," I found myself whispering to Neuhoff.

"How?" asked Neuhoff. "I don't like leaving any poor devil to a fate like that. But anybody who leaves these logs will get sucked in himself. These marshes are bottomless."

Again and again came the agonized cries. I dropped out of the column and let the marching troops pass me. With the help of a soldier, I removed a loose pole from the bridge. We heaved the heavy log as hard as we could into the direction of the sinking man. The cries ceased and for a few moments we could hear the man splashing and struggling to reach the pole. We could see nothing through the darkness, and there was something uncanny in hearing a human being fighting for his life with every bit of strength he had left. He again shouted. There was a gurgling sound and I felt every hair on my body crawl. Then all was quiet. Dead quiet.

Heinrich Haape, German medical officer

German Difficulties

It was appallingly difficult country for tank movement—great virgin forests, widespread swamps, terrible roads, and bridges not strong enough to bear the weight of tanks. The resistance also became stiffer, and the Russians began to cover their front with minefields; it was easier for them to block the way because there were so few roads.

The great motor highway leading from the frontier to Moscow was unfinished—the one road a Westerner would call a "road". We were not prepared for what we found because our maps in no way corresponded to reality. On those maps all supposed main roads were marked in red, and there seemed to be many, but they often proved to be merely sandy tracks. The German intelligence service was fairly accurate about conditions in Russian-occupied Poland, but badly at fault about those beyond the original Russian frontier.

Such country was bad enough for the tanks, but worse still for the transport accompanying them—carrying their fuel, their supplies, and all the auxiliary troops they needed. Nearly all this transport consisted of wheeled vehicles, which could not move off the roads, nor move on it if the sand turned into mud. An hour or two of rain reduced the Panzer forces to stagnation. It was an extraordinary sight, with groups of them strung out over a hundred miles stretch, all stuck—until the sun came out and the ground dried.

General Blumentritt

Information concerning Russia was comparatively scanty. We had in our possession the captured archives of Holland, Belgium, Greece, Jugoslavia and even of the French General Staff, but none of these countries was any better informed about the Russians than we were. The information concerning the troops we would first meet on the border was fairly correct, but we had no statistical data as to the future potentialities of this vast state. Of course, during our first six months' advance we found out a lot more.

Colonel-General Franz Halder, Chief of the General Staff

I realized soon after the attack was begun that everything that had been written about Russia was nonsense. The maps we were given were all wrong. The roads that were marked nice and red and thick on a map turned out to be tracks, and what were tracks on the map became first-class roads. Even railways which were to be used by us simply didn't exist. Or a map would indicate that there was nothing in the area, and suddenly we would be confronted with an American-type town, with factory buildings and all the rest of it.

Field-Marshal von Rundstedt,
G.O.C.-in-C., Army Group South

Bolski was not particularly amused.

"What do distances matter to us?" he demanded.

"A hell of a lot," Kageneck growled. "As much as they meant to Napoleon."

"Nonsense!" said Bolski scornfully. "This is the twentieth century and we have Adolf Hitler for a leader—not Napoleon."

"So what?" asked Jakobi.

"We have the greatest army and the greatest military leader of all time. Distance means nothing to-day." He was encouraged to greater heights of oratory: "Let us not forget: we are not a spear thrown haphazardly into space, which may or may not find the target. We are the sword of the new Germany, wielded by the best hands, and when called upon are always ready to cut and thrust until our enemies are completely destroyed."

Heinrich Haape

No More Castles

We did not waste time looking for accommodation. In France castles and mansions had been ours for the asking. The small wooden huts of the East held little appeal, particularly in view of the ubiquity of certain "domestic pets". Consequently our tactical headquarters lived almost the whole time in tents and the two command wagons which, together with a few wartime *Volkswagen* and the vehicles of the wireless section and telephone exchange, carried our other ranks when we changed location. I myself slept in a sleeping-bag in the small tent I shared with my A.D.C., and do not remember having used a proper bed more than three times throughout this Panzer drive. The one man with any objection to living under canvas was our senior military assistant, who preferred to sleep in his car. Unfortunately he had to leave his long legs sticking out through the door, with the result that he could never get his wet boots off after a rainy night.

General Erich von Manstein, G.O.C. LVI Panzer Corps

The First Reserves

We were forty in our wagon. All day long we hung in the openings, the sliding doors right back, and tried to see as much as we could of the landscape flitting by. Positions went by rank: first a row sitting on the floor, with their legs dangling out; then a row on a narrow board, leaning themselves on the diagonally placed barrier; behind these standing room—the gallery—leaning on the shoulders of those in front. It worked jolly well like that, only one or other of the front seats turning round swearing when one of the gallery trod on his fingers. On the other hand, one could hardly speak of harmony at night. When a chap stirred in his sleep, his cheesy toes would dig into another man's nose, and when that one jerked his head away he would ram another fellow in the belly, so he in turn would wake up and start taking it out of yet another.

Washing, too, was a business. When the train halted, every man looked to the chance of cleaning up, but you could never go far from the train; nobody could tell you whether it was there for minutes or hours. Nor were there any privies; at every halt the chaps squatted along the line with their trousers down and tried to reduce the necessary business to the minimum of time. If the whistle blew, there would be faces scarlet with a final effort and trousers pulled up on the run. You also had to see you

weren't counted a deserter; none of the swine up above
would ever admit that it was a job of that sort made you
miss the bus.

We touched Breslau and entered Poland. Children and
womenfolk surrounded the train, begging for bread. It
was a foreign lingo now, but their gestures were
understandable enough. We gave them food and still had
enough for ourselves.

Once the train halted bang in the heart of a little town;
men and women alike flocked down in curiosity, and the
children came right up to us, but as the train had not
halted for some hours that meant we had to take full
advantage of the halt, so in no time the whole train was
flanked by a row of naked backsides and the Poles
scurried their children out of range.

We crossed the Soviet frontier at Przemysl, and saw
the first extensive damage. The formerly Russian part of
the place had been badly hit. This was where the attack
had begun. We were silent as we passed this destruction.
An impression of the great misery which this war was
going to inflict was forced on us. Hopeless piles of ruin,
fireplaces sticking out of the rubble, grim reminders
indeed; houses cut in two, revealing all the intimacies
of each floor; iron girders snapped like matches, beams
shattered, collapsed walls, utter confusion, where once
had been normal life; the labour of centuries in a few
short hours turned to illusion.

On we went, past ruins, crashed trees and shell craters.
Here and there were the first corpses of tanks, death-
dealing steel beasts shattered by steel. The farther we
went, the more frequent this wreckage was; over there
one obviously just bogged in the marsh, here one off
which a mine had ripped the giant tracks, now another
decapitated, minus its conning tower. Of how many
destroyed lives could these dead monsters have told?

We began to reflect rather gloomily. Our thoughts
turned to home. A sunset like this brought heartache;
I could have howled. Then one of the chaps began singing
to himself. It was a gloomy tune, but others joined in,

humming at first. Soon we had all picked it up and that tune soared strongly against the monotonous roll and beat of the train's wheels on the rails. Lost in dreams, one felt one's eyes trying to penetrate the sombre shadows of the endless ghost-ridden expanses of this foreign land. What did lie ahead?

Benno Zieser

Russian Prisoners

We suddenly saw a broad, earth-brown crocodile slowly shuffling down the road towards us. From it came a subdued hum, like that from a beehive. Prisoners of war. Russians, six deep. We couldn't see the end of the column. As they drew near the terrible stench which met us made us quite sick; it was like the biting stench of the lion house and the filthy odour of the monkey house at the same time.

But these were not animals, they were men. We made haste out of the way of the foul cloud which surrounded them, then what we saw transfixed us where we stood and we forgot our nausea. Were these really human beings, these grey-brown figures, these shadows lurching towards us, stumbling and staggering, moving shapes at their last gasp, creatures which only some last flicker of the will to live enabled to obey the order to march? All the misery in the world seemed to be concentrated here. There was also that gruesome barrage of shouts and wails, groans, lamentations and curses which combined with the cutting orders of the guards into a hideous accompaniment.

We saw one man shuffle aside from the ranks, then a rifle butt crash between his shoulder-blades and drive him gasping back into place. Another with a head wound lost in bloodstained bandages ran a few paces out with gestures almost ludicrous in their persuasiveness to beg one of the nearby local inhabitants for a scrap of bread. Then a leather thong fetched him a savage lash round his shoulders and yanked him, too, back into place.

Another, a lanky fellow, a regular giant, stepped aside to pump ship, and when he too was forced back he could not stop nature and it all drenched the man in front, but he never even turned his head.

Stray dogs were legion, among them were the most unbelievable mongrels; the only thing they were all alike in was that they were thin. The Sheikh said one could have learned to play the harp on their ribs. That was no hindrance to the prisoners. They were hungry, so why not eat roast dog? They were always trying to catch the scary beasts. They would also beg us with gestures and *bow-wows* and *bang-bangs* to kill a dog for them. There it was, shoot it! And we almost always did; it was a bit of sport anyway, and at the same time it delighted those human skeletons. Besides, those wild dogs were a regular pest.

When we brought one down, there followed a performance that could make a man puke. Yelling like mad, the Russkies would fall on the animal and tear it in pieces with their bare hands, even before it was quite dead. The pluck they would stuff their pockets with, like tobacco, whenever they got hold of any of that—it made a sort of iron ration. Then they would light a fire, skewer shreds of the dog's meat on sticks and roast it. There were always fights over the bigger bits. The burnt flesh stank frightfully; there was almost no fat in it.

But they did not have roast dog every day. Behind the huts there was a big midden, a regular mountain of stinking waste, and if we did not look out they would poke about in it and eat such things as decaying onions, the mere sight of which was enough to turn you up. If one of us came near they would scatter like dung-flies. I once found one roasting dried pig's dung.

Benno Zieser

A German Prisoner

The day we arrived we were invited by Krassovsky to come to his headquarters. He was anxious to examine a German prisoner personally. One of our patrols had crossed the Dnieper for the express purpose of bringing in prisoners. Krassovsky had only one officer on his staff who spoke German fairly well, Commandant Fechner, and he was anxious that I should be present at the examination.

The prisoner was a Company Sergeant-Major, and with his horn-rimmed glasses, his fine hands and his slim figure, he seemed to be a man of some education and intelligence. On the way back he had tried to escape from our patrols by jumping from the boat into the Dnieper, but a blow from a rifle butt had prevented his escape. His head was bandaged, and blood trickled from his lips from time to time as he talked. He had lost his front teeth, which made it difficult for him to talk and difficult for us to understand him. He spoke with a strong Berlin accent.

"Your name, rank and unit?"

"Heinrich Fechner, Company Sergeant-Major of 147 Infantry Division."

"Fechner." General Krassovsky smiled. "No relation of yours, I suppose, comrade Fechner?"

I noticed that the man was listening intently. He seemed to understand Russian.

"Who is in command of your regiment?"

"General von Falz."

"What sort of a general?"

"Brigadier-General."

"What army does your unit belong to? What other units are there at Kriukov? Who commands them? What equipment have they?"

"I don't know."

"You mean you don't want to say."

"No. I really don't know."

"Do you speak Russian?"

"No."

"Do you understand Russian?"

"No."

"Good. Very well, tell him, comrade Fechner, that we

shall send him to Kharkov escorted by Cossacks."

The man turned pale and didn't wait for Krassovsky's words to be translated.

"Shoot me straight away," he said in Russian.

"Oh, so that loosens your tongue, eh? You do speak Russian, after all. And almost without an accent. Where were you born?"

"Lodz."

"So you're not German at all? You're Polish."

"I was born in 1908. Lodz was in Russian hands then."

"So much the worse for you. You're Russian, and you're fighting against us. You'll be hanged."

"Hang me then, but don't hand me over to the Cossacks."

"Lieutenant Petrov, call Cossack Lieutenant Kromov."

"Excellency, I'll talk. I'll answer your questions."

The prisoner swayed.

"Give the man a glass of water."

Within a short space of time we had all the information we wanted. The German attack was to begin at dawn the next day.

Ivan Krylov

Deserters

Sometimes the steppes would be white with the leaflets which our airmen dropped to the Soviet forces. These informed the Russians they should give up their senseless resistance and come over to us. The bottom part of the leaflets was detachable and counted as "Pass for officers or men up to fifty in number." There was the promise, in German and Russian, of "good treatment and an early return to your homeland after the war is over".

Most deserters showed us these passes when they came over. There were others who were only mastered at the cost of fierce fighting but who when beaten would suddenly pull out one of these passes, in a crumpled state, as if they thought they would prove trump cards and ensure them against any more worries.

However, those passes did not bring any of them any advantage whatsoever. They were only a propaganda trick; "Birdlime," said the Sheikh, "to catch stupid peasants." It bore the fine name of Psychological Warfare. Actually, all prisoners, without distinction, were marched to the nearest assembly camp, and there nobody cared two hoots whether they really were deserters or had fought us like furies to the last; though, it is true, there were a number of deserters kept at base for menial tasks. As a matter of fact, they had a far better time than any of us.

Benno Zieser

A Captured German Colonel's Diary: September 1941

Russia has double the population of Germany and is able to put twice the number of troops in the field.

There is no need for us to be in a hurry for Moscow. The fact that the Russians are throwing in more and more troops against us makes no difference to us. We will take Moscow when we want to.

The young people of both sexes are a great danger. They belong to the Bolshevist organization. Whenever these ragamuffins are discovered they must be detained and inquiries made at the burgomeister's office as to whether they are local residents. If they are not residents, they are to be arrested immediately, but they must not be shot before they have been interrogated by the Gestapo. Adults who are not local residents or who arouse suspicion must also be detained. The question of shooting them can be decided by each officer individually.

The Russians are very tenacious in defence and particularly skilful in constructing field fortifications.

In the Gaisin district the Russians discovered that our situation was serious, and for that reason they began to bomb us daily.

Only a reserve field battalion saved us from encirclement by counterattacking.

Young soldiers must remember that even during a

protracted war a soldier remains a soldier. Care must be taken that they do not get out of hand, otherwise we shall go downhill without noticing it with ever-increasing speed, as happened in the last war.

We cannot deny the Bolsheviks' courage and contempt for death. We have not been confronted by such an opponent hitherto.

As yet our troops have not been exterminating all prisoners and wounded. But the longer the war goes on, the more ruthlessly must we wage it. We will set aside all who were Bolsheviks, either officially or by virtue of their conduct. We will kill ten Bolsheviks for every German. Without attempting to prophesy—prophecy in wartime is always dangerous—and without using any fine language, I am bound to say the following: We are going to cross the Dnieper. We have no time to lose and must make short work of the Russians before the bad weather sets in. Obviously, we shall be exposed to attack by their cavalry.

The heavy fighting near Moscow has now been going on for three weeks. Apparently we are allowing the Russians to counter-attack and even to advance in some sectors. The situation at Leningrad looks very promising. But we must not forget that the Russians, unlike the French, are able to throw in more and more masses of men.

Conclusions:

1. Our communication lines have been considerably lengthened. Every bullet has to be brought by railway, then by motor transport and finally across country. Do not abandon ammunition under the influence of panic and do not waste it. Keep calm.

2. We have experienced a shortage of petrol and will continue to do so, as well as a shortage of supplies, provisions, etc. Actually the bread ration has already decreased to three hundred grammes. We are not receiving sugar or butter. Therefore food that has been seized must be dealt out economically.

3. We have only two lorries of necessary articles for the whole regiment. Everybody must send home for razor-blades and boot polish.

4. We shall soon enter the malarial region. Malaria is a very unpleasant disease, although not necessarily fatal. It is carried by mosquitoes. When we get twenty-one miles beyond the Dnieper there will no longer be any danger of malaria.

5. In future no leave will be granted except in special cases.

I leave it to those experts with sufficient leisure to clarify the future course of events.

Colonel Kress

A Prophecy

Shortly before sunset we heard the soft melody of a lute coming from the bower adjoining the house. Lammerding and I found an old Lithuanian seated near the house playing to a few soldiers. His long, snow-white beard made him look like an ancient bard. We asked him into the house to play for us. He sat by the fireplace, his hands quivering over his instrument. Officers and men stood about or leaned against the walls and doorway listening in silence.

As if out of distant depths that we could not at first comprehend came weird chords, first searching and appealing, then gradually developing into a coherent theme of exquisite melody, sad, almost melancholic, yet with no touch of morbidity. To me these plaintive melodies were the expression of the soul of a frontier nation, which had suffered subjection and bondage for many centuries. And then, gradually, the mood changed; turbulent and provocative tones grew into a throbbing and angry rhythm. The old man's face, which had been serene, as if no longer interested in worldly matters, was transformed. His eyes flashed with an inner fire and he started to sing in a foreign tongue. His voice was feeble with age, but true to every note. It seemed that he was conveying the thanks of a nation that had regained its freedom.

Those who followed the German Army and took over administration of Lithuania made a sad blunder when they failed to recognize this cry for freedom and did not call upon the help of these people in the fight against the Reds. There was a reservoir of goodwill waiting to be tapped. Instead it was dammed up by short-sighted oppression.

Some of the soldiers who had been listening to the old man took the opportunity to have a look at the inside of the farmhouse. The massive stone oven in the centre of the living-room amused them; it was about twenty feet square, had an open fireplace and a number of apertures in which stood primitive-looking pots. The thick walls of the oven divided the house into semi-enclosed rooms.

"Hey, Uncle!" called one of the soldiers. "You must have a big family. Why do you want an oven as big as this?"

The old man smiled. He knew enough German to understand what they were getting at. "Will you be in Russia this winter?" he asked in his thin voice.

"Perhaps."

"Then you will find out! And perhaps you won't laugh."

Heinrich Haape

The German forces pressed on. In spite of all the space which they could play with, the Russians were cutting it fine by the late summer—Leningrad was besieged and Moscow, the holy city, was almost within sight of the most forward German elements. But there was a late summer of quite exceptional wetness, and on 12 September the first snow fell.

The Fall of Kiev

On 26 September the Battle of Kiev was brought to a successful conclusion. The Russians surrendered.

665,000 men were taken prisoner. The Commander-in-Chief South-west Front and his chief of staff fell in the last phase of the battle while attempting to break out. The Commander of the Fifth Army was among the prisoners captured. I had an interesting conversation with this officer, to whom I put a number of questions. "When did you learn that my tanks had penetrated behind you?" "About the 8th of September." "Why did you not evacuate Kiev at once?" "We had received orders from the Army Group to evacuate the area and withdraw eastwards and had already begun to do so, when we received contrary orders to turn about and defend Kiev in all circumstances." The carrying out of this second order resulted in the destruction of the Kiev Army Group. The enemy was never to make the same mistake again. Unfortunately, though, we were to suffer the direst calamities as a result of just such interference from higher levels.

The Battle of Kiev was undoubtedly a great tactical victory. But whether great strategic advantages were to be garnered from this tactical success remained questionable. It all depended on this: would the German Army, before the onset of winter and, indeed, before the autumnal mud set in, still be capable of achieving decisive results? It is true that the planned assault on Leningrad had already had to be abandoned in favour of a tight investment. But the O.K.H.* believed that the enemy was no longer capable of creating a firm defensive front or of offering serious resistance in the area of Army Group South. The O.K.H. wanted this Army Group to capture the Donetz Basin and reach the River Don before winter.

But the main blow was to be dealt by the reinforced Army Group Centre, with objective Moscow. Was there still sufficient time for this to succeed?

General Heinz Guderian, G.O.C. Panzer Group 2

The steel ring that would tighten on Moscow was to

* The Army High Command.

be the greatest pincer movement of all time. We on the left flank were to be the claw of the pincers that would surround Moscow from the north-west, while the right flank of the Army Group was advancing on Kaluga and Tula and would squeeze the capital city from the south-east.

But the rain continued—rain such as this part of Russia had never in living memory experienced at this time of the year. So the Russian peasants told us. We marched on, but it got colder and colder and we were soaked through and depressed. The roads became quagmires and we thought bitterly of the winter clothing that had been promised us.

Heinrich Haape

On 2 October the Führer announced that the drive to Moscow would be "the last decisive battle of this year", and on the 6th the assault began. Three days later Molotov proclaimed a state of siege in the city, and on the following day the Government, with the exception of Stalin himself, packed its bags and moved eastwards to Kiubyzhev. Heavy industrial plant was transferred en masse to Siberia. The German advance continued along the whole front, and before long the forward troops were within easy reach of Moscow.

The Evacuation of Moscow

In the early days of the war our people had to be told what the Nazis were, and with other writers I was asked to describe with hatred the horrible thing that was hanging over our land. On the second day of the war I began to write for the Vakhtangov Theatre the play *Welcome Arms*. Its theme concerned a second European front.

The play was written in two months, and then during the period of heavy air raids, when we slept in the theatre, we rehearsed. One night I went home. A bomb hit and destroyed the theatre and until the next afternoon I was thought to have perished. But actually I was already rewriting my burned manuscript from memory. We began to rehearse again elsewhere, but the day before the première was billed, the company was given short notice to evacuate to Omsk in Siberia, for the position in Moscow was becoming critical.

Boris Voyetekhov

Among the mountains and pine forests there is spread out the beautiful capital of the Urals, Sverdlovsk. It has many fine buildings, but I want to tell you of the two most remarkable buildings of the whole area. Winter had already come when Sverdlovsk received Comrade Stalin's order to erect the two buildings for the plant evacuated from the south. The trains packed with machinery and people were on the way. In its new home the war factory had to start production, and it had to do so in not more than a fortnight. Fourteen days—not an hour more! It was then that the people of the Urals came to this empty spot with shovels, bars and pickaxes: students, typists, accountants, shop assistants, housewives, artists, teachers. The earth was like stone, frozen hard by our fierce Siberian frost. Axes and pickaxes could not break the stony soil. In the light of arc-lamps people hacked at the earth all night. They blew up the stones and the frozen earth, and they laid the foundations. Comrade Sivach, the grey-bearded decorator from the Sverdlovsk theatre, and his team were leading.

People's hands and feet were swollen with frostbite, but they did not leave work. Over the charts and blueprints, laid out on packing-cases, the blizzard was raging. Hundreds of trucks kept rolling up with building materials.

Rapidly the steel structures rose from the ground. . . . On the twelfth day, into the new buildings with their glass roofs, the machinery, covered with hoarfrost, began to arrive. Braziers were kept alight to unfreeze the machines. . . . And two days later, the war factory began production.

V. Ilyenkov

On to Moscow

Two days after we had left Butovo, late in the afternoon, the first snow fell in heavy flakes on the silently marching columns. Every man's thoughts turned in the same direction as he watched the flakes drop on the slushy roads. The first manifestations of winter! How cold and how long would the winter be? The black soil immediately dissolved the white flakes as if sucking them in, but as the late afternoon frost set in and snow fell more thickly, the countryside took on itself a white mantle. We watched it uneasily.

But by the evening we had reached the upper Dnieper and were lying exactly seventy-five miles from Vyasma and one hundred and seventy miles west of Moscow. Facing us across the river, which was narrow at this point, lay a strong line of Russian bunkers. Next morning we launched our assault across the river and by 6.30 a.m. the Russian defensive system was in our hands and the enemy was in full retreat. We thrust towards our next objective—the town of Sychevka.

The weather deteriorated. It became colder and snowed the whole day. But the snow did not remain for long. It was churned into the black earth, into which our vehicles sank deeper and deeper. The troops hauled and pushed the wheels of the transport; the gallant little *panje* horses sweated and strained; at times we had to take a brief ten-minute rest from sheer exhaustion; then back to the transport, our legs in black mud up to the knees. Anything to keep the wheels moving. To make up for lost time, and in a desperate race against the weather that we knew would worsen, we marched the night through and reached the area north of Sychevka on 11 October.

Heinrich Haape

And now, when Moscow itself was almost in sight, the mood both of commanders and troops changed. With amazement and disappointment we discovered in late October and early November that the beaten Russians seemed quite unaware that as a military force they had almost ceased to exist. . . . Skilfully camouflaged strongpoints, wire entanglements and thick minefields now filled the forests which covered the western approach to Moscow.

One began to hear sarcastic references to the military leaders far away in Germany. The troops felt that it was high time our political leaders came and had a look at the front. Our soldiers were over-tired now, our units under strength. This was particularly so among the infantry, where many companies were reduced to a mere sixty or seventy men. The horses, too, had suffered grievously and the artillery had difficulty in moving its guns. The number of serviceable tanks in the Panzer divisions was far below establishment. Since Hitler had believed that the campaign was over, he had ordered that industry at home cut down on its production of munitions. Only a trickle of replacements reached the fighting units. Winter was about to begin, but there was no sign of any winter clothing to be seen anywhere.

By mid-November the mud period was over and frost heralded the approach of winter. Both the roads and the open country were now passable for vehicles of all kinds. Tractors extricated the heavy artillery from the mud far behind the front and one gun after another was towed forward. It happened, however, that in the process of dragging these guns out of the ground into which many had became frozen fast, a number of them were literally torn to pieces.

General Blumentritt

Winter

Then the weather suddenly broke and almost overnight the full fury of the Russian winter was upon us. The thermometer suddenly dropped to thirty degrees of frost. This was accompanied by heavy falls of snow. Within

a few days the countryside presented the traditional
picture of a Russian winter. With steadily decreasing
momentum and increasing difficulty the two Panzer
groups continued to battle their way towards Moscow.

                                               General Blumentritt

On 13 November we awoke and shivered. An icy blast
from the north-east knifed across the snowy countryside.
The sky was cloudless and dark blue, but the sun seemed
to have lost its strength and instead of becoming warmer
towards noon as on previous days, the thermometer kept
falling and by sundown had reached minus twelve degrees
Centigrade.

The soldiers, who up to now had not regarded the light
frosts too seriously, began to take notice. One man who
had been walking outside for only a short distance without
his woollen *Kopfschutzer* or "head-saver" came into the
sick bay. Both ears were white and frozen stiff.

It was our first case of frost-bite.

We gently massaged the man's ears, taking care not
to break the skin, and they thawed out. We powdered
them and covered them with cotton-wool and made a
suitable head-dressing. Perhaps we had managed to save
the whole of the ears; we should have to wait and see.

This minor case of frost-bite was a serious warning.
The icy winds from Siberia—the breath of death—were
blowing across the steppes; winds from where all life
froze, from the Arctic ice-cap itself. Things would be
serious if we could not house ourselves in prepared
positions and buildings, and I stopped to think of the
armies marching on Moscow across open country at this
very moment. All that those men had received so far were
their woolen *Kopfschutzers*; the winter clothing had still
not arrived. What was happening to the men's feet, for
the ordinary army boot retained very little warmth?

Then, too, the thermometer showed only twelve degrees
below zero. Temperatures would drop to minus twenty-
four degrees—minus thirty-six degrees—minus forty-eight
degrees—perhaps even lower. It was beyond com-

prehension—a temperature four times colder than a deep freezer. To attempt any movement without warm clothing in those conditions would be sheer suicide. Surely the older generals had been right when, after the battle of Vyasma and Bryansk, they had counselled: "Dig in for the winter." Some of them were men with experience of Russia during the 1914-1918 War. At the most they had said, continue the war through the winter only with a few thoroughly equipped and well-provisioned divisions. Make the big push in the spring.

If only the battle for Moscow had started fourteen days earlier, the city would now have been in our hands. Or even if the rains had held off for fourteen days. If—if—if. If Hitler had started "Barbarossa" six weeks earlier as originally planned; if he had left Mussolini on his own in the Balkans and had attacked Russia in May; if we had continued our sweeping advance instead of stopping at the Schutsche Lake; if Hitler had sent us winter clothing. Yes, if, if, if—but now it was too late.

Those Arctic blasts that had taken us by surprise in our protected positions had scythed through our attacking troops. In a couple of days there were one hundred thousand casualties from frost-bite alone; one hundred thousand first-class, experienced soldiers fell out because the cold had surprised them.

A couple of days later our winter clothing arrived. There was just enough for each company to be issued with four heavy fur-lined greatcoats and four pairs of felt-lined boots. Four sets of winter clothing for each company! Sixteen greatcoats and sixteen pairs of winter boots to be shared among a battalion of eight hundred men! And the meagre issue coincided with a sudden drop in the temperature to minus twenty-two degrees.

Reports reached us that the issue of winter clothing to the troops actually advancing on Moscow had been on no more generous scale. More and more reports were being sent to Corps and Army Headquarters recommending that the attack on Moscow by a summer-clad army be abandoned and that winter positions be

prepared. Some of these reports were forwarded by
Central Army Group to the Führer's Headquarters, but
no reply or acknowledgment ever came. The order
persisted: "Attack!" And our soldiers attacked.

Heinrich Haape

Moscow Tram-stop

There was a deathly silence all round. In front of us
lay the tramway shelter and the telegraph poles silently
pointed the way to the great city beyond the curtain of
snow.

"Let's walk across and have a look at that tramway
station," Kageneck said. "Then we can tell Neuhoff that
we were only a tram ride from Moscow."

We walked silently down the road to the stone shed.
There was not a movement around us as we stopped and
stared at the wooden seats on which thousands of
Muscovites had sat and waited for the tram to clang down
the road from Moscow.

There was an old wooden bin attached to one wall.
I felt inside and dragged out a handful of old tram tickets.
We picked out the cyrillic letters, which by now we knew
spelled *Moskva*.

Slowly we trudged back to the car. Kageneck broke the
silence and spoke for both of us: "It must fall, yet . . .
I wonder. . . ."

Fischer turned the car round and we headed back along
the white road.

The snow was falling a little more heavily now.

Heinrich Haape

Every soldier outside Moscow knew that this was a
battle for life or death. If the Russians succeeded in
defeating us here, there could be no hope. In 1812 Napoleon had at least returned with the shattered remnants
of his Grand Army. In 1941 the choice for the Germans
was only to hold fast or to be annihilated. Russian

propaganda took the form of postcards, dropped from the air. These bore crude pictures of the snow-covered Russian plains dotted with the corpses of German soldiers. Such propaganda made no impression on our troops.

General Blumentritt

On Leave from Russia

"At first it was fine," went on Rudolf. "We swept on, adding towns and villages by the score. Then the troops began to get stale. Do you know how we behaved to the civilians? Shall I tell you?" he asked. We didn't reply before he began his story.

"We behaved like devils out of hell," he said. "We have left those villagers to starve to death behind us, thousands and thousands of them. How can you win a war in this way? Do you think they won't revenge themselves somehow? Of course they will."

"You mean you leave nothing behind? No homes, no food, no animals?"

"Those are the orders," said Rudolf. "Just to leave enough for the occupying troops."

"It's utter madness," said Heiner. "Whoever gave such orders are out of their minds. Surely not the generals?"

"No," said Rudolf. "The Russian front is really in the hands of the S.S., the generals have little to say. It is Hitler's revenge for being told he couldn't win a war against Russia. He is trying to prove all the army officers wrong."

We sat in an awful silence for a moment. Then Rudolf went on to tell us more details of the partisans behind their lines.

"We shoot the prisoners on the slightest excuse," he said. "Just stick them up against the wall and shoot the lot. We order the whole village out to look while we do it, too."

"Yes," said Dr. Schmitt. "And I have heard too that

Hitler ordered that every officer or political commissar made prisoner on the Eastern Front was to be shot immediately after questioning."

Rudolf jumped up. "No," he declared, "you are wrong there. The officers are not shot after questioning. I, at least, have seen that that's not true."

"Calm down," said Dr. Schmitt. "I only said 'ordered', I didn't say it was being carried out. Hitler signed a secret document to have it done, but the high Army officers are refusing to carry the order out. That is one reason why Hitler is getting so wild and allowing the S.S. and the Gestapo terrible powers in the villages after you have passed on."

"My God," said Rudolf. "If it is really true, then everything is lost. Not only the Russian war, but the whole war."

Heiner made a sign to Dr. Schmitt not to say anything more on that subject, but Rudolf would go on talking.

"You can't imagine what happens behind the lines. We had orders to try and clear partisans out of a wood. We combed that wood for two days in the most bitter weather. But no partisans. I was just about to withdraw my troops, when suddenly whistles began to blow, and the wood was full of Russians in a second. They were in such a terrible condition, however, that we beat them off. They had been lying in holes in the ground covered only with straw and brushwood and had had no food or drink, indeed they must scarcely have dared to take breath. They were so cold their limbs would not move properly when the order came to attack us."

"The courage of desperation," said Dr. Schmitt. "Men in those conditions will do anything."

"They do do anything," said Rudolf. "As terrible things as we do to them. When we passed through another village where the partisans had caught some of our troops we found men stripped naked except for their steel helmets which still stuck on their heads. A long line of them were tied together and water had been poured over them until they had frozen into a solid block of ice. You see, it's a vicious circle. We hate them, they hate us, and on and on it goes, everyone getting more and more inhuman."

Rudolf's last words echoed round the room. No one spoke. I put out a hand and touched Dr. Schmitt lightly; he was sitting quite close to me. He looked up and saw that I wanted him to try to help Rudolf.

"Yes," he said slowly, as if coming out of a coma. "It *is* a vicious circle."

"Another of our mistakes was in the Ukraine," said Rudolf, now a little calmer. "I was one of those who marched in to be received, not as a conqueror but as a friend. The civilians were all ready to look on us as saviours. They had had years of oppression from the Soviet. They thought we had come to free them. Does it sound absurd? Perhaps it does. What did we do? Turn them into slaves under Hitler. Worse, we deported their women for labour in Germany, and did not bother if they were married or single, had children or not. To add insult to injury we forced every woman and girl to undergo medical inspection. Ninety-nine per cent of the unmarried girls were virgins, but we took no notice of that, just ordered one and all to line up for medical inspection as though they were prostitutes. After inspection a clean medical report was made in their labour books, then they were loaded into wagons and transported to work for the Fatherland."

In the deep silence that followed I was very near to tears. To try and overcome them I hastily refilled the glasses and offered one to Rudolf to cheer him up.

"Come on, Rudolf, try and cheer up, we are together for only a short time. Come on," I pleaded.

Dr. Schmitt and his wife also took glasses, and Hermann and Heiner. We lifted them, and perhaps stupidly, but anyway with the best intentions, we began to hum an old German drinking song. "Drink, dear brother, drink, and let worry look after itself." (*Trink, Brüderlein, trink, lasse die Sorgen zu Haus!*)

Rudolf took the glass and stared at me and said, "You can take my word for it, Else, if the Russians should ever

knock at this door and only pay back one half of what
we have done to them, you wouldn't ever smile or sing
again!"

Else Wendel, housewife

Rejoining One's Unit

The cart track led past the charred remains of a cottage,
now no more than foundations of walls with charred and
shivered beams sticking oddly out of the cinders. In many
places the mass was still smouldering, thin smoke coiled
slowly up into the air. A few paces farther, I saw some
military graves. The earth was freshly turned, the crosses
new. *Tenth Company,* I read. My heart shrank. My own
company. *Rifleman Georg Haunstein.* Didn't know him.
Must be a new chap. *Corporal Dieter Hufnagel.* Must
be one of the heavy machine-gunners. *N.C.O. Karl
Mansch.* A stranger. Then a lot more I did not know.
But stop, this one—was that not the fellow who had collected those prisoners' rings? And there was Habacher,
too, one of the real front-line veterans. So Habacher too
had now been knocked out. When Habacher had to shoot
that commissar he said afterwards he was sure the
commissar would have his revenge. *Hartman, Kulbeck,
Strangel.* Strangel was in my platoon, a lad bubbling over
with good spirits and humour.

Racked with anxiety, I now ran through all the names
on the remaining crosses, and found another and yet
another whom I knew. Then my breath caught in my
throat. I bent low to see it clearly. The letters swam in
front of me. It could not be! *Corporal Willi Scholz.*

Our Willi! I stared at the rough lettering in sheer
dismay, and my thoughts began a mad whirl. How cold
and supercilious that lettering did look, the second *l* was
partly smudged, somebody had corrected it, started first
to put *h*—for *Wilhelm,* I suppose. They thought Willi
could not possibly be his baptismal name, till someone
must have said: "Yes, that was his name all right, *Willi.*"
How I hated that cursed cross! I felt I could have flung

the thing into the smoking ruins of the house to feed the flames.

The tin hat set on the cross was a bit crooked, just a little bit, precisely the way he had always worn it; it had always been a bit on the large side for him. I took it down. My hands shook. In the leather band inside was scratched *W. Scholz*, in Willi's own hand. But it was not at all easy to read, the leather was smeared with dark brown stains. Blood. Dried blood. And at the side the tin hat had a hole, with the usual sharp, in-bent edges, and they too were dark brown, like the patches on the leather.

Benno Zieser

RETREAT FROM MOSCOW

In mid-November the Russians, jealous for their holy city, counter-attacked both north and south—at Kalinin and Tula. They counter-attacked also in the south, and retook Rostov-on-Don before the month was out. On 1 December they successfully mounted a major operation at Tula, and the threat to Moscow was removed for ever. Twelve days later von Bock, the Army Commander, was relieved because of his failure and was succeeded by List. By mid-December the Germans were in retreat along the entire front, and on the 19th the Führer decided that drastic measures were required—he relieved von Brauchitsch and took supreme command of the armies himself.

A bombshell burst on 8 December—Japan was at war with America! It seemed like an act of senseless bravado. Did we not already have enough enemies? Was not the position on the Russian front serious enough—an army without winter clothing facing an enemy with allies? Must we be at war with a hostile world?

Then came reports that fresh Siberian troops, equipped with superb winter clothing, were attacking our lines on both sides of Kalinin. Stalin must have had a secret agreement with Japan for some time past, otherwise how dared he withdraw these divisions from the East?

Over the Volga the Siberian troops came, and threw themselves against our 127 and 162 Divisions. The Volga was no longer a barrier—it was completely frozen over; an army could have marched across it. Desperately I prayed that the Russians would not break through and set the whole front aflame. It was a selfish prayer; at any moment I feared the instruction would be issued: "All leave cancelled." I wanted to be away before the order was given.

. . . .The retreat from Moscow had begun.

It was a retreat that involved the entire German Army from before the capital. Three armies were falling back from the rich prize and were being hammered as they went by Marshal Zhukov and his hordes of warmly clad reinforcements.

For our ill-equipped troops, retreat in many instances spelt death. Death with the thermometer standing at fifty degrees below zero. Fiercely, the wind from the far steppes of Asia continued to blow, driving the loose snow and ice before it. The highways could no longer be recognized except as lanes of hard-packed snow. During the blizzards it was cold, bitterly cold, but when the clouds cleared and the sun hung low in the sky it was colder still. It was as if the sky itself had frozen into a crystal of cold lead. Death came with icy pinions and stood at our elbow. But our troops fought him just as, again and again, they formed up and fought the Russians. They retreated across the snow desert with their faces to the enemy.

Every day we fought bitterly, threw back the Russians with bloody losses to themselves and every evening disentangled ourselves from the grip of the enemy so that we could warm our frozen bodies in the shelter of some deserted hamlet.

In this unearthly cold, in which the breath froze and icicles hung from nostrils and eyelashes all day long, where thinking became an effort, the German soldiers fought—no longer for an ideal or an ideology, no longer for the Fatherland. They fought blindly without asking questions, without wanting to know what lay ahead of them. Habit and discipline kept them going; that and the flicker of an instinct to stay alive. And when the soldier's mind had become numb, when his strength, his discipline and his will had been used up, he sank into the snow. If he was noticed, he was kicked and slapped into a vague awareness that his business in the world was not finished and he staggered to his feet and groped on. But if he lay where he had collapsed until it was too late, as if forgotten he was left lying at the side of the road and the wind blew over him and everything was levelled indistinguishably.

We fought our way southwards towards Staritsa, and on 22 December found ourselves back in Vassilevskoye. We had arrived there at the end of our sweeping march through Poland and Russia with practically a full battalion of eight hundred men. The fighting strength of the battalion was now 189 men, including officers and N.C.O.s. It had shrunk pitifully, but was still battleworthy.

Heinrich Haape

Only for a few hours each day was there limited visibility at the front. Until nine o'clock in the morning the wintry landscape was shrouded in a thick fog. Gradually a red ball, the sun, became visible in the eastern sky and by about eleven it was possible to see a little. At three o'clock in the afternoon dusk set in, and an hour later it was almost completely dark again.

Supplies were usually short. Only a few railways ran into the area behind the front. These were frequently cut by the partisans. The water froze inside the boilers of the engines, which were not built to withstand the Russian climate. Each engine could draw only half the normal number of wagons. Many of them became stuck for days on end in the snow and ice. Our urgent requests for artillery shells could scarcely be met. Yet in order to encourage the soldiers on the Eastern Front trainloads

of red wine were shipped to us from France and Germany.
The anger of a unit which received a trainload of wine
instead of the shells it urgently needed can be readily
imagined. Even as wine such a cargo was frequently
useless. At forty degrees Centigrade below zero, not an
unusual temperature, it had often frozen in transit, burst
its bottles, and all that remained were chunks of red ice.

Defensive positions which offered shelter to their
occupants were almost non-existent. This resulted in a
tactical development whereby both sides fought bitterly
for possession of the scattered villages where there was
at least some cover to be found against the cruel cold.
A further result was that both sides shelled these villages
and set fire to the wood and thatch houses in order to
deprive the enemy of the relief which they provided. There
could be no question of digging in; the ground was frozen
to the consistency of iron.

General Blumentritt

The Christmas Present

Little Becker and I walked on together in silence; there
was nothing to say. The wind blew up and drove the snow
and flakes of ice past us in almost horizontal lines.
Fortunately the wind was at our backs. Kageneck and
Lammerding came out of a house and rejoined us when,
about an hour later, we came to a small hamlet. *Oberst*
Becker and von Kalkreuth followed them, got into their
jeep, covered themselves with blankets and drove off.

Stolze joined us and asked Kageneck, "What's
happening?"

"A hell of a lot. It's a bastard," replied Kageneck
bitterly. "The enemy has broken through at Vassilevskoye
and nobody knows his head from his arse at the moment.
The Russians might be anywhere—at our backs, on our
flanks, or even in front of us. We'll have to send our flank
patrols."

"Through those snowdrifts?" asked Stolze.

"It will have to be done," Kageneck replied.

"And what about the rest of the front?" Stolze asked. "Surely it can't be as bad as this everywhere?"

"We're retreating from Moscow along the whole of the Central Army Group front," said Kageneck. "Three German armies, all with their backs turned on Moscow."

Lammerding took up the tale: "The situation has deteriorated to an alarming extent."

"And the foulest part of it all," Kageneck burst out, "is that nearly all our generals have been relieved of their posts."

"Brauchitsch?" asked Stolze.

"Yes."

"Guderian?"

"Yes."

"Von Bock?"

"Yes."

"Kluge?"

"Field-Marshal von Kluge is practically the only one of the old brigade left. He's taken the Central Army Group from von Bock. Strauss has been relieved of command of 9 Army; Rundstedt's gone; so has Hoth; even Auleb has had 6 Division taken away from him."

"Then who the hell is our commander now that all the generals have been sent into the desert?" demanded Stolze. He grabbed Kageneck by the arm and for a moment we all stopped while the blizzard swept round us.

"We have a Christmas present, gentlemen," said Kageneck. "A new commander."

"Who is it?" Stolze demanded urgently.

Kageneck pulled his *Kopfschutzer* firmly round his ears and looked hard at Stolze: "*Gefreiter* Adolf Hitler has assumed complete command of the entire German Wehrmacht."

Heinrich Haape

Winter Clothing—a Solution

Now we had an opportunity to equip our men with

more winter clothing. Kageneck ordered that the seventy-three dead Russians be carried to the village and stripped of their felt-lined boots and warm clothing.

But the bodies were frozen stiff. And those invaluable boots were frozen to the Russians' legs.

"Saw their legs off," ordered Kageneck.

The men hacked off the dead men's legs below the knee and put legs, with boots still attached, into the ovens. Within ten or fifteen minutes the legs were sufficiently thawed for the soldiers to strip off the vital boots.

Stolze had captured his own little personal booty. In hand-to-hand combat he had killed a Russian commissar and he came up to me, his face beaming beneath a wonderful fox-fur cap that he had taken from the dead commissar. I was lavish in my admiration of the prize. Stolze turned to his orderly: "If ever anything happens to me, see to it that the doctor gets this cap. Understand?"

"*Jawohl, Herr Oberleutnant,*" said the orderly with a grin. . . .

. . . . Stolze's body lay in a barn at the eastern end of the village—among the 10th Company men he had loved so well, men, who, after his death, had shown how close had been the bond between them. They had not dug a grave in the snow for him. They did not trust the Staritsa Line and wanted to inter his body in a proper German war cemetery behind the lines. They laid out his body on a long narrow sledge, rested his head on a pillow and folded his hands across his chest. This improvised bier was placed in the open barn in such a way that if we had to evacuate our positions in a hurry they could take him along at a moment's notice, either by hitching a horse to the sledge or pulling it themselves. They had gone to all this trouble in spite of dead weariness, hunger and long hours of danger and strain. Stolze could have had no finer tribute.

Black rafters stuck out from the thick snow on the roof of the barn like badly decayed teeth. Inside it was still light enough to pick out details. Gently I pulled back the ground-sheet that covered Stolze's body and powdery grains of snow rolled to the ground. Like sculptured marble, Stolze lay on the sledge. His eyes were closed and there was a suspicion of a smile on his mouth. If winter lasted for ever, I thought, Stolze's body would lie embalmed like this until the end of time.

Stolze's orderly was waiting for me outside. He saluted and said: "*Herr Oberleutnant* Stolze ordered me to give *Herr Assistenzarzt* this fox-fur cap."

Heinrich Haape

Scorched Earth

The retreating army marched against a back-drop of flame. Special "scorched-earth commandoes" were organized to carry out Hitler's adaptation of Stalin's earlier policy. But our men carried it out more thoroughly than ever the Russians had done. The night shone red as buildings, whole villages, broken-down vehicles, everything of any conceivable value to the enemy, went up in flames. Nothing had to be left to the Red Army—and nothing was left. We marched with the flames licking our footsteps, marched day and night, with only short halts, for we well knew that we were the rearguard of the army that had fallen back from Kalinin; there were no troops between us and the pursuing Russians.

On the evening of 29 December we had crossed the Volga at Terpilovo; we marched the whole of that night, right through the next day and the next night, with the Russians on our heels. But if our spur was the enemy, the whip that flayed us as we marched was the unholy cold. Like mummies we padded along, only our eyes visible, but the cold relentlessly crept into our bodies, our blood, our brains. Even the sun seemed to radiate a steely cold and at night the blood-red skies above the burning villages merely hinted a mockery of warmth.

For long periods at a stretch each man was conscious

only of the man who walked in front of him as the shrunken grey column marched ceaselessly towards Staritsa.

And silently with our column went the sledge carrying Stolze's body. The 10th Company men had captured a horse from the Reds for the sole purpose of pulling the sledge. But on the afternoon of 30 December a flight of six Heinkel 111s flew over us from the south, turned and came at us in a shallow dive. We threw ourselves off the road, into snowdrifts or into the ditch. Some men stood up and shouted, "We're German!"; others swore as they dived for cover. But the Heinkels came in and dropped their bombs. In our winter clothing and in our rearguard position, the airmen's mistake was understandable. The bombs exploded, throwing up showers of snow and frozen earth, but nobody was hit. But a near-miss had killed the horse and shattered the sledge carrying Stolze's body. The half-smile was still on the big fellow's face when the 10th Company men went to retrieve the corpse, which was as stiff as a gun-barrel and unharmed. With shovels, Stolze's men set to work to enlarge a bomb crater which would act as a grave for their dead leader, for there was no other sledge they could commandeer.

Then the Heinkels regrouped and came in for another attack. The six men in the burial party threw themselves into the grave on top of Stolze. Another cluster of bomb-craters appeared in the snow and the Heinkels set course southwards. From fragments of the smashed sledge the men fashioned a cross for Stolze's grave and the gallant warrior was left to his rest beside the road of retreat from Moscow.

Heinrich Haape

2

EIGHTH ARMY VERSUS
AFRIKA KORPS

*In February 1941 the war in North Africa and Egypt
was about to enter into a new and critical phase. Hitler
decided to send German troops to North Africa to stiffen
his hard-pressed Italian allies. These soldiers and their
commander were to write a page in history, together with
their opponents, the British desert forces later christened
the Eighth Army.*

AN OBSCURE GENERAL ARRIVES

"DETACHMENTS of a German expeditionary force under an obscure general, Rommel, have landed in North
Africa."

The announcement was perfunctory but rather
interesting. It had been issued in an Intelligence summary
by the British High Command early in March 1941.

Lieutenant Heinz Werner Schmidt, Afrika Korps

In view of the highly critical situation with our Italian
allies, two German divisions—one light and one
Panzer—were to be sent to Libya to their help. I was
to take command of this German Afrika Korps and was
to move off as soon as possible to Libya to reconnoitre
the ground.

The middle of February would see the arrival of the first German troops in Africa; the movement of 5 Light Division would be complete by mid-April and of 15 Panzer Division at the end of May.

The Italian motorized forces in North Africa were to be placed under my command, while I myself was to be subordinate to Marshal Graziani.

In the afternoon I reported to the Führer, who gave me a detailed account of the situation in Africa and informed me that I had been recommended to him as the man who would most quickly adapt himself to the altogether different conditions of the African theatre. The Führer's chief adjutant, Colonel Schmundt, was to accompany me for the first stage of my tour of reconnaissance. I was advised to start by assembling the German troops in the area round Tripoli so that they could go into action as one body. In the evening the Führer showed me a number of British and American illustrated papers describing General Wavell's advance through Cyrenaica. Of particular interest was the masterly co-ordination these showed between armoured land forces, air force and navy.

General Erwin Rommel

It was not then known that Rommel had given his Afrika Korps special desert training in Germany. On a sandy peninsula in the Baltic, he had found terrain which approximated to that in Libya and there had worked out tactical and maintenance problems. The troops had lived and worked in over-heated barracks and artificial sandstorms, and on strictly rationed water and limited food. After this 'hot-house' training they were ready for desert action when they stepped off the ships at Tripoli.

The New Broom

Before von dem Borne, the Chief of Staff, had an opportunity of checking the number of officers present, Rommel entered unexpectedly. The officers snapped to attention. Von dem Borne announced resonantly, "Staff Officers and Panzer Regiment officers ready for the conference!" I was surprised at what seemed rather an informal way of "reporting". (Normally in the German Army the General would be advised briefly how many officers, and from which units, were present, how many were absent, and so on.) But without further ceremony Rommel launched himself into his address:

"Gentlemen," he said, "I am pleased to know that after strenuous days the gentlemen of the 5th Panzer Regiment are now in Tripoli almost up to full strength. With the arrival of your Panzers the situation in North Africa will be stabilized. The enemy's thrust towards Tripolitania has been brought to a standstill. Our reconnaissance units [a battalion of armoured cars] under Lieutenant-Colonel von Wegmar have reached the Italians' advanced positions on the Gulf of Sirte at El Agheila, and have morally and materially strengthened the front. It is our task to restore the confidence of the Italian people in their arms. and to bolster up the fighting spirit of our allies."

Rommel paused between sentences, clenching his fists with elbows bent and thrust slightly forward. That powerful chest, those energetic facial gestures, and his abrupt, precise, military manner of expressing himself clearly indicated a resolute will. The officers, all standing, listened intently to his review of the situation.

Rommel raised his voice. He shook his fist lightly.

"We *must* save Tripolitania from the attack of the British Army. We *will* hold them."

Lieutenant Heinz Werner Schmidt

Lili Marlene

Vor der Kaserne, vor dem grossen Tor
Steht eine Laterne, und steht sie noch davor.
Wenn sich die späten Nebel drehn,
Bei der Laterne woll'n wir stehn
Wie einst Lili Marlene
Wie einst Lili Marlen'.

The Desert

The war in Africa is quite different from the war in
Europe. It is absolutely individual. Here there are not
masses of men and material. Nobody and nothing can
be concealed. Whether in battle between opposing land
forces or between those of the air or between both it is
the same sort of fight, face to face; each side thrusts and
counter-thrusts. If the struggle were not so brutal, so
entirely without rules, one would be inclined to think of
the romantic idea of a knight's tourney.
Lieutenant Schorm, Afrika Korps, diary, 16 April 1941

Two main considerations governed warfare in the
Libyan-Egyptian desert: supply, and the balance of "mobile striking power"—a term which may be used to
cover the combined power of tanks, anti-tank guns and
field artillery working together as a common force. The
chief geographical factor influencing tactics in this desert
is that, except at El Alamein near Alexandria and at El
Agheila on the border of Tripolitania, there are no
defensive positions that cannot be outflanked. At both
these places secure flanks are provided by narrow
bottlenecks—between the Mediterranean and the Qattara
Depression in one case, and the Great Sand Sea in the
other. Everywhere else there is an open desert flank, the
cause of constant anxiety to the commander who has not
superiority in mobile striking power. Even the most
gallant infantry cannot hold fixed positions in this desert
when once enemy armoured forces have outflanked them.
Then, if they are not to be cut off, they must withdraw
and keep on withdrawing until wear and tear of supply
difficulties reduce the enemy's superiority in armoured
and mobile forces to such an extent that he loses control
of the open desert flank. Their only alternative is to
establish themselves behind a fortified perimeter covering
a water-point and harbour like that at Tobruk.

THE FIRST BLOW: 30 MARCH 1941

We went for the little fort in the desert, and the British positions round it, from three directions. The engagement was sharp but lasted only a couple of hours. We took the British commander, Major-General Gambier-Parry, in his tent. The haul of prisoners numbered almost three thousand. We had a further spectacular success. A mobile force of motor-cyclists caught up with the British column moving eastward across the desert below the Jebel Akhdar nearby, and to their astonishment held up the two heroes of the British advance to Benghazi: Lieutenant-General Sir Richard O'Connor, who had just been knighted for his successes against the Italians, and Lieutenant-General Sir Philip Neame, V.C. So we had three generals in the bag.

Mechili landing-ground was littered with destroyed planes. British machines swooped down to attack it afresh at short intervals. At the height of one assault, "my" Fieseler Storch dropped in out of the sky. Out stepped Rommel, smiling buoyantly, fresh from a personal reconnaissance of the desert scene.

The command trucks of the captured British generals stood on a slight rise. They were large, angular vehicles on caterpillar tracks, equipped inside with wireless and facilities for "paper" work. We christened them "Mammoths" then, but I did not realize that these useful trucks would be used by Rommel and his staff and commanders right through the long struggle that was now beginning in the desert.

Rommel inspected the vehicles with absorbed interest after a brief interview with the captured British generals. He watched them emptied of their British gear. Among the stuff turned out he spotted a pair of large sun-and-sand goggles. He took a fancy to them. He grinned, and said, "Booty—permissible, I take it, even for a General." He adjusted the goggles over the gold-braided rim of his cap peak.

Those goggles for ever after were to be the
distinguishing insignia of the "Desert Fox".
Lieutenant Heinz Werner Schmidt

Rommel Writes to His Wife

3 April 1941

Dearest Lu,

We've been attacking since the 31st with dazzling
success. There'll be consternation amongst our masters
in Tripoli and Rome, perhaps in Berlin too. I took the
risk against all orders and instructions because the
opportunity seemed favourable. No doubt it will all be
pronounced good later and they'll all say they'd have done
exactly the same in my place. We've already reached our
first objective, which we weren't supposed to get to until
the end of May. The British are falling over each other
to get away. Our casualties small. Booty can't yet be
estimated. You will understand that I can't sleep for
happiness.

Rommel

TOBRUK

*Weakened and faced by a new and determined foe,
the British withdrew eastwards with celerity and not
without some disorder. They left behind them a citadel
destined to prove a thorn in the flank of their enemies.*

Seven weeks after the capture of Cyrenaica 9 Division
was fleeing helterskelter for Tobruk with Rommel in close
pursuit.

Vehicles shouldered each other crazily on the crammed
roadway. To keep fleeing was the only thought. Some
of the battered transport broke down and was abandoned.
Some of the division were overtaken and made prisoner.
In Nazi prison camps Australians came to talk of the
"Breakfast Battalion". Its commander, perhaps under the
delusion that he was still engaged in leisurely manoeuvring

with his militia company somewhere back in Australia, ordered the battalion to "stop for breakfast". His officers demurred, pointing out that Nazi scout cars were only a few miles away. The colonel repeated serenely that "the battalion would stop for breakfast". Those of the companies who could manage it disobeyed and kept on fleeing. The colonel and about a hundred of his men stopped for breakfast. For the next four years they partook of that meal in Nazi prison camps: a long time to stop for breakfast.

The tide had turned against the impudent force that occupied Cyrenaica. Rommel recaptured Benghazi. Six days after, 9 Division and the remnants of a British armoured division reached Tobruk. The Benghazi Derby was over. In Tobruk they turned to stand before Rommel and all that he had to hurl against them.

That was the day before Good Friday. But the troops came to call it Black Friday.

Eric Lambert

Churchill on Tobruk

I have never known Churchill at a loss on any question of pure strategy; naturally enough, the service representatives would often have to press him to reject or alter a solution he proposed when the right decision on grounds of pure strategy was unacceptable for lack of resources or for reasons of time and space—which were perhaps not Winston's strongest suit. On grounds of pure strategy Winston was therefore arguing passionately—I never knew him overrule—for the retention of Tobruk. When Winston asked for my opinion, I supported his desire to hold on, not because it was his idea but because it seemed to me to offer absolutely the only hope of stopping the rot. I pointed out that though there would indeed be difficulties for the Navy and Air Force in supplying and supporting Tobruk, these difficulties on our side, even though our forces were inadequate, would be as nothing to the fears and uncertainties of the enemy when he came to advance far beyond a by-passed Tobruk, with our forces there threatening his communications while they were at extreme stretch across hundreds of miles of desert. The alternative for Rommel would be to devote so large a part of his force to the investment and capture of Tobruk that with what was left he would find it impossible to advance farther into Egypt. To leave a force in Tobruk, on that first occasion, to threaten Rommel's tenuous communications seemed the one chance left of giving pause to an otherwise victorious enemy who at that time looked like stopping nowhere short of Alexandria or Cairo.

Winston greeted this support for his own ideas with unfeigned delight. And at once he found the right phrase for Tobruk: "A sally port," he said, pronouncing this with his slight lisp between the "s" and the "a". He rolled the phrase round his mouth and repeated it. "Yes, a sally port, a sally port; that is what we want, that is the thing to do with them. The farther he advances the more you threaten, the more he has to fear. That is the answer, a sally port. . . ."

Air Vice-Marshal Arthur Harris

The Siege Begins

There'll be no Dunkirk here. If we should have to get out, we shall fight our way out. There is to be no surrender and no retreat.

General Morshead, G.O.C. Tobruk garrison

The final count showed more than forty thousand men inside the perimeter. On 12 April there were some five thousand Axis prisoners, and 35,307 British, Australians and Indians, but many of these were not front-line troops. There were far more Ordnance, Army Service Corps and medical personnel than the garrison needed; five British engineer companies, which had been working on roads

and installations throughout Cyrenaica; hundreds of Air
Force ground staff, and a number of stragglers.
Fortunately the fighting units had reached Tobruk in good
order, and they were now joined by two urgently needed
regiments of Royal Horse Artillery, which were rushed
up from Egypt.

Before the end of April some twelve thousand troops
and airmen and more than seven thousand prisoners of
war were withdrawn from Tobruk by sea and the final
streamlined garrison—stripped down to essential personnel—from early May to late August averaged little
more than twenty-three thousand and fell as low as
22,026 in July. Of these nearly fifteen thousand were
Australians and about five hundred were Indians. The
rest came from Great Britain.

Chester Wilmot

All our energies and ingenuity were required to guard
effectively the twenty-five miles of the perimeter, at any
point of which the Germans might have attacked. The
defence lines were in the form of a semi-circle, whose
radius was about ten miles, with Tobruk as the centre.
Within this area we, in the tanks, had to be prepared to
move at a moment's notice to any part of the perimeter
which was threatened.

Cyril Joly

The First Attacks: Amateur Gunners

On this morning our Transport Officer was in command
of the guns and, when the first enemy vehicles appeared,
Battalion H.Q. said he could engage them. The guns had
no sights but we got direction by squinting down the
barrel, and range by trial and error. As it happened, a
British artillery colonel was there and he gave us expert
advice. Our gun drill wasn't very good and our fire orders
would have shocked the R.H.A., but we got the shells
away. When the vehicles were about five hundred yards

out, the T.O. called, "All ready boys, let 'er go." The first shell fell short. "Cock 'em up a bit, boys," said the colonel. We did, and the second shot fell dead between the two leading vehicles. We kept on firing and they disappeared in a cloud of dust—and stayed out of range for the rest of the day.

Sergeant E. D. Rule

Repulse

There was terrible confusion at the only gap as tanks and infantry pushed their way through it. The crossing was badly churned up and the tanks raised clouds of dust as they went. In addition, there was the smoke of two tanks blazing just outside the wire.

Into this cloud of dust and smoke we fired anti-tank weapons, Brens, rifles, and mortars, and the gunners sent hundreds of shells. We shot up a lot of infantry as they tried to get past, and many, who took refuge in the anti-tank ditch, were later captured. It was all I could do to stop the troops following them outside the wire. The Germans were a rabble, but the crews of three tanks did keep their heads. They stopped at the anti-tank ditch and hitched on behind them the big guns, whose crews had been killed. They dragged these about a thousand yards, but by then we had directed our artillery on to them. They unhitched the guns and went for their lives. That was the last we saw of the tanks, but it took us several hours to clean up small parties of infantry who hadn't been able to get away.

Major J. W. Balfe

Disillusionment

The information distributed before the action told us that the enemy was about to withdraw, his artillery was weak and his morale had become very low. We had been led to believe that the enemy would retire immediately on the approach of German tanks. Before the beginning of the third attack* the regiment had not the slightest idea of the well-designed and executed defences of the enemy, nor of a single battery position, nor of the terrific number of anti-tank guns. Also it was not known that he had heavy tanks. The regiment went into battle with firm confidence and iron determination to break through the enemy and take Tobruk. Only the vastly superior enemy, the frightful loss and the lack of any supporting weapons, caused the regiment to fail in its task.

Afrika Korps officer

25 April 1941

Things are very warm in front of Tobruk. I shan't be sorry to see more troops arrive, for we're still very thin on the long fortress front. I've seldom had such worries—militarily speaking—as in the last few days. However, things will probably look different soon.

. . . . Greece will probably soon be disposed of and then it will be possible to give us more help. Paulus is due to arrive in a few days. The battle for Egypt and the Canal is now on in earnest and our tough opponent is fighting back with all he's got.

Rommel

Stukas

It was an ordinary Libyan day, furnace-hot, with a glare that was like a knife across the eyes. Striking the stone-littered surface of the desert the light quivered vaporously. The sky was the colour of smoke. It was motionless. The sun was seen through it like a coin in a dim pool.

But there was life in that sky.

Six Platoon sat in their pits. They were not the men who, attired correctly and uniformly, had marched around the roads of Palestine or stalked the streets of Jerusalem and Tel Aviv in quest of adventures. Their shorts were

* The one on 14 April.

bleached to a dirty yellow and their boots were worn to whiteness by the sand. Gone was the slouch hat; in its place they wore the round steel helmet, painted yellow. Those who had discarded their shirts showed skins as brown as the wood in the butts of their rifles. Their eyes were keener, their faces leaner, their lips drawn finer.

For the umpteenth time, Dooley Franks wiped an oily rag over the Bren gun and covered it carefully with an empty sandbag, and for the thousandth time Tommy Collins, his "Number Two", checked the magazines. Sergeant Lucas glanced approvingly along his Italian Breda machine-gun. Corporal Percy Gribble fingered a boil on his neck. Andy Caine amused himself with a chameleon he kept on the end of a piece of string. Dick Brett shovelled some fallen sand out of a pit. The whole platoon busied itself in a casual sort of fashion. Then, with one accord, they stopped and looked upwards.

There was a faint pulsing in the sky.

"Here the bastards come!" said Dooley.

The pulsing became a trembling, the trembling became a hum.

Then suddenly the noise of the dive-bombers burst out of the blue like a snarl.

"Here they are!" cried Dick, and pointed to the east.

They came out of the sun, black and evil-looking. Stukas. Their curiously shaped wings were like those of hawks, poised to drop on their prey. There were two flights of them. One flight peeled off, dwindling in the direction of the invisible town.

The world became all noise. Around them the Bofors guns coughed out a torrent of explosions and the sky flowered with little white pom-poms of smoke. Farther back the heavy anti-aircraft brayed hideously upwards.

One by one the black shapes came earthwards, as if they hurtled down a gigantic slide. The shrieks of their downward passage pierced the sound of exploding bombs. The earth around the Australians vomited upwards in great black clouds.

The air became a fog of yellow dust and black smoke

and through the frightful din came faintly the cries of men. Tortured ears rejected the concussions and grew dulled, hearing the bombing as muffled convulsions of the earth.

Then, as suddenly as it began, the raid ceased. The anti-aircraft fire dwindled to isolated bangs. The noise of the Stukas grew fainter and fainter in the distance. Human voices carried through the drifting smoke. One of the voices called, high-pitched and urgent:

"Stretcher-bearer!"

Forms came running through the haze.

"You all right, Dick?" Andy called.

"I'm all right," said a dazed Dick. But echoes of the bombing still thundered in his ears.

"They got a couple from Three Section."

Gradually the smoke was clearing.

Six Platoon came out of their pits to discover who were their two latest casualties. Dick clambered across the parapet and made towards the wadi where men were already gathered. Leaping across a trench, he noticed a figure huddled against its side. For a moment he thought it to be a corpse; but it was unmarked and a faint regular trembling ran through it.

"Who's that?" he called.

The figure raised its head slowly. Percy Gribble's chalk-white face stared up at him dimly. The lips moved but said nothing. Dick turned and hurried away. He felt as though in seeing what he had he was guilty of something shameful.

The two dead men had been placed on stretchers. Neither of them was well-known to Dick. One was a small grey man approaching middle age who had joined the battalion only a few days before it left Palestine. His remains formed an unnatural heap beneath a blanket through which the blood oozed. The other lay uncovered, his eyes looking up sightlessly to the sky. None of Six Platoon had known him very well either. He had been a big, fair, smiling young fellow, always pleasant, but shy. All they knew about him was that he had been a motor mechanic and had a young wife to whom he wrote every day. He was not marked, but his clothes hung from him in a thousand small tatters where the blast had ripped across his body.

Watched by the men of Six Platoon, the stretcher-bearers bore the dead men slowly down the wadi. Andy Caine gazed expressionlessly after them.

"That's that," he said.

Eric Lambert

Rommel Breaks Through

When the fog lifted we saw about thirty tanks lined up near R2—half a mile to the west of us. The tanks dispersed, four or five going to each of the posts near by. Infantry followed in parties of about sixty. As they got within range we opened up and they went to ground, but four tanks came on. Their machine-guns kept our heads down and their cannon blasted away our sandbag parapets. The sand got into our M.G.s and we spent as much time cleaning them as we did firing them, but we sniped at the infantry whenever we got a chance. Our anti-tank rifle put one light tank out of action, but it couldn't check the heavier ones, which came right up to the post. We threw hand grenades at them but these bounced off, and the best we could do was to keep the infantry from getting closer than a hundred yards.

After about an hour of this fighting the tanks withdrew, but about ten o'clock more came back. They drove through the wire and one even cruised up and down over our communication trench dropping stick bombs into it. We held their infantry off most of the morning, but eventually under cover of this attack they got into one end of the post, where the Bren crew had all been wounded. Then the Germans worked along the trench while the rest of us were still firing from the other pits. By this time more than half our chaps—we'd only had fifteen—had been killed or wounded, and the Germans got command of the post before we survivors realized what had happened. Just then our artillery began shelling it heavily and the German tanks must have been driven off. So there we were, Germans and Aussies stuck in the post together with shells falling outside. A Jerry sergeant said, "I don't know who'll be the prisoners—you or us. We'd better wait awhile until the shelling stops." When the shelling stopped more Germans came in and the sergeant said, "You're the prisoners." And we were.

Corporal R. McLeish

Rommel at the Front

Rommel in these days was always present in person when any attack went in against a point on the Tobruk perimeter—not with the staff of the attacking formation, but with the front-line troops. Often, to the annoyance of the tactical staff, he would give orders in person on the spot, changing plans to meet the situation. His subordinate commanders found this a real thorn in the flesh, and resented it bitterly.

We left the Mammoth at Advanced H.Q. and drove off in the usual little battle party—the two open cars and the armoured car, Aldinger, Berndt, and I with the General.

A report had come in that the Australians in the sector facing the Italians had been feverishly active during the night. Rommel wanted a precise picture of the situation now, and so went to see in person. As we approached the sector, we thought it completely calm and were ready to conclude that the reports of enemy activity overnight had been, as so often before, exaggerated by our allies. Even the enemy artillery in Tobruk seemed quiet.

But the puzzle was soon solved: we found not a single Italian in the whole sector, barring a few isolated artillery batteries in the rear, entirely unprotected by infantry. We peered cautiously over a rise and were met by the sight of hundreds of discarded sun-helmets gaily decorated with multi-coloured cocks feathers—Bersaglieri helmets. Otherwise, not a thing. It dawned on us that the

Australians must have "collected" the entire battalion of our allies during the night.

Rommel hurriedly ordered up a scratch assortment of troops from Acroma to act as a stop-gap in the denuded sector. Then he issued a sharp order . . . to the effect that he would, in future, expect the immediate execution of officers who showed cowardice in the face of the enemy.

Lieutenant Heinz Werner Schmidt

The Australians: An Appreciation

The Australians, who are the men our troops have had opposite them so far, are extraordinarily tough fighters. The German is more active in the attack, but the enemy stakes his life in the defence and fights to the last with extreme cunning. Our men, usually easy-going and unsuspecting, fall easily into his traps, especially as a result of their experiences in the closing stages of the European campaign.

The Australian is unquestionably superior to the German soldier: 1. In the use of individual weapons, especially as snipers. 2. In the use of ground camouflage. 3. In his gift of observation, and the drawing of correct conclusions from his observation. 4. In using every means of taking us by surprise.

Enemy snipers achieve astounding results. They shoot at anything they recognize. Several N.C.Os of the battalion have been shot through the head with the first bullet while making observations in the front line. Protruding sights in gun directors have been shot off, observation slits and loopholes have been fired on, and hit, as soon as they were seen to be in use (i.e. when the light background became dark). For this reason loopholes must be kept plugged with a wooden plug to be taken out when used so that they always show dark.

Major Bellerstedt, O.C. 2nd Battalion, 115th
Motorized Infantry Regiment

Our opponents are Englishmen and Australians. Not

trained attacking troops, but men with nerves and toughness, tireless, taking punishment with obstinacy, wonderful in defence. Ah well, the Greeks also spent ten years before Troy.

Lieutenant Schorm, diary, 6 May

Courtesies of War

We didn't know what sort of reception we'd get, as almost any truck which came near the perimeter in daylight used to get shelled. But I stood on the bonnet, holding up a big Red Cross flag and hoping for the best. They didn't fire a shot. When we were four hundred yards south of R7 we stopped the truck and I went forward with a stretcher-bearer named Keith Pope, and our padre, Father Gard, followed along behind us. I still had a flag, and when we were about two hundred and fifty yards from the post, a German stood up with another flag like mine.

He shouted what sounded like: "*Halten Minen*." We could tell we were on the edge of a minefield because we could see the bodies of thirteen of our chaps lying there. A couple of Jerries came out with an electrical mine-detector and guided a lieutenant and a doctor out to us. I told the officer we wanted to pick up our dead and wounded. He replied in English, "Very well, but only one truck and only two men at a time. You must not come closer than this. We will send your wounded out."

They brought four wounded and let the truck come up to take them away. Then they carried out the bodies of fifteen dead and helped us with those in the minefield. I told the doctor we were four short and he replied that three of our wounded had been taken away in ambulances early that morning; another taken prisoner. When the last of our dead had been brought to us, the lieutenant told me we were not to move until they were all back in the post and had taken in their flag. He went back; his men went below. He lowered his flag and I lowered mine. I saluted him, and he saluted back, but he gave me the salute of the Reichswehr, not of the Nazis. Our armistice was over.

Sergeant W. Tuit

Inside Tobruk: After Five Months

It is August of that same year. Tobruk, and its miles of trench, are quiet for the moment in the glowing dusk. The floor of the wadi is level and spacious; this is a well-known spot. It is several miles behind the Red Line, and they call it Happy Valley. Some say it should be Bomb-happy Valley, for it escapes the attention of neither dive-bombers nor Nazi guns. Perhaps, originally, it was Bomb-happy Valley. Who knows for certain? So many tales have been told around it already, for, like all places where men live, die and work together, it has its legends.

Down the wadi comes a file of men. They march slowly, out of step, and mostly in silence. The dull clink of their weapons is clear in the evening air. At first their faces look all the same, burnt deep, with several days of beard, their eyes red-rimmed with the whites gleaming, cheeks hollowed, lips straight and grave. Their shirts and shorts are stiff like canvas with mingled dust and sweat, and streaked again with the sweat of that day. Their legs are bare and burnt almost black; their boots are worn pure white. Some who still have them wear their tunics, for the air will soon be deathly cold; and their headgear is, as before, motley: a steel helmet, a crumpled slouch hat and an Italian pith helmet. Their packs, haversacks and ammunition pouches have become as white as their boots, and their weapons gleam dully in the spots where they have worn, for they have had five months of use.

They are a strange spectacle. They were once ordinary men, but now they do not belong among ordinary men; in the city they would seem like a vision. Their sameness is not only that of their dark brown faces, their silence, their fatigue, for they have shared together, for many months, the most abysmal, the most terrible of human emotions; each has in turn, and in his own way, been a hero, a panting coward, an entity with a mind crying its anguish at death. And while each has shown to his fellows most of his deepest self, each hugs to himself, grimly and pitiably, what is left. No one of them will ever be quite the same again.

As he reaches a turn in the wadi, Henry Gilbertson stops, turns round and says, "B Company—halt!"

They gather in close, for it has become very dark.

Eric Lambert

Bugs—Anti-British

All day we lay in a dug-out just big enough for three Diggers and me stretched out. Four feet above us was a roof of corrugated iron resting on sleepers and over that sandbags, earth and bits of camel-bush, which made the top of the dug-out just one more piece of desert to German snipers scanning the level plain from five hundred yards away. The late afternoon sun beat down on the sandbags. We were clammy with sweat. The wind died away and dust stopped drifting in through the small air vent and the narrow low doorway that led to the crawl trench outside. The air was heavy with dust, cigarette smoke and the general fug we'd been breathing in and out for the past thirteen hours. We waited for darkness when we could stretch our legs and fill our lungs with fresh, cool air, and the troops could crack at the Hun who had been lying all day in his dug-out, too.

. . . I woke about seven in the evening and started to scratch. I seemed to be itching all over—the itchiness of being dirty. You get that way after the flies and fleas have been at you all day. You don't know whether you've been bitten or not, and you just scratch as a matter of routine. In the far corner Mick was doing a bit of hunting. He had his shirt off. Seriously, deliberately he ran his thumb nail under the seam and a slow smile of success spread across his face. "Got you, you little—— That makes four less, anyway!"

Chester Wilmot

Bugs—Anti-German

Nothing new. The heat's frightful, night time as well as day time. Liquidated four bugs. My bed is now standing in tins filled with water and I hope the nights will be a little more restful from now on. Some of the others are having a bad time with fleas. They've left me alone so far.

Rommel

The Lost Men

We have immense fun over "the lost men". Wherever you go in the desert, you come across little pockets of men camped by their vehicles: they are invariably unshaven, cheerful, and brewing up tea in a petrol tin. Similarly they can *always* tell you which way to go ("Y Track, sir? Straight on till you get to the Rifleman's Grave; can't miss it, sir"; or: "Barrel Track, mate? W'y you just come from it.") Nine times out of ten they give you the directions wrong. They appear to belong to nobody, and seem perfectly contented to camp out in the blue. Arthur has now decided that they are all deserters from Wavell's first campaign. He is planning for both of us to go "missing" one day. Then we will ensconce ourselves in a jolly little camp, and spend our days waving people in the direction of the Diamond Track, or the Gebel Something-or-other.

C.O., 1st Battalion, Black Watch

The Navy Runs In Supplies

Then above the roar of engines, wind and sea, from the rear gun-platform an officer shouts through a megaphone, "Stand by. Action stations." We wait again. Then: "Stand by, Enemy aircraft."

Suddenly we're snatching at the nearest rail or bulkhead as the destroyer heels over in a wild zigzag and seems to leap forward. On the slippery deck the cargo slides crashing into the scuppers and spray drenches everything.

Above the turmoil that voice again: "Stand by. Blitz barrage." Behind us a great white swath of wash is even more tell-tale than before, but they'll have seen us now and the only way to trick them is to zigzag. I look across at *Havock*—a great stream of black smoke is pouring from her funnels. Then we hear the bomber's drone and *Havock*'s guns stab the darkness with red flashes. She rolls over in a ninety-degree turn and a hundred yards or so ahead of her a great white water-spout tells us that the Stuka has missed its mark.

Out of the darkness ahead we see two pin-points of light, the harbour lights of Tobruk, shielded from the air but visible to us. We slacken speed. There is no wash now, and a welcome cloud cloaks the moon and other bombers cannot see us.

But they are over Tobruk and are going for the harbour. We can hear the muffled crack of the ack-ack guns and see the flashes of bursting shells high in the sky; only the "heavies" are firing, so apparently the bombers are well up.

We slip in between the lights, past the black ghosts of wrecks, under the lee of the white sepulchre of a town. The ack-ack is still speeding the raider home, but another is coming in—lower. The Bofors are firing too, so it must be well under ten thousand feet. But we have no time to think of the fireworks display above us. As *Decoy* stops moving two barges and two launches come alongside. Troops clamber over the side, pitching their kitbags ahead of them. Unloading parties swarm aboard and slide ammunition down wooden chutes into one barge, while the rest of the cargo is dumped anyhow into the other. As soon as the troops are off, the crew start bringing wounded aboard in stretchers.

They are getting a warm farewell. One stick of bombs screams down on the south shore of the harbour; the next is closer—in the water five hundred yards away. The old hands continued working, unworried, but some of the new ones, like us, pause momentarily, shrinking down behind the destroyer's after-screen. From the man with the megaphone comes a sharp rebuke—"What are you stopping for? Those bloody bombs are nothing to do with you."

Chester Wilmot

Winston Churchill to General Morshead

To General Morshead from Prime Minister England. The whole Empire is watching your steadfast and spirited defence of this important outpost of Egypt with gratitude and admiration.

While Tobruk held on, Rommel's main force drove on to the east. Wavell's counter-attack in June on the Egyptian frontier was a failure. There the 88 mm. A.A. gun established its formidable reputation in an anti-tank role. General Auchinleck assumed command of the British forces, and the Eighth Army as such was born.

In constructing our positions at Halfaya and on Hill 208 great skill was shown in building in batteries of 88 mm. guns for anti-tank work, so that with the barrels horizontal there was practically nothing to be seen above ground. I had great hopes of the effectiveness of this arrangement.

Rommel

On the second day, 16 June, thrust and counter-thrust around Capuzzo ended in stalemate. The enemy still held Halfaya, and twenty miles south-west in a series of running skirmishes his 5th Tank Regiment, with superior numbers and fire-power, forced 7 Armoured Brigade back across the frontier. Rommel mustered every tank he could to press home his advantage. One column, with seventy-five tanks of the 5th Regiment, carried its outflanking movement twenty miles into Egypt south of Halfaya. Simultaneously another column fought its way through

nearer the coast towards Halfaya. Threatened by these
two moves, the Anglo-Indian forces, which had held
Capuzzo for nearly two days, had to withdraw, leaving
on the battlefield a large number of disabled, but
recoverable, British tanks.

It had been a disastrous three days. Captured German
documents (secret German military reports and not
propaganda) allege that 143 British tanks were destroyed.
This was a slight exaggeration, for the actual British losses
were 123. However G.H.Q. admitted later that "two-
thirds of the British armour was out of action" after the
battle, and it did not claim that the Germans had lost
more than fifty tanks. The battle had been decided by
two factors—a new German anti-tank weapon and
Rommel's bold handling of his armour. The weapon was
the 88 mm. A.A. gun, used for the first time (on the
frontier at least) in an anti-tank role. Rommel had only
twelve of these, but, if German official documents are
to be believed, they knocked out seventy-nine British
tanks—one for every twenty rounds they fired.

At the two German frontier positions that held, eight
of these guns destroyed thirty-six British tanks. The tanks,
firing a 2-pounder with an effective range of eight hundred
yards at most, were no match for the 88 mm. with its
20-pound shell that could knock out an 'I' tank at a range
of a mile. In these positions the 88 mm. guns were dug
in flush with the ground and so well camouflaged that
the British tank crews did not even know what had hit
them.

MALTA

*Throughout the war in North Africa, the island of
Malta was a constant thorn in the side of the Axis. The
outcome of the desert battle depended largely on the rate
of reinforcement achieved by both sides, and air and
submarine attacks from Malta on the convoys supplying
Rommel were a serious hindrance to him. The Italians*

*had been attacking Malta to little effect since June 1940,
but in January 1941 the Luftwaffe joined in, trying to
destroy Malta's offensive capacity and starve it out by
attacks on the island itself and on the Allied convoys
supplying it. The crisis of the battle came in the spring
of 1942, when Malta's strength was almost neutralized
and its power to resist greatly weakened.*

The Luftwaffe Attacks

The drone of the bombers was getting louder now as
they approached Gozo Island, just north of Malta.
Squadrons of Me. 109s could be seen spreading out to
the left and to the right, slightly above. Much higher up
in the clear, bright blue, a coop top flashed in the sun
revealing the presence of a top cover of enemy fighters.
From this higher group two squadrons took more definite
shape and, breaking away from the others, advanced
towards the island at a very fast clip. Over St. Paul's Bay,
near the north tip of Malta, they spread out wide into
pairs, and in that position roared over the island at some
ten thousand feet.

. . . . More guns barked near St. Paul's Bay. The flak
burst in among the leading bombers, and some of the
bursts were white. More ack-ack batteries cracked and
in a few seconds all the guns of that part of the island
were slamming away. Up in the sky the white bursts were
being outnumbered by brown-black ones, their closeness
intensifying the speed of the enemy planes that were now
like groaning spiders crawling through peppered blue.

Then the gaggle began to split.

One wave turned east and flew out over the sea. The
second swung west and crossed the pilots' line of vision,
while the third kept on for the centre of the island. Now
the three prongs resembled a giant leaf-rake in the sky.

. . . . From one of the leading bombers in the centre
group a jet of white smoke spouted from the starboard
engine, followed by black. The maimed Junkers turned
to its left and ploughed into another. There was a

simultaneous flash that snuffed out like an altar candle. The pressure of the explosion chewed and pushed at the waves of black flak ahead of it, encircling and rolling up wave upon wave until suddenly the whole of it burst into a gigantic ball of flame, and the enemy bombers shattered into a million pieces and were no more than the flak. Two Spitfires dived through the murk, zoomed up again and were lost to sight. Me.s weaved back and forth, some in the flak, but most of them above it.

. . . . The east wave came in from the sea and hit Sliema, Valetta and the harbour first. The 88s held their incredibly vertical dives till they were about four thousand feet from the earth, then, synchronized by gyroscope with the bomb release, were pulling up in a back-breaking climb, twisting and weaving crazily towards the sea again. Meanwhile, others dived and bombs plummeted into the ground, and the dust and sand spouted like geysers. In a few minutes that part of the island, nearly eight miles away, was going up and down, while the rumbling crept along and through the earth like an approaching earthquake, the tremor reaching the feet of the watching pilots. The centre wave was starting its dive. The west group was turning and diving. Then all hell broke loose. . . . A thousand flashes of orange, red and purple were pipping the ground and the dust rose and spread to blot out the far side of the island. Overhead, the west wave was screaming in, the whine of the brakes so close now, unhindered, unopposed. Aircraft, near enough to see the big black crosses edged in white, were milling in, mad, anxious, in ones and twos, trying not to be the first, nor yet the last.

. . . . And the first bombs were leaving the bellies of the crazy diving planes of the west wave; strings of small bombs dribbling end over end, big bombs, black and shooting down in their tantalizing arc. [Wallace] had seen many bombs drop before, heard a good many more, but never did he realize that they dropped with such ferocity, such complete certainty and yet with no apparent control, falling like loose shale from an unpropped mine just before it finally caves in. There were big bombs, singly and in pairs, small ones in strings, all black, screaming and whistling in that hideous flat curve across the hill town of Rabat, over M'dima, the ancient capital of Malta, the vicious arc ending at the foot of the hill which was Takali aerodrome, the whistling straining, like high winds over iced wires in winter, all ending in rumbling explosions.

Charles MacLean

The Ordeal of *Penelope*

Thursday, 26 March 1942

Ju. 87s were employed for the first time on the Grand Harbour area. H.M.S. *Penelope,* lying at Hamilton Wharf, her bows south, was damaged forward and aft by near misses, causing the flooding of all compartments below the two foremost mess decks and a number of compartments aft, and also putting A and B turrets out of action. The forward near miss lifted all the decks forward, resulting in the straining of most of the watertight doors.

The after near miss caused severe blast-damage to the after superstructure, waist screens and watertight doors.

. . . . The keel plate had been bent upwards for a distance of thirty feet in a large dent six to eight feet deep. At the centre of this dent, the keel plate and lower plate were cracked across for a distance of twelve feet.

It was decided that *Penelope* must sail as soon as possible.

A scheme of first-aid repairs was devised. This subsequently proved thoroughly efficient and capable of rapid execution.

It was estimated that the repairs would take four weeks if too many raids did not take place.

Saturday, 4 April

This was a black day. From 11.15 a.m. to 7.40 p.m. heavy and sustained attacks were made on *Penelope*.

In the first raid a near miss damaged the dock caisson, and the dock started to leak. The dock pump was put out of action and only got going again at 11 p.m.

Another near miss struck the dockyard wall on the port side of *Penelope,* abreast of the quarter deck. This bomb hurled great piles of masonry and debris on to the quarter deck, the 4-inch gun deck and boat deck. Other bombs blew large stones from adjacent buildings on to the upper deck. So after "dinner" it was a matter of all hands to remove the rock garden from the ship.

It was during the last attack on this day that a bomb hit *Penelope*'s port after brow and exploded just beneath it. Many hundreds of small holes were made in the port side aft in all compartments. The port outer shaft was punctured with three large and several smaller holes.

Some damage was done to the propellers. Fires broke out in the Captain's store and in some of the port after cabins.

This extra damage entailed a lot more repair work. I sent an appeal to the Army for welders. A prompt response was made and five sappers, qualified welders, joined the ship at 9.30 a.m. on Easter Sunday.

They worked with great skill and endurance.

Easter Sunday, 5 April

Another black day. Three heavy attacks on *Penelope* were made at 7.55 a.m., 11.25 a.m. and 5.05 p.m. *Penelope* made a signal to the Vice-Admiral, Malta: "We take a poor view of Hitler's Easter eggs." The Vice-Admiral replied: "I agree. They are not even like the curate's." The raids in each case were made by large formations attacking in waves. Each raid lasted about an hour. A huge bomb hit the dock abreast of the starboard side of the bridge. Large blocks of masonry and debris were thrown up as high as the bridge, which looked like the Mappin Terrace. The direct route between the ammunition lighter and the ship was blocked. To add to the difficulties a lighter with five hundred rounds was hit by a bomb and another lighter had to be quickly

loaded. The dock was flooding rapidly, the water rose
to twenty-one feet and there was a danger of the ship
coming off the blocks. When the last raider had passed,
the dockyard electricians gave us the blessed news that
the pumps would soon be working. At 7.24 p.m. I
reported to the Vice-Admiral: "Pump is working again
and water has been lowered by eighteen inches—Atta
pump."

Wednesday, 8 April

At 3.45 a.m. the hands commenced ammunitioning and
working dock machinery.

At 8.15 a two-hour mass attack on *Penelope* began,
and a bomb hit the starboard brow, making hundreds
of holes in the starboard side forward. Only the most
serious could be patched in the time and all the remainder
had to be plugged with wooden pegs (the ship looked
rather like a porcupine when she sailed).

There was a total of seven separate and heavy raids
that day. The A.A. ammunition situation was acute
throughout the day. The guns were firing 4-inch shells
faster than they could be fused and embarked.

At the end of daylight raiding there was no 4-inch and
very little close-range ammunition on board for the sea
passage.

It had been intended to put a lighter with five hundred
tons fuel alongside, but there were so many delays that
at 4 p.m. I decided to wait no longer but to get the ship
out of the dock and alongside Canteen Wharf to oil. This
move was a tricky business as the tugs had been
sunk—but Mr. Murphy, the pilot, handled the ship with
skill.

The enemy redoubled his efforts and the fifth and sixth
raids were intense. I am convinced that it was in the main
the resolute firing of the ship's guns which defeated the
enemy's aim and saved the ship. During the sixth raid
the Gunnery Officer was killed. I myself received a flesh
wound in an undignified place, and had to go to the
dockyard dressing station.

This left Lieutenant Hamilton temporarily in command and in control of the guns.

I have in previous reports remarked on the outstanding ability of Lieutenant Hamilton.

In the course of this last raid he was at his best—fought off the raid magnificently and then dealt brilliantly with the ammunition situation.

The ship had no 4-inch ammunition left and we were due to sail in two hours.

Captain A. D. Nicholl, H.M.S. Penelope

After successfully dodging further air attacks, Penelope *reached Gibraltar on 10 April.*

AFRICA: THE PENDULUM SWINGS BACK

Meanwhile, throughout the summer and autumn of 1941, both armies in North Africa built up their forces. It appeared that the British would be ready to strike first, and in fact the Eighth Army under General Cunningham attacked on 18 November, with initial success. For the first four days the two Corps—XXX and XIII—fought brilliantly, but trouble followed at Sidi Rezegh.

"It has come in a way we did not expect," wrote a German officer on Afrika Korps H.Q., "and there's hell let loose. On the evening of the 18th, while I was still continuing my afternoon sleep, there came a telephone call summoning me to pack my kit immediately. Position: the enemy is attacking with very strong forces in the southern sector." Actually, by this time the leading column was near El Gobi—fifty miles west of the frontier.

Sidi Rezegh: The Battle Begins

I woke the next morning to the certain knowledge that there would be fierce and desperate battles all day. Without my own bedding, with a crew who were not yet used to my ways and fads, almost smothered by the fug under the tarpaulin which had been necessary to keep off the rain which beat down all night, I could not have been less ready for instant and exhausting action. My beard was at the most uncomfortable stage of its growth, my clothes were damp and foul-smelling, my face and hands cold and numb. I left the operator to complete the net and walked over to Kinnaird's tank. I was such a picture of misery and despondence that Kinnaird, despite his many anxieties, grinned and said, "Cheer up, Tony. You're still alive. It could be worse. But you've come just at the right moment. Here are the others, and these are the orders. 7 Armoured and the Support Group are already being attacked from the north-west. We have got to get to them. But as far as is known both 15 and 21 Panzer are between us and them. So we shall have a bloody battle before we can even give them any help. Right—we move off in five minutes."

Within a few minutes of starting the reports began to come in, all telling the same story of tanks and anti-tank guns on the escarpments to the east and south-west of Sidi Rezegh, preventing us from moving to join the desperate battle on the airfield.

All morning the battles swayed forwards and backwards round the airfield and the high ground to the north. While 7 Armoured and the Support Group beat off the first attacks, we and 22 Armoured fought to get through to them.

I lost all count of time, and only the growing aches of my empty stomach and the parched dryness of my mouth indicated the passage of the hours. I lost, too, all count of the casualties in my squadron and the losses which each tank claimed to have inflicted on the enemy. The early battles were fought in the mist of the damp of the sodden ground evaporating in the sun. Later a dark pall of smoke and dust overhung the whole battlefield, hiding friend and foe alike. In the turmoil and confusion it was miraculous that more mistakes were not made in shooting against friends. Gradually we pushed the

Germans farther and farther back, with the loss of many
tanks on both sides. My own tank was penetrated by a
shot which spent itself in the effort of piercing the armour
and only fell to the floor at my driver's feet, doing no
damage. There was a momentary relief of the tension
when, referring to the many rumours of the desperate
methods the Germans were reputed to be resorting to
in their search for metals, he remarked, "Not bad for
bloody church railings, I calls it."

Cyril Joly

Confusion

By now it was pretty dark and we joined up with the
Brigadier (Davy) and some of our tanks and most of
our N.H. guns and huddled together in a "night leaguer". As we collected, I looked back and could see our
foes doing likewise about one and a half miles to two
miles behind us, silhouetted against the remaining lights.
We made our usual type of huddle, with trucks inside
and our guns, etc. on the perimeter . . . I had no
overcoat—nothing but what I stood in; same for Dick
except, poor devil, he was in shorts and a jersey. It was
horribly cold by then. We were three windy cats all the
time and kept walking out to listen. We could hear distant
sounds of a lot of tanks moving, but otherwise quiet—a
good many Verey lights going up from the foe. About
9.30 we heard the unmistakable noise of tanks, so we
all took post on our guns, etc. One could see two hundred
to three hundred yards in the moonlight. First came a
single tank about one hundred and fifty yards on our
north: when it had just passed us it fired a Verey light
towards us but I don't think it saw us for its own dust.
A few minutes later about twelve tanks followed the first
and again fired a light. This waiting was awful, and we
all breathed a sigh as they passed. This lot turned south
after passing us. Then a number more approached,
obviously on a line to meet us. Not a nice moment. Before
they arrived a truck stopped about sixty yards away and

a man approached us with a tommy-gun. A party of four led by John Cookson went to meet and challenge him. He was a German and we hauled him in. His truck drove away towards the oncoming tanks and I think warned them. Anyhow, a few minutes later they appeared alongside us and I heard our Brigadier shout, "If they fire a light, shoot." They fired a light which fell into our middle. Then each party let fly with everything which would bear on our foe. My and Dick's guns were on the far corner from them and we could not shoot.

We all started our engines and got going. Our truck would not start. We tried for about twenty seconds but "no go". The Sergeant-Major shouted, "Let's get on another"—so we hopped out and jumped on a passing Bofors gun and tractor and rode out of the hotch-potch, everyone going off in every kind of direction. We went like hell for about two miles. I was clinging to the back of the tractor expecting to be jolted off under the gunwheels. Actually I scrambled on to the top. After about two miles we came on a stopped truck which was Ted Key's. One of our guns drew alongside. So Ted, the Sergeant-Major and I got on to it and, in company with our Bofors friends, continued south. The afternoon's push of the German tanks and column had been south of us and towards the east, i.e. behind us. As we went we could see their lights on each side of us and had to keep a sharp look out in case we bumped into one of their night leaguers.

Captain W. Williamson

Brewed Up

"Driver, halt," I ordered. "Gunner, 2-pounder— traverse left—on—tank—German Mark III—eight five zero yards. Fire." I watched Basset carefully turn the range-drum to the right range, saw him turn to his telescope and aim, noticed out of the corner of my eye that King was ready with the next round, and then the tank jolted slightly with the shock of the gun firing. Through the

smoke and dust and the spurt of flame I watched intently
through my binoculars the trace of the shot in flight. It
curved upwards slightly and almost slowly, and then
seemed to plunge swiftly towards the target. There was the
unmistakable dull glow of a strike of steel on steel. "Hit,
Basset! Good shot! Fire again," I called. Another shot and
another hit, and I called, "Good shot; but the bastard
won't brew."

As I spoke I saw the flame and smoke from the
German's gun, which showed that he was at last
answering. In the next instant all was chaos. There was
a clang of steel on the turret front and a blast of flame
and smoke from the same place, which seemed to spread
into the turret, where it was followed by another dull
explosion. The shock-wave which followed swept past me,
still standing in the cupola, singed my hands and face and
left me breathless and dazed. I looked down into the
turret. It was a shambles. The shot had penetrated the
front of the turret just in front of King, the loader. It had
twisted the machine-gun out of its mounting. It, or a
jagged piece of the torn turret, had then hit the round
that King had been holding ready—had set it on fire.
The explosion had wrecked the wireless, torn King's head
and shoulders from the rest of his body and started a
fire among the machine-gun boxes stowed on the floor.
Smoke and the acrid fumes of cordite filled the turret.
On the floor, licking menacingly near the main
ammunition stowage bin, there were innumerable small
tongues of flame. If these caught on, the charge in the
rounds would explode, taking the turret and all in it with
it.

I felt too dazed to move. My limbs seemed to be
anchored, and I wondered vaguely how long I had been
standing there and what I ought to do next. It was a
miracle that the explosion had left me unharmed, though
shaken. I wondered what had happened to Basset and
bent into the cupola to find out. Shielded behind the gun
and the recoil guard-shield, Basset, too, had escaped the
main force of the explosion. The face that turned to look

at me was blackened and scorched and the eyes, peering at me from the black background, seemed to be unnaturally large and startlingly terrified. For once Basset's good humour had deserted him, and the voice which I heard was shaking with emotion.

"Let's get out of 'ere, sir. Not much we can do for King, poor bastard!—'e's 'ad it and some. An' if we 'ang around we'll catch a packet too. For Gawd's sake let's —— off quick."

At last I awoke from my daze. "O.K., Basset. Tell Newman to bale out, and be bloody quick about it."

As Basset bent to shout at the driver the tank was struck again, but this time on the front of the hull. When the smoke and dust cleared, Basset bent again to shout at Newman. A moment later he turned a face now sickened with horror and disgust and blurted out:

" 'E's ad it too, sir. It's took 'alf 'is chest away. For ——'s sake let's get out of 'ere." In a frenzy of panic he tried to climb out of the narrow cupola past me, causing me to slip and delaying us both. Through my mind there flashed the thought that the German would still continue to fire until he knew that the tank was knocked out, and as yet no flames would be visible from the outside. Inside the turret there was now an inferno of fire.

Without knowing how I covered the intervening distance, I found myself lying in a small hollow some twenty yards from my stricken tank, watching the first thin tongues of flame and black smoke emerging from the turret top.

Cyril Joly

First Round to Rommel

The wide plain south of Sidi Rezegh was now a sea of dust, haze and smoke. Visibility was poor and many British tanks and guns were able to break away to the south and east without being caught. But a great part of the enemy force still remained inside. Twilight came, but the battle was still not over. Hundreds of burning vehicles, tanks and guns lit up the field of that *Totensonntag*. It was long after midnight before we could get any sort of picture of the day's events, organize our force, count our losses and gains and form an appreciation of the general situation upon which the next day's operations would depend. The most important results of the battle were the elimination of the direct threat to the Tobruk front, the destruction of a large part of the enemy armour and the damage to enemy morale caused by the complete ruin of his plans.

Rommel

At about 10.30 hours on the 24th Rommel put himself at the head of 21 Panzer Division, and drove off at a furious pace. Late that afternoon he reached the Wire,* with the whole Afrika Korps stretched out behind him over forty miles of desert, and 7 Armoured Division and 1 S.A. Division stampeding in all directions. Rommel's bold move had thrown 30 Corps into complete disorder, and according to British accounts General Cunningham wanted to retire at once into Egypt. . . . But very fortunately for the British, General Auchinleck had arrived at Eighth Army Headquarters; he disagreed with Cunningham, and ordered the continuation of the offensive. This was certainly one of the great decisions of the war; Auchinleck's fighting spirit and shrewd strategic insight had saved the "Crusader" battle and much else besides.

General von Mellenthin

General Auchinleck was convinced that his attack should be pushed home in spite of the initial reverse of Sidi Rezegh and Rommel's counter-stroke. He replaced General Cunningham with General Ritchie, and the offensive continued. For a few days each side struggled for the advantage in confused fighting, then the British

* The Frontier (Ed.)

*once more went forward. On the night of 25/26 November
the New Zealanders captured Sidi Rezegh. Tobruk was on
the point of relief.*

The Wandering General

The Mammoth, now carrying all the most senior
officers of the Panzer Group, drove on to the wire fence.
Unfortunately, no way through could be found, and it
was impossible to make one. Finally, Rommel grew
impatient. "I'll take over myself," he said, and dismissed
the A.D.C., who had been directing the vehicle up till
then. But this time even Rommel's legendary sense of
direction did not help. To make matters worse, they were
in an area completely dominated by the enemy. Indian
dispatch riders buzzed to and fro past the Mammoth,
British tanks moved up forward and American-built
lorries ground their way through the desert. None of them
had any suspicion that the highest officers of the German-
Italian Panzer Group were sitting in a captured command
vehicle, often only two or three yards away. The ten
officers and five men spent a restless night.

During the days that followed, Rommel continued to
drive from one unit to another, usually through the British
lines, in order to deal with the continually recurring crises.
On one occasion he went into a New Zealand hospital,
which was still occupied by the enemy. By this time no
one really knew who was captor and who captive—except
Rommel, who was in no doubt. He inquired if anything
was needed, promised the British medical supplies and
drove on unhindered. He also crossed an air strip
occupied by the British, and was several times chased
by British vehicles, but always escaped.

The Relief of Tobruk: 27 November 1941

One more determined concerted heave would do it. The
honour of making the junction went to the 19th N.Z.
Battalion and a squadron of the 44th R.T.R., commanded

by an Irish giant of the Royal Tanks, Major "Stump" Gibbon. Led by seventeen Valentines rumbling along through the night, the 19th Battalion made excellent progress. Unseen tanks, moving at night, are demoralizing enough, because of the noise; but when backed up by determined bayonets, the attack becomes terrifying. German resistance collapsed like a house of cards; and the junction with the men of Essex and, most appropriately, more Valentines of Royal Tanks, finally took place on Ed Duda at one o'clock in the small hours of 27 November. The news, awaited so anxiously throughout the free nations, flashed round the world. Nowhere was it so welcome as in the Anzac countries. The Australians had held Tobruk, tenaciously and with typical offensive spirit for many months of hard fighting and harder living; one battalion still remained to share in the "fight out". And the New Zealanders had finally forged the link on Ed Duda. Significantly, both thrusts were supported by determined Valentine crews of the Royal Tanks and good gunners.

If the 19th Battalion got the limelight, 6 N.Z. Brigade made an equally solid contribution by clearing their area in stubborn night fighting. The New Zealanders now occupied a big bulge stuck on the end of the Tobruk corridor. The corridor provided access to the base supplies and facilities; limited access only, because through movement was restricted to night and hampered by minefields. So into Tobruk went New Zealand wounded and Army Service Corps units; and also 13 Corps Headquarters (General Godwin-Austen is credited with announcing his entry by the signal: "Tobruk and I both relieved").

Brigadier Clifton

The Afrika Korps withdrew, the British followed. Rommel first stood for five days at Gazala, and then pulled back again. Benghazi was occupied by the Royal Dragoons on Christmas Eve; the garrisons left far behind at Bardia and Halfaya were overcome a few days later.

*On 7 January 1942 Rommel withdrew to his old lair at
El Agheila on the Bay of Sirte. Two weeks later, on 21
January, he started to advance again against the over-
extended Eighth Army. He pushed on for a month,
regaining most of his lost ground as far as Gazala, where
an equilibrium was established until May.*

THE SECRET OF THE AFRIKA KORPS

The terrific armoured battles in the Western Desert
cannot be understood without some reference to the
weapons and equipment on both sides. Contrary to the
generally accepted view, the German tanks did not have
any advantage in quality over their opponents, and in
numbers we were always inferior.

To what, then, are we to ascribe the brilliant successes
of the Afrika Korps? To my mind, our victories depended
on three factors—the superior quality of our anti-tank
guns, our systematic practice of the principle of *Co-
operation of Arms,* and—last but not least—our tactical
methods. While the British restricted their 3.7 in. anti-
aircraft gun (a very powerful weapon) to an anti-aircraft
role, we employed our 88 mm. gun to shoot at tanks as
well as aeroplanes. In November 1941 we only had
thirty-five 88s, but moving in close touch with our Panzers
these guns did terrific execution among the British tanks.
Moreover, our high-velocity 50 mm. anti-tank gun was
far superior to the British 2-pounder, and batteries of
these guns always accompanied our tanks in action. Our
field artillery, also, was trained to co-operate with the
Panzers. In short, a German Panzer division was a highly flexible formation of all arms, which always relied on
artillery in attack or defence. In contrast, the British
regarded the anti-tank gun as a defensive weapon, and
they failed to make adequate use of their powerful field
artillery, which should have been taught to eliminate our
anti-tank guns.

General von Mellenthin

THE SECOND RETREAT

On 27 May 1942 Rommel attacked. The British line extended from Gazala (held by 1 South African Division) in the north, to Bir Hacheim, held by the Free French in the south. Rommel raced below Bir Hacheim and swung up into the centre of the Eighth Army. The latter's defensive positions behind the outflanked Gazala Line, notably the Knightsbridge Box, suffered heavy attacks, which were at this stage repulsed. Rommel next pierced the Gazala Line from its rear, and built up a bridgehead in an area known as "The Cauldron".

Gazala: The Knightsbridge Box

The Knightsbridge Box was selected by the O.C. 2nd R.H.A. as a "pivot of manoeuvre". The term conveyed little to any of us, involving as it did a technique which was as foreign to our mobile methods as is an anchorage to a fleet in action. The orders were to select and prepare a defensive position to be contained by the 2nd R.H.A., C Battery Northumberland Hussars (Anti-Tank), two troops of the 43rd L.A.A. Regiment, the 3rd Coldstream Guards and one company of the 2nd Scots Guards.

The area given for choice of position was one of fifty square miles, and here had to be formed a long-stop somewhere behind the Gazala Line, which was a string of similar positions between the sea and Bir Hacheim. The area chosen was a small plateau. It could only be overlooked from a distance and could not be looked into. A shallow depression in the middle gave bare cover for the troops of I Battery commanded by Major Blacker and L Battery commanded by Major Livingstone-Learmonth. After three days' reconnaissance this small saucer was discovered about six miles east of the centre of the Gazala Line. It was pear-shaped, about half a mile long and a quarter of a mile wide, but it possessed the outstanding advantage that the gun positions and the "observation" were in one and the same area and could be defended simultaneously by the troops available. Standing alone on this very ordinary looking bit of sand one wondered at the circumstances which made it necessary to enclose it in such a way as to prohibit its occupants all possibility of manoeuvre. It seemed like anchoring battle-ships in mid-ocean. Such thoughts were forgotten as the battle developed with increasing intensity around it—sometimes nearer, sometimes farther, closing in as the days went by—until at the end it became a fortress of the first importance, at least in one's own eyes, when the chances of escape had diminished and all guns were firing "charge one".

On 26 May rumour on a high level was offering odds against a German attack. The following morning, with admirable daring and efficiency, Rommel turned our southern flank, south of Bir Hacheim, with tanks in force. After a long march, he overran our outpost screen and surprised an armoured brigade at breakfast. It was a bad start for us. There followed some exciting days. First, the attempts of the enemy to attack and overrun our position. Heavy enemy shelling was accompanied by infantry attacks which were repeatedly repelled by our fire. Our observation was good, especially to the south, where the attacks were made, and a life-time of "practice" shooting could be fulfilled in an hour. The attacks were soon followed by enemy tanks, who approached up the steep escarpment to the north. These were accounted for by the Northumberland Hussars, who used their new guns to great effect.

Brigadier L. Bolton

The First Check

After a peaceful breakfast on 27 May, a great deal of gun fire developed to the south and the noise of battle approached rapidly. I very soon got orders to proceed to "The Bobble", a feature just west of the Box on which the 2nd R.H.A. O.P. was situated and which it was deemed important to hold. I went with my party of four

6-pounder guns, which we knew very little about and had never fired. On my way I put up an old fox which cheered me considerably: later he was to return past my truck as the battle got too close to be healthy.

My first view of the enemy was when about sixty-five tanks appeared in a cloud of smoke and dust over a crest about sixteen hundred yards distant. My guns opened fire—one of them later claimed a hit—but it soon became obvious that we had no chance of stemming the avalanche, and, after a lot of waving of blue flags—the guns carried no wireless—I was ordered to make my way back to the Box. This manoeuvre was accomplished without loss, although one gun had been put out of action by a solid shot earlier on. As we skirted round the north side of the Box, under the Escarpment, we fired a lot of rounds at about twelve hundred yards into this mass of German tanks and vehicles, which continued north and sat on a ridge about two miles from the Box. The advance tanks and guns were followed by an enormous quantity of "soft" vehicles, which for the rest of the day made an excellent target for the R.H.A. batteries. Inside the Box it was hardly a picnic; shells from guns and tanks landed at very regular intervals, but, strange to say, our losses were nil; our strenuous efforts to get underground more than paid a dividend.

About 6 p.m. a German tank attack developed on our front, the tanks climbing the Escarpment, halting on meeting the minefield, getting turret-down and raking the whole area with machine-gun fire, very unpleasant for those being shot at, but remarkably ineffective. We had two guns put out of action temporarily, and two portees burnt, but when the attack was eventually beaten off, the fires in the Box indicated that the other units had suffered more than we had.

Major R. I. G. Taylor

As our position proved for the present impregnable to the enemy, Rommel decided to ignore it. Thousands of German vehicles parked within easy range of our guns, but as a rule we had neither the time nor the ammunition to engage them. Rommel came himself to see, and his lone tank, stationary at about three thousand six hundred yards' range, made good shooting for one of the L Battery O.P.s. The tank was visited frequently by German staff cars and Storch aircraft, and the O.P. officer "split" a twenty-five yard bracket on it several times, but this only made it move a few hundred yards each time.

Brigadier L. Bolton

British armoured forces counter-attacked, but in spite of their new tanks suffered severely at the hands of a more skilful commander.

Grants in Action

Now a shiver went through me. From out of the dip emerged rank after rank of the new tanks—a good sixty in all. They came at us with every muzzle blazing.

I got my right gun into action. It stopped one tank. Several others were burning. But the bulk of them came on relentlessly. What was wrong with my left gun, I wondered? It was silent, its muzzle still drooping to the ground. I leaped from my trench despite the stuff whistling all round and raced to the gun.

Two of the crew were sprawled on the ground. The breech of the gun was shattered. The loader lay beside a wheel, bleeding from a machine-gun bullet in the chest. "Water, water," he gasped.

A fresh salvo burst beside the gun. Tanks were obviously attacking it at almost point-blank range. To stop there meant death.

I dropped prone, and tried to cradle the head of the wounded man in my arms.

He shook his head at me.

"I'll carry you to my trench—there's water there," I shouted in his ear. He shook his head again. To my consternation, he heaved himself to his feet and half stumbled, half ran towards my slit-trench.

Now the tanks were right on top of the front lines in the sector to my right. I scrambled back towards my trench. Muller was not there. I dragged the wounded gun-number halfway into the hole with me. My Italian water-bottle, half-full of coffee, lay there, and I thrust it into the man's shaking hand. He drank greedily, and then sagged back, dead. His legs dangled in the hole; his torso lay twisted on the rim of it.

Shell-bursts were now erupting all round. Was I alone out here now? As I wondered this, there came a reply from behind, where Sergeant Weber was firing my third gun. He pumped out shell after shell. But there was little help in his valour.

Twelve tanks swung at us to neutralize this menace. Their guns blazed insistently at us, and they came straight on.

I dropped my glasses and rolled to the bottom of my trench, where Muller had spread a blanket. I dragged it over myself in ineffectual protection. The toes of the dead man's boots dangled six inches from my eyes.

The earth trembled. My throat was like sandpaper. This, then, was the end. I had escaped at Sidi Rezegh. But now this was it. My fiancée would be told: "With deep regret we have to inform you that. . . ." She would read that I had died a hero's death for the Fatherland. And what would it mean? That I was just a bloody mess in the sand at an unidentified spot near an unimportant point in the desert called Acroma.

A tank crunched by at the edge of my trench. I heard an English voice calling. Was it a man in the tank, or an infantryman following up with bayonet fixed?

A blanket is not much good against a bayonet. But perhaps they would not see me. Perhaps I should just lie here and go mad. Perhaps I should be killed by a shell. Perhaps another tank would crush me.

The minutes crawled by. I now heard German voices. Apparently the British were rounding up prisoners in my own sector. And here was I in the trench.

Firing had ceased. After perhaps a quarter of an hour

I heard the tanks rolling off towards the south. Silence descended on the battlefield. But I still lay there like a sleeping man.

When I lifted my head the sky had dimmed from its brassy afternoon glare. Evening was coming. I saw no sign of life all round. Then I was startled by a figure that burst like a jack-in-the-box from a slit-trench some way back. It was my man Muller.

He had an anguished expression on his face. "Are you well, *Herr Oberleutnant*?" he called to me. And he added oddly, "I am not."

"Get down here," I ordered Muller. "We shall wait until it is dark before we move."

"*Herr Oberleutnant,*" said Muller, "that venison was just ready when the Tommies came."

As soon as darkness had fallen on the battlefield Muller led me back to the wadi, where the gazelle had been roasted. A haunch, still warm, lay on a sheet of iron there. Muller's flask still held coffee. We tore off hunks of the tasty but exceedingly tough meat and swallowed it.

I can still remember the feeling of the juice running down from the corners of my mouth. It was good to be alive. That sense of futility and the inevitability of death that had overwhelmed me in the slit-trench had gone. The will to live is strong in us.

Lieutenant Heinz Werner Schmidt

Rommel takes Stock

I will not deny that I was seriously worried that evening. Our heavy tank losses were no good beginning to the battle (far more than a third of the German tanks had been lost in this one day). 90 Light Division under General Kleemann had become separated from the Afrika Korps and was now in a very dangerous position. British motorized groups were streaming through the open gap and hunting down the transport columns which had lost touch with the main body. And on these columns the life of my army depended.

However, in spite of the precarious situation and the difficult problems with which it faced us, I looked forward that evening full of hope to what the battle might bring. For Ritchie had thrown his armour into the battle piecemeal and had thus given us the chance of engaging them on each separate occasion with just about enough of our own tanks. This dispersal of the British armoured brigades was incomprehensible. In my view the sacrifice of 7 Armoured Division south of Bir el Harmat served no strategical or tactical purpose whatsoever, for it was all the same to the British whether my armour was engaged there or on the Trigh Capuzzo, where the rest of the British armour later entered the battle. The principal aim of the British should have been to have brought all the armour they had into action at one and the same time. . . . The full motorization of their units would have enabled them to cross the battlefield at great speed to wherever danger threatened. Mobile warfare in the desert has often and rightly been compared with a battle at sea—where it is equally wrong to attack piecemeal and leave half the fleet in port during the battle.

Rommel

The tank battles around us had not gone our way. In spite of our new tanks with the bigger armament and thicker armour, the 88 mm. dual-purpose gun was proving deadly. Time and again our tanks were led on to them by the withdrawal of the enemy, who then engaged them over open sights at two or three thousand yards' range and took heavy toll.

Brigadier L. Bolton

Bir Hacheim

Having destroyed a British brigade which lay across their communications to the west, the Germans next attacked Bir Hacheim in strength. After a defence which commanded Rommel's unqualified admiration, the Free French had to withdraw.

On the night 1-2 June, 90 Light Division and the Trieste moved against Bir Hacheim. They crossed the minefields without heavy casualties, thus shutting off the fortress from the east.

After our summons to surrender had been rejected, the attack opened at about midday. The Trieste from the north-east and 90 Light from the south-east advanced against the fortifications, field positions and minefields of the French defenders. With our preliminary barrage there began a battle of extraordinary severity, which was to last for ten whole days. I frequently took over command of the assault forces myself and seldom in Africa was I given such a hard-fought struggle. The French fought in a skilfully planned system of field positions and small defence works—slit trenches, small pill-boxes, machine-gun and anti-tank gun nests—all surrounded by dense minefields. This form of defence system is extraordinarily impervious to artillery fire or air attack, since a direct hit can destroy at the most one slit trench at a time. An immense expenditure of ammunition is necessary to do any real damage to an enemy holding a position of this kind.

It was a particularly difficult task to clear lanes through the minefields in face of the French fire. Superhuman feats were performed by the sappers, who suffered heavy casualties. Working under the cover of smoke-screens and artillery fire, they were frequently forced to sap their way direct through to the mines. Our victory was in a great measure due to their efforts.

Under non-stop attacks by our Luftwaffe (from 2 June up to the capture of the last French positions on the 11th, the Luftwaffe flew thirteen hundred sorties against Bir Hacheim) the French positions were attacked in the north by mixed assault groups drawn from various formations and in the south by 90 Light Division. Attack after attack came to a halt in the excellent British defence system.

During the first days of our attack on Bir Hacheim the mass of the British forces kept astonishingly quiet. Their only move was on 2 June against the Ariete, who resisted stubbornly. After a counter-attack by 21 Panzer Division, the situation quietened down again. British raiding parties from the area south of Bir Hacheim were continually harrying our supply traffic, to our great discomfort. Mines were laid on the desert tracks and attacks made against our supply columns. The British Motorized Group "August" particularly distinguished itself in this work, We were forced to use armoured cars and self-propelled guns for convoy protection.

Rommel

The battle still hung in the balance, both armies having suffered reverses. The British forces were still largely intact, and on the night of 4 June XXX Corps was to attack to drive a wedge into the Cauldron.

Away in the desert south of Knightsbridge, where the forces concentrated for the attack, an Indian Army officer observed that "the moon was late and the night was chill. A great quiet hung over the desert. A few tanks took station ahead followed by Bren-carriers. Behind them the lorry-borne infantry formed up. The men wore their greatcoats; while they waited they sat around their trucks. . . . The old moon climbed the sky and the night passed. At ten minutes to three the night exploded with the shock of heavy guns. The earth rocked. . . ."

The Battle for the Cauldron

All vehicles were lightened and precious possessions thrown away. A spare pair of boots, a cherished battery for a wireless, spare kit—they all went, and every drop of water that could be procured was carried in their place. All that night of 4-5 June the men stood to, and at about 2 a.m. they fired a long programme of concentrations on areas where the enemy were thought to be.

Then off in the moonlight, westwards—just such a silent move as when the Regiment trekked at speed, a little over a year previously, to the help of Tobruk. As dawn broke, and shortly after passing Bir 180, the Brigade Group topped the western lip of the Cauldron and were received with heavy and accurate fire. At once the guns dropped into action and each group shook out, guns in the centre, anti-tank and machine-guns on the flanks, vehicles and remaining infantry in rear.

After a short, fierce gun duel the enemy shelling ceased, and as the sun rose our tanks poured through the guns and joined battle with the German tanks over to the west. By about 10.00 hrs. the battle had become more or less stabilized, and from a commanding position on the escarpment in the H.L.I. area Captains Barber and Chadburn of the 426th Battery, on O.P. duty in their Honey tanks, could see down into the Cauldron proper, which was seething with German troops of all arms. It was an O.P. officer's dream. Fortunately they had plenty of ammunition and tremendous execution was done until the H.L.I. were counter-attacked by tanks and forced to withdraw. Captain Barber's Honey had a track blown off and had to be towed out by Captain Chadburn's.

About midday the tanks broke off to refuel, bringing with them the tattered remains of the H.L.I. Regiment, who had found themselves caught in daylight between the opposing tank forces. Each tank had its load of badly wounded men, a grim and weary lot. Their colonel, blood pouring down his face, passed through three times collecting what was left of his men.

The enemy shelling went on all day, though as long as our tanks and O.Ps held the high ground to the west the Germans were unable to overlook our gun positions. But since the ground was paved with stone slabs digging was impossible, and each shell took a heavy toll.

Towards evening a reinforcement battalion started to arrive and take up position in the Cauldron in the rear of the Support Group, and as dusk fell the Armoured Brigadier came up and told the leaders of the Support Group that he was withdrawing the tanks and that the Group was to "stand and fight where they were to the

last man and the last round". He promised to be back
with his armour at first light on the 6th, but the tanks
ran into trouble in their leaguer area and could not return.
This completely altered the situation on the morrow, for
it meant that we lost possession of the high ground to
the west.

British gunner

*The attack had gone astray, and the Germans counter-
attacked with devastating success.*

Few knew what was now our main object, for the
original plan of attack had been thwarted and turned
against us. The troops who had set out that morning in
darkness were now being smashed and decimated and split
and driven in flight, overrun and captured, pursued and
harried, shelled and dive-bombed, encircled and crushed
by armoured forces.

Antony Brett-James

As darkness approached, the fighting intensified, the
shelling increased and brew-ups flared up all round. At
last light a Jat battalion drove out to take up a position
on the ridge six hundred yards in front. It was caught
as it was deploying; all the officers were killed and what
was left melted away. The night was very dark and every
man on the guns "stood to" in view of the infantry attack
that had seemed to be boiling up when darkness fell.

As the tanks rumbled off to their rallying point, quiet
descended on the Cauldron and it was possible to take
stock of the situation. All ammunition was brought up
and spread round the guns. The wounded were loaded
up in fifteen-hundredweights and sent off eastwards. The
men had a substantial, though cold, meal. Most of the
guns were still in action, but many had been hit, and gun
detachments were made up to at least three men per
gun. . . .

On the left the Baluchis, commanded by a most capable
and phlegmatic colonel, had dug in and prepared to meet

any onslaught. In rear as night fell Gurkhas could be seen digging in hard, and on the right rear another infantry battalion seemed to be arriving. There was also a company of those most excellent and experienced machine-gunners the Northumberland Fusiliers, who in the days of peace had challenged the Abbasia gunners at every sport. One of their officers, just arrived back from Cairo, brought a very opportune parcel of food and drink. Arriving at dusk in the midst of heavy shelling, he threw it out and drove off to his company.

The night passed quietly enough with spasmodic shelling, and at dawn everyone brewed up and had a good breakfast. The day had every promise of being exciting and the Gunners were thrilled at the certain prospect of a tank shoot. They wanted badly to get their own back for the shelling they had had to put up with, for the incessant dive-bombing and for all the good chaps dead. . . .

Meanwhile the Germans had been massing their tanks and lorried infantry in the gap a few thousand yards westwards. As the dawn spread quickly over the desert the shelling started once more and our guns answered back. Our O.Ps attempted to get forward on to the high ground again but in the absence of our own armour found it already occupied by German tanks, with of course *their* O.Ps. More and more German tanks appeared in the west and spread round the position in a double ring, shooting up the F.O.Os in their Honey's, but remaining just out of range of our 25-pounder solid shot. They gave the impression of hounds holding a stag at bay, but not daring to go in.

Suddenly at 8.30 a.m. the enemy fire was concentrated on Birkin's battery, then into the Baluchis. The German tanks moved in, making for E Troop of 425th, and a brisk and deadly exchange took place. Then, as the dust and smoke cleared away, the enemy withdrew, leaving ten tanks behind, knocked out a few hundred yards from the guns of 425th Battery. The Gunners were delighted and settled down to await the next attack. It was not long in coming. The enemy moved farther west, to attack the units on 425th's left flank. A few minutes of intense small arms and machine-gun fire—and then dead silence. The position had been overrun. A handful of men were seen staggering off under heavy escort. This left 425th Battery with an exposed flank, and a hasty rearrangment had to be made. But a little later Stukas flew over the position and the ring of purple smoke sent up by the enemy to show his forward positions to the planes made it clear that the box was now completely surrounded.

Never for a moment did the shelling stop. Casualties became heavier and heavier. Vehicles were burning everywhere. The enemy with their guns just out of sight could direct their fire with great accuracy on the mass of men and vehicles and guns in the Cauldron below. Captain Bennett, hit through the leg, arrived at the Command Post to report his troop position untenable. Three of his gun detachments had been knocked out, but the guns themselves were intact. B.S.M. Hardy and a driver were immediately despatched in a quad to pull the guns in four hundred yards, a feat which they accomplished most gallantly in spite of heavy machine-gun fire.

Ammunition was now running short, particularly A.P., and orders were given for all fire to be held until the attack came in to close quarters. The position was exceedingly unhealthy and on the left flank had every prospect of soon becoming untenable. It was suggested to Colonel de Graz, commander of the Support Group, that the whole force should move back to the Knightsbridge Ridge, some three and a half miles to the east, and so have its flanks assured on the minefield before it was completely surrounded. But in view of the orders given him, he would not contemplate it.

More and more enemy tanks kept spreading round the area and presently a large column many miles long (actually the German 90 Light Division) appeared from the south behind the position, thus sealing the fate of this luckless brigade.

About 10 a.m. there was a very welcome lull—but it was short-lived. Down came the shells again, and a number of the Command Post staff were hit.

The Germans could now observe our every move. At about this time Colonel de Graz and Colonel Seely held a small conference at the Regimental Command Post, roughly in the centre of the box, and though there were only some ten people present the enemy at once started shelling.

The next attack came in very quickly and soon German tanks had overrun the infantry battalion in the rear and were nosing about amongst the burning vehicles round the Bir. Captain Trippier and his Northumberland Hussars were quite magnificent. Under heavy fire they man-handled their anti-tank guns across to try to safeguard our rear, but they were all knocked out. He then drove back with his truck full of badly wounded men to report that he had not a man left. As he spoke a shell exploding beside him wounded him severely. Events moved quickly now and amazing things happened as the fighting raged at close quarters. A sergeant of the Recce Regiment with what was left of his section leaped on a German tank, trying to ram hand grenades through the turret. They were killed to a man. The machine-gun fire was intense. Cartridge boxes went up in a sheet of flame. Four lorry loads of Germans in British three-tonners drove straight past the guns untouched. A staff car and two generals drove up to the Command Post, and as the gunners jumped at it, accelerated and got away. The doctor and his orderly worked unceasingly in a murderous fire round the Command Post, which was a shambles of dead and wounded. As the gun detachments were killed signallers, drivers and Northumberland "Geordies" crawled over to take their places.

Colonel Seely, who had been constantly on the move around his Regiment in his Honey tank, encouraging the men by his splendid example, arrived at 426th Battery Command Post during the early afternoon and suddenly observed three German infantry lorries appearing over the escarpment about a thousand yards north of F Troop. The German infantry jumped out, but before they could get into action with their light automatics they were met by the concentrated fire of F Troop, the 6-pounder anti-tank guns of the Northumberland Hussars and the small arms of the Recce Regiment. In a few moments the lorries were in flames and the scattered German survivors rounded up.

About 3 p.m. the Germans were attacking the right of the position. Of the anti-tank guns one only now remained, but there was no one to man it until a young lance-bombardier, with one arm blown off at the elbow, crawled out in a vain attempt to reach it. Colonel de Graz walked over from his blazing and useless vehicle, but was killed immediately as he tried to fire the anti-tank gun. Communication still remained. For sixteen hours the Signal Sergeant had sat in his vehicle keeping on the air to Brigade. The second-in-command spoke to the Brigadier and told him that if he would get some ammunition through with some tanks, we could hold out until dark. The Brigadier wished him luck, but at that moment the vehicle was hit and up it went.

As evening approached, everywhere the German tanks were moving in. The Indian Infantry Brigade was completely overrun—there was nothing left. Nearly every vehicle was burning and heavy smoke obliterated the sky. Still the South Notts Hussars held out and kept the tanks at bay. Guns were facing every direction—wherever a tank could be seen working up through the smoke. Solid shot tore up the ground all round. As a last desperate measure it was decided to move the guns of Captain Pringle's E Troop to the rear, despite the enemy's immediate reaction to any sign of movement.

The quads drove up and the men—all that were left of them—leapt to hook in the guns. But before they had gone two hundred yards all four of the quads went up in flames. Major Birkin, hurrying to see what could be done, had his armoured car hit by an A.P. shot and his invaluable B.S.M. Hardy killed beside him. By the time

he had regained his remaining A Troop, of which only
two guns were still in action, the enemy tanks were on
top of the position and the gallant fight of the 425th
Battery was over.

Down in the hollow, Alan Chadburn's guns were still
intact, but on all sides the German tanks were closing
in, machine-guns blazing. Colonel Seely and Bish Peal,
his adjutant, who had continued to ply indomitably about
the battlefield, had their tank hit and set on fire. Both
died later in enemy hands. The end was very near now.
426th Battery Command Post fell to the advancing tanks;
and though in a last defiant gesture Chadburn's F Troop
scored two direct hits at eight hundred yards they could
do no more. The groups of British prisoners appearing
over the escarpment put further firing out of the question,
and the survivors of 426th Battery turned sadly to their
final task—the battering of their gun sights. For a few
moments more the air sang with machine-gun bullets; then
all was quiet, and that deep silence that descends on a
battlefield when the contest is over spread over the
Cauldron.

British gunner

*12 June was the day on which the vast battle of Gazala
was finally lost. The British armour met disaster and the
Knightsbridge Box was evacuated.*

By nightfall the British armour was only a shadow of
its former strength, and the desert was strewn with the
wrecks of Grants, Crusaders and Stuarts which, since the
Eighth Army had been driven off the field, were
irrecoverable, even when the damage was slight. The
German tanks had broken through the main line of
defence covering the road between Gazala and Tobruk
and several miles of the escarpment between Knightsbridge and El Adem were in their hands.

The Victors Sum Up

The C.-in-C., coming from the sector of 15 Panzer Division (Via Balbia), says that although part of the rearguard of 1 S.A. Division has been captured, the bulk of the Gazala formations have got away; therefore 21 Panzer Division was ordered at noon to pursue the enemy by swinging east of Tobruk.

. . . . Messages from 90 Light say that although local penetrations have been made in the east and west sectors of the El Adem Box, enemy resistance is on the whole unbroken. The three German reconnaissance units report that in the area south and south-east of El Adem they have thrown back enemy reconnaissance forces. Italian XX (Motorized) Corps is assembling around Knightsbridge, Italian X and XXI Corps are moving east through the Gazala position.

Enemy situation. The enemy has succeeded in evading our pincer movement and is escaping from the Gazala position. These forces (1 S.A. Division and 50 British Division) and the armoured brigades—no longer fit for battle—of 1 and 7 Armoured Divisions are assembling on the Libyan-Egyptian frontier; air reconnaissance confirms continuous movements from Tobruk eastwards; wireless intercept has confirmed that 1 S.A. Division and 50 Division together with the two armoured divisions are on the frontier [this was not entirely correct, but the reports are given as I made them at the time]. Therefore in the Tobruk zone we can reckon on 2 S.A. Division only, with 11 and 29 Indian Brigades in the outer approaches of the fortress.

C.-in-C.: "It is my intention to take Tobruk by a *coup de main*. For this purpose the outlying area of Tobruk, south and east of the Fortress, must be gained without delay, and the British Eighth Army pressed away farther to the east."

General von Mellenthin

A plan was proposed for a wholesale British withdrawal eastwards, but General Auchinleck opposed this.

Tobruk must be held and the enemy must not be allowed to invest it. This means that Eighth Army must hold the line Acroma-El Adem and southward and resist any enemy attempt to pass it. Having reduced your front by evacuating Gazala and reorganized your forces, this should be feasible and I order you to do it.

Auchinleck to Ritchie

The Prime Minister was urging a firm stand, the Eighth Army Commander was optimistic, but General Auchinleck then began to have doubts.

The conditions required for good maintenance were absent, and it is reasonable to conclude that the defences had indeed fallen into considerable neglect, that their detailed layout was largely unknown, and that they were very much in a state of being nobody's business.

A British Brigadier

Although I have made it clear to you that Tobruk must not be invested I realize that its garrison may be isolated for short periods until our counter-offensive can be launched. With this possibility in mind you are free to organize the garrison as you think best and to retain whatever administrative services and stocks of all sorts you consider necessary either for the service of the garrison or to assist the counter-offensive.

Auchinleck to Ritchie

Had I seen this order I should not have been content with it.

Winston Churchill

The Fall of Tobruk: 20-21 June

At 05.00 [20 June] I stood with Rommel on the

escarpment to the northeast of El Adem; Battle Headquarters had been set up there and when daylight came we had excellent observation as far as the Tobruk perimeter. Promptly at 05.20 the Stukas flew over. Kesselring had been as good as his word and sent hundreds of bombers in dense formations; they dived on to the perimeter in one of the most spectacular attacks I have ever seen. A great cloud of dust and smoke rose from the sector under attack, and while our bombs crashed on to the defences, the entire German and Italian Army artillery joined in with a tremendous and well co-ordinated fire. The combined weight of the artillery and bombing was terrific, and as we soon realized, had a crushing effect on the morale of the Mahratta battalion in that sector. The Stukas kept it up all day, flying back to the airfields at Gazala and El Adem, replenishing with bombs, and then returning to the fray. On this occasion the Air Force bombing was directed through the Operations Section of Army Headquarters, with very fruitful results.

After a time the assault engineers released orange smoke as a signal that the range should be lengthened, and at 06.35 the report came back that the wire had been cut in front of Strong Point 69. Group Menny, and the infantry of the Afrika Korps, now attacked the forward line of bunkers and made rapid progress against feeble resistance. At 07.03 Group Menny reported that a whole company of Indians had been taken prisoner, and by 07.45 a wide breach had been made and about ten strong points had been taken. Bridges were laid across the anti-tank ditch and the way was prepared for the tanks to enter the perimeter.

The weak resistance of the defenders was due primarily to the bombardment, and paradoxically to the excellent concrete shelters built by the Italians. Under the crushing weight of bombs and shells the Indians were driven below ground, where they were relatively secure, but could not bring any fire to bear on our attacking troops, who followed closely behind the barrage. Another important factor was the weakness of the defenders' artillery fire. There seems to have been a complete lack of co-ordination of the various batteries; a few South African guns were firing during the break-through, but apparently the 25th Field Regiment R.A., which was in immediate support of 11 Indian Brigade, did not fire until 07.45. The guns of this regiment had been sited in an anti-tank role, and it appears that they were relying on the medium artillery to bombard the perimeter gap, and the German troops assembling beyond it. But the mediums remained silent, and it was not until 08.45 that the Afrika Korps reported that the enemy's fire was "increasing", particularly that of the "heavy calibres". I well remember our surprise, when watching the battle that morning, at the small volume of fire put down by the Tobruk artillery. Meanwhile Rommel had gone forward to take direct command of the break-through.

General von Mellenthin

General Ritchie to General Klopper, G.O.C. Tobruk Garrison

Army Commander: Every day and hour of resistance materially assists our cause. I cannot tell tactical situation and must therefore leave you to act on your own judgment regarding capitulation.

Report if you can extent to which destruction P.O.L. effected.

G.O.C.: Situation shambles. Terrible casualties would result. Am doing the worst. Petrol destroyed.

Army Comd.: Whole of Eighth Army has watched with admiration your gallant fight. You are an example to us all and I know South Africa will be proud of you. God bless you and may fortune favour your efforts wherever you be. . . .

Surrender

After his message that he was "doing the worst", which

went in clear about 06.30, General Klopper sent out *parlementaires* under the white flag to the enemy forces lying east and west of his position with an offer to surrender. A huge white flag was hauled up over 6 Brigade Headquarters by some native drivers and "a sort of cry or moan," wrote one observer, "went up from the South African Police. It gave an extraordinary impression of anguish and misery."

Rommel Enters Tobruk

At 05.00 hours on 21 June, I drove into the town of Tobruk. Practically every building of the dismal place was either flat or little more than a heap of rubble, mostly the result of our siege in 1941. Next I drove off along the Via Balbia to the west. The staff of 32 British Army Tank Brigade offered to surrender, which brought us thirty serviceable British tanks. Vehicles stood in flames on either side of the Via Balbia. Wherever one looked there was chaos and destruction.

At about 09.40 hours, on the Via Balbia about four miles west of the town, I met General Klopper, G.O.C. 2 South African Infantry Division and Garrison Commandant of Tobruk. He announced the capitulation of the fortress of Tobruk. He had been unable to stave off the defeat any longer, although he had done all he could to maintain control over his troops.

I told the General, who was accompanied by his Chief of Staff, to follow me in his car along the Via Balbia to Tobruk. The road was lined with about ten thousand prisoners of war.

On arrival at the Hotel Tobruk, I talked for a while with General Klopper. It seemed that he had no longer been in possession of the necessary communications to organize a break-out. It had all gone too quickly. I instructed the South African general to make himself and his officers responsible for order among the prisoners, and to organize their maintenance from the captured stores.

Rommel

Twenty-five thousand men and enormous quantities of supplies fell into Rommel's hands. Before the day ended, Hitler had promoted him Field-Marshal. We all celebrated—with captured tinned fruit, Irish potatoes, cigarettes and canned beer.

For a day or so we rejoiced in the blessings of the British Naafi. It was a pleasure to snuffle round the field-kitchens, where pork sausages and potatoes, so long a rarity, were being fried. There was British beer to drink, and tinned South African pineapples for dessert.

We spurned our own rations, especially *"Alte Mann"*,* with distaste and contempt. Instead we gloried in Australian bully beef, of which the Australians were as sick as we were of *"Alte Mann"*. It was some time, however, before we could find ourselves agreeing with the sentiments expressed in captured enemy letters, which were far from extolling the deliciousness of bully. When conditions permitted, we used to send home parcels of Australian bully. It was regarded in Germany as a luxury.

Lieutenant Heinz Werner Schmidt

The fall of Tobruk made an enormous impression in Berlin and throughout Germany. Public spirits rose at once to a peak not experienced since the conclusion of the Battle of France in 1940. Rommel was the man of the day to whom nothing seemed impossible. Perhaps we can win the war after all, everybody said, and gave themselves up to jubilation over a victory which they really felt was a victory.

Arvid Fredborg, Swedish journalist

Post-Mortem

As things turned out, I don't think the scratch garrison of Tobruk had a hope of survival. The garrison was not strong enough, and insufficient time was available to sort

* *Alte Mann*—Italian sausage, labelled A.M.

things out and get the defence organized properly. Air
support, through no fault of the gallant Desert Air Force,
was quite inadequate, and the enemy were in a position
to form up and lay on their attack without interference.
There were some hard things said about the South
Africans after the capitulation, but I could never myself
blame that division; they never had a chance. Under
Montgomery at Alamein and before, the South Africans
conducted themselves magnificently.

Much petrol, transport and supplies fell into Rommel's
hands, and it was this that no doubt persuaded the
German Commander, and eventually Hitler, that the
capture of the Nile Valley was now a practical proposition.

Major-General Sir Francis de Guingand

*Urgent conferences were held at Rommel's head-
quarters to consider further action.*

A grave decision had to be made now. In the original
plan agreed upon between Hitler and Mussolini at the
end of April, it was laid down that after Rommel had
taken Tobruk, the *Panzerarmee* would stand on the
defensive on the Egyptian Frontier, and that all available
aircraft and shipping would then be diverted to the attack
on Malta. With the fall of the island our communications
would be secure, and an advance to the Nile could follow.
On 21 June Field-Marshal Kesselring flew to Africa, and I
was present at his conference with Rommel in our Command Vehicle. Rommel insisted that he must follow up his
victory without waiting for an attack on Malta, but
Kesselring pointed out that an advance into Egypt could
not succeed without full support from the Luftwaffe. If this
were given, the Luftwaffe would not be available for
operations against Malta, and should the island recover,
Rommel's communications would be in serious jeopardy.
Kesselring maintained that the only sound course was to
stick to the original plan, and postpone an invasion of
Egypt until Malta had fallen.

Rommel disagreed emphatically and the discussions became exceedingly lively. He admitted that the *Panzerarmee* had suffered heavily in the Gazala battles, but maintained that Eighth Army was in far worse plight and we now had a unique opportunity for a thrust to the Suez Canal. A delay of even a few weeks would give the enemy time to move up new forces and prevent any further advance. The two commanders failed to reach agreement, and before leaving, Kesselring made no secret of his intention to withdraw his air units to Sicily.

Rommel had made up his mind irrevocably. The vanguard of the Afrika Korps was already on its way to the frontier, and on the evening of the 21st Rommel sent off a personal liaison officer to put his views before Hitler. He also signalled to Rome, and assured the Duce that "the state and morale of the troops, the present supply position owing to captured dumps, and the present weakness of the enemy, permit our pursuing him into the depths of the Egyptian area". Rommel carried the day with Hitler, in spite of the reasoned and powerful objections of the Italian General Staff, the German Naval Staff, Field-Marshal Kesselring, and also General von Rintelen, the German military attaché in Rome. Hitler signalled to Mussolini that "it is only once in a lifetime that the Goddess of Victory smiles", and the fateful decision was made to postpone the Malta attack until September, and throw everything behind Rommel's invasion of Egypt.

General von Mellenthin

The Last Invasion

On the evening of 23 June the advance guard of the Afrika Korps crossed the Egyptian frontier. Rommel's aim was to outflank the formidable minefields and "boxes" which the British had built up in the frontier area, but in fact Ritchie had already decided to fall back to Matruh. During the next twenty-four hours our advance guard made a sensational advance of over a hundred miles and reached the coast road between Matruh and Sidi Barrani. The morale of the troops was high and the victories of the past month went far to balance the strain and exhaustion of incessant fighting at the height of a desert summer. Tank strength, however, was ominously low, for there had been many breakdowns in the march from Tobruk, and the Afrika Korps entered Egypt with only forty-four Panzers.

Our advance on 24/25 June met with little interference from British ground forces, but was exposed to heavy and determined attacks by the Desert Air Force; the pace of the advance was outstripping our available fighter cover and we had to pay a heavy toll in casualties; indeed from the moment we entered Egypt the writing was on the wall as far as air support was concerned. Rommel never again enjoyed the advantage of air superiority, and the enemy's air forces grew with terrifying strength.

General von Mellenthin

On 25 June General Auchinleck decided that the precarious position of his forces was such that he must assume personal responsibility for the battle, and he himself relieved General Ritchie. He made up his mind to halt the enemy in the area between Matruh and Alamein. The area which was to prove critical was due south of Matruh: Minqa Qaim, occupied by seven New Zealand battalions newly arrived from Syria.

Minqa Qaim

The general situation was extremely vague, and I could see no merits in the position we stood in, though I knew of no better and could not see one. We moved on to the ground on the late afternoon of the 26th and dug in that night and until nine o'clock next morning. On top of the escarpment the solid rock was within eighteen inches of the surface, and it was not possible to do very much.

Soon after midday we could see that the enemy had worked round the right flank of the Division. There was a steady thudding of gunfire, much dust and the smoke of many explosions and burning vehicles, and occasionally the distant mutter of automatics, but we could form little idea of what was happening. Everything remained quiet with 5 Brigade but we could see that 4 Brigade was heavily engaged and that the enemy was steadily moving east of us. North of 5 Brigade the great enemy mass remained out of range. We moved headquarters to a safer area with the 22nd Battalion.

Early in the afternoon Division informed us that General Freyberg had been wounded. Inglis had taken command and Jim Burrows had taken over 4 Brigade.

. . . . I was called to Division for a conference about eight o'clock that evening. We stood in a group at the back of the command truck. Inglis said that all attacks had been repulsed so far, but the enemy was fairly round behind us and we obviously were in a grave position. The going to the south was reported bad, the only sure going was due east, which meant that we must make a break through.

Brigadier Kippenberger

The entire 2 New Zealand Division lined up in their vehicles and prepared to make a mad dash for safety.

. . . . The trucks were packed to the limit and the hundreds of men whom they could carry were crammed on to the fighting vehicles. Men were hanging on wherever there was standing room, squeezed inside the gun quads, on the guns themselves, on carriers and anti-tank portées, everywhere imaginable. The loading was completed in a quiet and orderly manner and I walked round to check up. I found about twenty men still unaccommodated and they followed me round while I found places for them one by one.

Brigadier Kippenberger

Break-Out

At last, well after midnight, we started to move forward, the column led by the C.R.A. 4 Brigade had not completed its attack, but we were forced to begin the break-out so that we should have a long enough period of darkness in which to get well clear of the enemy. We passed slowly through 4 Brigade's old area. There was little small-arms fire ahead of us, and later we learned that 4 Brigade had done tremendous execution with the bayonet.

We had gone only a short distance past the original forward posts when the scouting carriers moving just ahead of the column halted. A moment later the darkness in front exploded into fire. Tank shells and machine-gun bullets poured into the column, and a number of our vehicles burst into flames, illuminating the whole area. We remained halted in reality for only a few seconds, uncertain what to do. Then the C.R.A. roared out from his jeep, "Follow me." Several of us in the leading vehicles did so, and we drove hard right, i.e. south, skirting the enemy tanks. The whole column followed. The going was poor, but any thought of cautious driving was abandoned. We had gone about five hundred yards when more enemy tanks immediately in front of us opened fire. We halted again, and our predicament was obviously much more serious this time. Many of the leading vehicles went up in flames, a single shell in some cases going through two or three trucks in line.

My recollections are a little vague at this point; but I remember that, with no alternative, we started up and drove straight into the enemy's fire. I can well imagine the feelings of those tank crews when they saw an irresistible tide of vehicles and guns bearing down upon them. Trucks were still exploding in flames, but nothing could have halted that onrush, the product more of instinct than of command. The air was so heavy with dust and smoke that one could do nothing but follow the vehicle in front into the thick blanket ahead. A number of unfortunate men were thrown off motor-cycles

or tossed out of trucks. Their death was certain, for
vehicles behind had no chance of avoiding them.

Lieutenant-Colonel G. P. Hanna

Escape

My car was jammed on all sides and could not move.
I told Ross and Joe to get out and for a moment we lay
flat on the ground. Many others had done the same. A
few seconds later I saw the truck ahead of us turning to
the left, and beyond it quite clearly saw John Gray
standing with his head through the roof of his car and
pointing in the same direction. "We'll give it a go, Ross,"
I said. "Very good, sir," he replied, as polite as ever. We
scrambled back and followed the trucks ahead, all bolting
like wild elephants. For a few moments we ran on amid
a pandemonium, overtaking and being overtaken by other
frantic vehicles, dodging slit trenches, passing or crashing
into running men, amid an uproar of shouts and screams.
I recognized the men as Germans, pulled out my revolver
and was eagerly looking out for a target when suddenly
there was silence and we were out running smoothly on
level desert. We were through.

Brigadier Kippenberger

The wild flare-up which ensued involved my own battle
headquarters, which lay to the south. . . . Soon my
headquarters were surrounded by burning vehicles,
making them the target for continuous enemy fire at close
range. I had enough of this after a while and ordered the
troops, with the staff, to move back south-eastward. The
confusion reigning on that night can scarcely be imagined.
It was impossible to see one's hand before one's eyes.
The R.A.F. bombed their own troops, German units were
firing on each other, the tracer was flying in all directions.

Rommel

*One more grave blow was to fall upon the Eighth Army
before the battle came to an end: X Corps, already*

deprived of 2 New Zealand Division, which had fought its way to Alamein and was busy sorting itself out, took a beating on the Fuka escarpment and struggled back minus eight thousand prisoners. As General Auchinleck watched his battered army stream into the Alamein positions, there was little hope to be found in anyone's mind.

The Middle East situation is about as unhealthy as it can be, and I do not very well see how it can end.
                    General Sir Alan Brooke, C.I.G.S., diary, 28 June

Panic

General Gott was in his Armoured Command Vehicle (A.C.V.), the first I had seen. He came out at once and walked a few yards clear of it. "Inglis has gone to Cairo," he said, and handed me a letter. It was a short note from General Corbett, then General Auchinleck's M.G.G.S. I remember very clearly the opening sentence: "The Chief has decided to save Eighth Army." The note then went on to say that the South Africans would retire through Alexandria and the rest of us down the desert road through Cairo.

I asked what was meant by the first sentence. "It means what it says—he means to save the Field Army," the General said. He went on to explain: a general retirement and evacuation of Egypt was in contemplation and Inglis had gone to Cairo to arrange for the evacuation of 2 N.Z.E.F. rear installations and hospitals; he supposed we would go back to New Zealand. I protested that we were perfectly fit to fight and that it was criminal to give up Egypt to twenty-five thousand German troops and a hundred tanks (disregarding the Italians)—the latest Intelligence estimate—and to lose as helpless prisoners perhaps two hundred thousand Base troops. Strafer replied sadly that N.Z. Division was battle-worthy but very few other people were and he feared the worst.

Inglis returned on the afternoon of the 30th, nothing

else of importance having occurred in his absence, and I returned to 5 Brigade. He drew a vivid picture of the confusion he had seen on the Cairo road and of the prodigious "flap" in Cairo itself. This was the time of the famous Ash Wednesday when Middle East and B.T.E. (it was customary to say "Middle East", meaning Middle East Headquarters, and B.T.E., meaning "Headquarters, British Troops in Egypt") were said to have burned many of their records and the Navy left Alexandria in haste. Paddy Costello, later one of our best divisional intelligence officers, was always very upset that the elaborate draft he had prepared for a handbook on the Italian Army was destroyed at this time. We heard all sorts of peculiar and perhaps libellous stories, such as the one that all the reserve store of binoculars had been thrown into Alexandria Harbour, but despite General Gott's warning I do not remember that we were particularly depressed. We thought it too bad to be true.

Brigadier Kippenberger

It is nonsense to talk of the Alamein "Line". When the Riflemen heard the suave voice of the B.B.C. announcer reporting that the Eighth Army had reached the Alamein "Line", they looked round at the empty desert, indistinguishable from the miles of sand to east and west, and commented as only Riflemen can.

Rommel is Stopped

On the morning of 30 June Rommel formed his plan for piercing the Alamein Line. Strictly speaking there was no such thing as an "Alamein Line", although the gap between the Qattara Depression and the sea was filled by a number of boxes. He decided that the Afrika Korps should make a feint in the direction of the Qattara Depression, but should move on the night of 30 June/1 July to a position about ten miles south-west of El Alamein station. We believed that the British X Corps, with 50 Division and 10 Indian Brigade, was holding the

Alamein Box and a position to the south-west of it at
Deir el Abyad. We thought that XIII Corps with 1
Armoured Division, 2 N.Z. Division, and 5 Indian
Division was holding the southern sector of the line,
between the Qaret el Abd Box and the Qattara
Depression. Rommel decided to repeat the tactics which
had served him so well at Matruh; under cover of the
darkness the Afrika Korps was to penetrate between the
boxes at Alamein and Deir el Abyad and get in the rear
of XIII Corps. 90 Light Division was to swing south of
the Alamein Box and cut the coast road to the east of
it—exactly the same orders as at Mersa Matruh. If we
could once get our troops in rear of the British, Rommel
was convinced that their defence would collapse.

In view of our experiences at Matruh I think that this
plan offered a real hope of victory. The German forces
were too weak for any heavy fighting, but they were still
capable of manoeuvre. It is quite possible that if Rommel
had got his divisions across the British rear, they would
have been stampeded once more into a headlong flight.

Unfortunately Rommel's theory was never put to the
test. . . . The Afrika Korps was late—its night move from
El Quseir to the concentration area near Tell el Aqqaqir
was delayed by broken ground—and when it advanced on
the morning of 1 July the corps found that there was no
box at Deir el Abyad, but that the enemy was holding
a box three miles farther east at Deir el Shein. It might
have been possible for the Afrika Korps to by-pass the
Deir el Shein Box and continue its move into the rear
of XIII Corps, but in that case another enemy
position—actually held by 1 S.A. Brigade north of
Ruweisat Ridge—would have had to be eliminated.
General Nehring decided to attack Deir el Shein, and
when Rommel came up later that morning he approved
of this decision.

On the afternoon of 1 July the Afrika Korps broke
into the Deir el Shein Box, and after very severe fighting
destroyed 18 Indian Brigade. But we lost eighteen tanks
out of fifty-five, and the fighting edge of the Afrika Korps

was finally blunted. 90 Light advanced during the afternoon, and attempted to by-pass the El Alamein Box; it ran into a crescent of fire from 1, 2, and 3 S.A. Brigades and their supporting artillery, and was thrown into confusion not far removed from panic. Rommel himself went to 90 Light to try and urge the division forward, but the volume of fire was so heavy that even he was pinned down.

On 3 July Rommel abandoned the hope of getting in rear of XIII Corps, and sought to use the Afrika Korps, 90 Light, and Littorio for a concentrated thrust round the Alamein Box. We suffered a sharp reverse that morning when the New Zealanders came out of their box at Qaret el Abd, attacked Ariete Division, and captured all their artillery. Nevertheless, Rommel ordered the main attack to go in on the afternoon of 3 July, and under cover of a heavy bombardment the Afrika Korps made a determined attempt to advance. Some ground was gained on Ruweisat Ridge, but with only twenty-six tanks it was impossible to break through. When darkness fell Rommel ordered the Panzer divisions to dig in where they stood; everyone realized that the offensive which opened on 26 May, and which had achieved such spectacular victories, had at last come to an end.

That night Rommel signalled to Kesselring that he had been forced to suspend his attack "for the time being". This check was all the more disappointing because our air reconnaissance reported that the British fleet had left Alexandria, and that there was much traffic *en route* from Egypt to Palestine. We had just failed.

General von Mellenthin

The Afrika Korps slowly but inevitably weakened for lack of reinforcements and supplies. Heavy fighting continued to rage around the Ruweisat Ridge, and what decision there was went to the British. By late July the inability of the Axis forces to make progress was worrying their commander, who by now was even more tired than his men.

18 July 1942

Dearest Lu,

Yesterday was a particularly hard and critical day. We pulled through again. But it can't go on like it for long, otherwise the front will crack. Militarily, this is the most difficult period I've ever been through. There's help in sight, of course, but whether we will live to see it is a question. You know what an incurable optimist I am. But there are situations where everything is dark. However, this period, too, will pass.

Rommel

26 August 1942

Dear Frau Rommel,

You'll no doubt be surprised at hearing from me from Africa. . . . The reason for my letter is to inform you about the state of the Marshal's health. Your husband has now been nineteen months in Africa, which is longer than any other officer over forty has stood it so far, and, according to the doctors, an astonishing physical feat. After the rigours of the advance, he has had to carry the immense responsibility of the Alamein front, anxiety for which has for many nights allowed him no rest. Moreover, the bad season has come again.

All this has, in the nature of things, not failed to leave its mark, and thus, in addition to all the symptoms of a heavy cold and the digestive disturbances typical of Africa, he has recently shown signs of exhaustion which have caused great anxiety to all of us who were aware of it. True, there is no immediate danger, but unless he can get a thorough rest some time, he might easily suffer an overstrain which could leave organic damage in its train.

The doctor who is treating him, Professor Dr. Horster of Würzburg University—one of the best-known stomach specialists in Germany—is constantly available to him for medical advice and to watch over his health. The Führer has been informed, and it has been agreed that he will

receive a long period of sick leave in Europe once the
future of this theatre has been decided. Until that time,
we will do everything we can to make his life easier and
to persuade him to look after himself. We prepare and
keep handy everything he needs for his health. I have
installed a small kitchen and obtained a good cook. Fresh
fruit and vegetables arrive by air daily. We fish, shoot
pigeons, obtain chickens and eggs, etc., in order to keep
his strength up.

                         Lieutenant Alfred Ingemar Berndt

3

PEARL HARBOR

When in 1940 most of the world expected Britain's collapse to follow that of the other Western colonial powers, Japan's imperial designs on south-east Asia, long cherished by the Army, the dominant force in Japanese society, suddenly seemed closer to realization. The European colonies were cut off and would be easy prey. Japan's former neutrality with regard to Europe turned to warmth towards Germany and Italy, with whom she came to an understanding. Vichy France was induced to give up bases in northern Indo-China.

A PACT IS SIGNED: BERLIN, 27 SEPTEMBER 1940

JAPAN recognizes and respects the leadership of Germany and Italy in the establishment of a new order in Europe.

Germany and Italy recognize and respect the leadership of Japan in the establishment of a new order in Greater East Asia.

Germany, Italy and Japan agree . . . to assist one another with all political, economic, and military means when one of the three contracting powers is attacked by a power at present not involved in the European War or in the Chinese-Japanese conflict. . . .

135

Germany, Italy and Japan affirm that the aforesaid terms do not in any way affect the political status which exists at present between each of the contracting parties and Soviet Russia.

President Roosevelt to Ambassador Grew in Tokyo: 21 January 1941

I believe that the fundamental proposition is that we must recognize that the hostilities in Europe, in Africa, and in Asia are all parts of a single world conflict. We must, consequently, recognize that our interests are menaced both in Europe and in the Far East. . . . Our strategy of self-defence must be a global strategy.

Ambassador Grew to Washington: 27 January 1941

A member of the embassy was told by my Peruvian colleague that from many quarters, including a Japanese one, he had heard that a surprise mass attack on Pearl Harbor was planned by the Japanese military forces, in case of "trouble" between Japan and the United States; that the attack would involve the use of all the Japanese military forces. My colleague said that he was prompted to pass this on because it had come to him from many sources, although the plan seemed fantastic.

Admiral Stark, Chief of Naval Operations, Washington, to Admiral Kimmel, C.-in-C. Pacific Fleet, Pearl Harbor: 13 January 1941

In my humble opinion we may wake up any day . . . and find ourselves in another undeclared war. . . . I have told the gang here for months past that in my opinion we were heading straight for this war, that we could not assume anything else and personally I do not see how we can avoid [it] . . . many months longer. And of course it may be a matter of weeks or days. . . . I have been moving Heaven and Earth trying to meet such a situation, and am terribly impatient at the slowness with which things move here.

The Axis Confer: Ribbentrop and Matsuoka, Japanese Foreign Minister, Berlin, 29 March 1941

Next, the R.A.M.* turned again to the Singapore question. In view of the fears expressed by the Japanese of possible attacks by submarines based on the Philippines, and of the intervention of the British Mediterranean and Home Fleets, he had again discussed the situation with General-Admiral Raeder. The latter had stated that the British Navy, during this year, would have its hands so full in the English home waters and in the Mediterranean, that it would not be able to send even a single ship to the Far East. General-Admiral Raeder had described the U.S. submarines as so bad that Japan need not bother about them at all.

Matsuoka replied immediately that the Japanese Navy had a low estimate of the threat from the British Navy; it also held the view, that in case of a clash with the American Navy, it would be able to smash the latter without trouble.

The R.A.M. replied that America could not do anything against Japan in the case of the capture of Singapore. Perhaps, for this reason alone, Roosevelt would think twice before deciding on active measures against Japan; for, while on the one hand he could not achieve anything against Japan, on the other hand there was the probability of losing the Philippines to Japan. For the American President, of course, this would mean a considerable loss of prestige; and because of the inadequate rearmament he would have nothing to offset such a loss.

In this connection Matsuoka pointed out that he was doing everything to reassure the English about Singapore. He acted as if Japan had no intention at all regarding

* *Reichaussenminister* (= Foreign Minister; i.e. Ribbentrop) (Ed.)

this key position of England in the East. Therefore it might be possible that the attitude towards the British would appear to be friendly in words and in acts. However, Germany should not be deceived by that. He assumed this attitude not only in order to reassure the British, but also in order to fool the pro-British and pro-American elements until, one day, he would suddenly open the attack on Singapore.

[Ribbentrop concluded by expressing his view that] Germany had already won the war. With the end of this year, the world would realize this. Even England would have to concede it, if she had not collapsed before then, and America would also have to resign herself to this fact.

Britain's fighting survival and the growing hostility of the United States towards Japanese expansion in China and Indo-China cooled the militarists' ardour for a while. Japan began negotiations with America in the spring of 1941, to try to secure the latter's acquiescence to her conquests by peaceful means. However, the United States Government was by now thoroughly aroused by Japan's advances, and economic sanctions were laid on her. Throughout the summer and autumn the talks dragged on, neither side being willing to give ground. The Japanese soon realized that they would not get what they wanted short of war. The military party, with General Tojo as Prime Minister, won complete control.

Manila: State of Readiness, 3 November

The idea of an imminent war seemed far removed from the minds of most. Work hours, training schedules, and operating procedure were still based on the good old days of peace conditions in the tropics. There was a comprehensive project on paper for the construction of additional airfields, but unfortunately little money had been provided prior to my arrival.

General Brereton, C.-in-C. U.S. Far Eastern Air Forces

Admiral Nomura, Japanese Ambassador in Washington,
contacts Foreign Minister Togo in Tokyo: 15 November
1941

. . . . He emphasized the firmness of the American
determination, the certainty that if Japan plunged into
the "southward venture" she would have to fight the United States as well as Britain, and the fact that in spite of
American involvements in the Atlantic the United States
could still throw its "main strength" into a Pacific war. He
gave his estimate that in Russia "the apex of German victories had been passed". And he ventured to suggest,
though he knew he would be "harshly criticized for it",
that his government use "patience for one or two months
in order to get a clear view of the world situation".

Foreign Minister Togo to Japanese Ambassador,
Washington: 16 November 1941

In your opinion we ought to wait and see what turn
the war takes and remain patient. However, I am awfully
sorry to say that the situation renders this out of the
question. I set the deadline for the solution of these
negotiations . . . and there will be no change. . . . Press
them for a solution on the basis of our proposals.

Admiral Stark, Chief of Naval Operations, to Admiral
Hart, Manila, and Admiral Kimmel, Pearl Harbor:
24 November

Top secret
Chances of favourable outcome of negotiations with
Japan very doubtful. This situation coupled with
statements of Japanese Government and movements of
their naval and military forces indicate in our opinion
that a surprise aggressive movement in any direction including attack on Philippines or Guam is a possibility.
Chief of Staff (Marshall) has seen this dispatch, concurs

and requests action, addresses to inform senior Army officers their areas. Utmost necessary secrecy in order not to complicate an already tense situation or precipitate Japanese action. Guam will be informed separately.

State Department to General Douglas MacArthur, C.-in-C. Far East: 27 November

Negotiations with Japan appear to be terminated to all practical purposes with only barest possibilities that Japanese Government might come back and offer to continue. Japanese future action unpredictable, but hostile action possible at any moment. If hostilities cannot, repeat cannot, be avoided the United States desires that Japan commit the first overt act.

Not only the Washington negotiations were used to screen Japanese intentions.

As November ran out, various other carefully planned devices of "deception" were put into effect—unfortunately with all too much success. The Japanese knew that they could not conceal their movement against Malaya, and doubtless were at pains not to do so; for by focusing all attention on the Gulf of Siam, this movement was in itself admirable "deceptive" cover for the operations elsewhere. Towards the end of November a programme of false radio traffic was begun, to mislead our radio trackers into placing the various ships and squadrons where they were not. It was announced that one of Japan's crack liners, the *Tatsuta Maru,* would sail for the Americas on 2 December to pick up Japanese nationals. This seemed to imply that the war must still be at least some weeks away. She actually did sail on schedule, carrying among others a score of Americans who were taking this last chance to get home—in happy ignorance of the fact that she was under orders to run out to the International Date Line and then return.

The Die is Cast

28 November. Domei informed the Japanese people to-day that American had submitted to Japan a note which was tantamount to "a sort of ultimatum", and which, by reiterating America's well-known principles, had brought the negotiations back to where they started eight months ago. "There is little hope of bridging the gap between the views of Japan and those of the United States," it declared. "There is little room for prolonging the negotiations, and just as little room for optimism." There was also the theme of the rest of the Press, and the mere fact that the Government had lifted the veil of secrecy surrounding the negotiations and had notified the people that they were face to face with "a sort of ultimatum" was in itself ominous.

The *Asahi* said: "The American memorandum is America's last word. The die is cast. A showdown has come, and the next few days will reveal which way the dice have fallen."

1 December. Foreign Minister Togo to-day rejected the American proposals as "fantastic, unrealistic and regrettable". In a formal statement issued by the Foreign Office, he said:

"The United States does not understand the real situation in East Asia. It is trying forcibly to apply to East Asiatic countries fantastic principles and rules not adapted to the actual situation in the world, and is thereby tending to obstruct the construction of the New Order. This is extremely regrettable."

Chief of Naval General Staff to C.-in-C. Combined Fleet, Admiral Yamamoto: 1 December

Japan, under the necessity of self-preservation, has reached a decision to declare war on the United States of America, British Empire and the Netherlands. The C.-in-C. Combined Fleet shall at the start of the war direct an attack on the enemy fleet in the Hawaiian area and

reduce it to impotency, using the 1st Air Fleet as the
nucleus of the attack force.

Chief of Naval General Staff to Admiral Yamamoto:
2 December

The hostile action against the United States of America,
the British Empire, and the Netherlands shall be
commenced on 8 December.* Bear in mind that, should
it appear certain that Japanese-American negotiations will
reach an amicable settlement prior to the commencement
of hostile action, all forces of the Combined Fleet are
to be ordered to reassemble and return to their bases.

Admiral Yamamoto to Pearl Harbor Task Force

Execute attack. 8 December designated as X day.

Japan Waits

7 December [6 December, U.S. time]. It was a bright,
warm, and pleasant December Sunday. But under the
circumstances, ominously quiet. The Press seemed to have
exhausted itself and for lack of any new developments
was devoid of any interest. Even the diatribes against
America and Great Britain had ceased. The only news
that caught my eye was a small item that Thai troops
were at last marching towards the south, and I made a
note of it for my next story. All Japan seemed to be
waiting for something.

Otto D. Tolischus, American journalist

DAY OF INFAMY

Sunday morning, 7 December 1941, I went to my

* 7 December in the United States, east of the International
Date Line (Ed.)

office, as I had done almost every Sunday since I entered the State Department in 1933. The faces of my visitors were grim. From all our reports it appeared that zero hour was a matter of hours, perhaps minutes.

During the morning I received a series of decoded intercepts consisting of fourteen parts of a long telegram from Foreign Minister Togo to Nomura and Kurusu. This was the answer to our proposals of 26 November. There was also a short message instructing the Ambassadors to present this to our Government, if possible to me, at one o'clock that afternoon. Here then was the zero hour.

The Japanese note was little more than an insult. It said that our proposal "ignores Japan's sacrifices in the four years of the China affair, menaces the Empire's existence itself, and disparages its honour and prestige". It accused us of conspiring with Great Britain and other countries "to obstruct Japan's efforts towards the establishment of peace through the creation of a new order in East Asia". It concluded by saying that, in view of the attitude of the American Government, the Japanese Government considered it impossible to reach an agreement through further negotiations.

The note did not declare war. Neither did it break off diplomatic relations. Japan struck without such preliminaries.

Towards noon Ambassador Nomura telephoned my office to ask for an appointment with me at one o'clock for himself and Kurusu. I granted his request.

A few minutes after one, Nomura telephoned again to ask that the appointment be postponed until 1.45 p.m. I agreed.

The Japanese envoys arrived at the Department at 2.05, and went to the diplomatic waiting room. At almost that moment the President telephoned me from the White House. His voice was steady but clipped.

He said, "There's a report that the Japanese have attacked Pearl Harbor."

"Has the report been confirmed?" I asked.

He said, "No."

While each of us indicated his belief that the report was probably true, I suggested that he have it confirmed, having in mind my appointment with the Japanese Ambassadors.

As I thought it over, I decided that, since the President's report had not been confirmed and there was one chance out of a hundred that it was not true, I would receive the envoys.

Nomura and Kurusu came into my office at 2.20. I received them coldly and did not ask them to sit down.

Nomura diffidently said he had been instructed by his Government to deliver a document to me at one o'clock, but that difficulty in decoding the message had delayed him. He then handed me his Government's note.

I asked him why he had specified one o'clock in his request for an interview.

He replied that he did not know, but that was his instruction.

I made a pretence of glancing through the note. I knew its contents already but naturally could give no indication of this fact.

After reading two or three pages, I asked Nomura whether he had presented the document under instructions from his Government.

He replied that he had.

When I finished skimming the pages, I turned to Nomura and put my eye on him.

"I must say," I said, "that in all my conversations with you during the last nine months I have never uttered one word of untruth. This is borne out absolutely by the record. In all my fifty years of public service I have never seen a document that was more crowded with infamous falsehoods and distortions—infamous falsehoods and distortions on a scale so huge that I never imagined until to-day that any Government on this planet was capable of uttering them."

Nomura seemed about to say something. His face was impassive, but I felt he was under great emotional strain. I stopped him with a motion of my hand. I nodded towards the door. The Ambassadors turned without a word and walked out, their heads down.

Nomura's last meeting with me was in keeping with the ineptitude that had marked his handling of the discussions from the beginning. His Government's intention, in instructing him to ask for the meeting at one o'clock, had been to give us their note a few minutes in advance of the attack on Pearl Harbor. Nomura's Embassy had bungled this by its delay in decoding. Nevertheless, knowing the importance of a deadline set for a specific hour, Nomura should have come to see me precisely at one o'clock, even though he had in his hand only the first few lines of his note, leaving instructions with the Embassy to bring him the remainder as it became ready.

It was therefore without warning that the Japanese struck at Pearl Harbor, more than an hour before Nomura and Kurusu delivered their note.

Cordell Hull, U.S. Secretary of State

Radar, a British invention, was being slowly developed by the Americans. They had a set at Pearl Harbor, exercise upon which was regarded as largely academic.

Thirty miles away at the Opana Station, Private Lockard had started to close down the radar set. Private Elliott protested. Although the "problem" was over, their relief had not come. Elliott wanted instruction in the operation of this fascinating gadget; why not keep it going and give him a chance to work it? Lockard consented, and Elliott sat down at the oscilloscope. Almost immediately there sprang up out of the dancing line of light a "blip" so big as to suggest that the machine must be out of order. Lockard displaced Elliott, tested the controls, found nothing wrong. There was the "blip" still shimmering before them, telling them that there was something out there bigger than they had ever picked up before and far beyond the greatest range at which they had ever previously got an indication. Bearing three degrees east of north, it was 137 miles away; and though the radar of that time afforded no means of telling just what it was, it looked like a lot of aircraft, perhaps as many as fifty or more.

Elliott was pretty excited about it. This was the best thing their new radar had done yet, and he wanted to send in a report. Lockard told him, in effect, not to be silly; the exercise was over and it was no more of their business. But Elliott insisted. Entertaining a grossly exaggerated idea of the real capabilities of the Information Center, he thought that this might be a bunch of Navy planes about which the Army knew nothing, and that if the report went in it might give Army a chance for a nice bit of practice in the technique of interception. Lockard finally told him to go ahead if he wanted to. The "blip" had been obediently recording the approach of the planes; they had come down to 132 miles and were still advancing at a fair speed. The direct telephone lines to the plotting board had been shut down by that time, but Elliott called the Center over the service line used for routine business. The operator said there was nobody there. But Elliott continued to insist, and the note of excitement in his voice bestirred the operator to say that he would find the officer and get him to call back. Violating orders, the operator left the switchboard to hunt up the lieutenant. Tyler called back. Lockard, answering the telephone, reported the news. It was all more or less incomprehensible to Tyler. Whatever these guys at Opana were seeing in their oscilloscope, Tyler had no means of knowing what it was. It might be anything. It might be a flight of Navy planes off a carrier. It might be . . . another flight of B-17s from the mainland. Probably was. Tyler told Opana to forget it, hung up, and stepped out into the fresh morning air. It was then about 7.20 a.m., just as the Navy was beginning to be really aroused over the submarine contact. Tyler found the morning pleasant, but with a good deal of low-hanging cloud, especially over the mountains.

Though snubbed from headquarters, Lockard and Elliot still thought they had made quite an interception, and continued to plot the advancing planes until, at about twenty miles out, the latter entered the "dead space" of the machine and the "blip" broke up among the echoes from the neighbouring heights. The two privates then secured the set and made a copy of their record to show their commanding officer. About 7.45 their relief appeared. Lockard and Elliott climbed into the car, made their way down the wood road to the highway, and set off for their barracks some nine miles away. As they tooled cheerfully along, they saw one of the trucks of their own Aircraft Warning company tearing up the road towards them. It appeared to have the accelerator on the floorboards; it was filled with their comrades from the company, and the men were apparently provided with full battle equipment. Lockard and Elliott honked politely. The truck thundered past without response. Lockard and Elliott thought it rather strange.

The first plane, a dive bomber, streaked in low over Pearl Harbor at 7.55 a.m., coming in from the south with its consorts behind it. Two reconnaissance float planes had been catapulted from the Japanese cruisers before them, but if they reached Oahu they were not observed. The first wave of the main body, 189 aircraft in all, had been flown off the carrier decks at 6.00 a.m., Hawaiian time. As they sighted the north point of Oahu, at ten minutes before eight, they split up. In accordance with sound air warfare doctrine, the first objective was the American defensive aviation. One dive bomber unit, swerving only a little to the right, went in from the north over the ranked and helpless Army fighters on Wheeler Field. Another, swinging wide around the west coast of the island, came up from the south against the Army bombers on Hickam Field and the Navy PBYs on Ford Island. Immediately behind these were forty torpedo bombers, launching their deadly missiles from a low altitude at the "sitting ducks" in Battleship Row. Fifty horizontal bombers were on the heels of the torpedo planes, in case the first should fail against nets or baffles; and after them all there came forty-five fighters, to put down any opposition which might get into the air or,

failing that, to polish off the remains at Wheeler and
Hickam, at Ford Island, Kaneohe and the Marine base
at Ewa.

The whole of this massive force was flung within the
space of a few minutes at virtually every prominent naval
and air installation on Oahu. The Japanese pilots knew
that an hour behind them a second wave of 171
aircraft—fifty-four horizontal bombers, eighty-one dive
bombers, and thirty-six fighters—was on its way in
support. But most of the damage was done within the
first quarter of an hour. The Ford Island air station and
the twenty-nine PBY patrol planes parked there was a
shambles within a few minutes, the planes blazing and
exploding. This one attack finished Ford Island, and the
Japanese did not return. The Marine field at Ewa, to the
westward, was worked over more methodically with dive
bombing and strafing; and at the end of a rather leisurely
fifteen minutes all the forty-nine planes there—fighters,
scout bombers and utility types—had either been totally
destroyed or put out of action. At Kaneohe, the Navy
patrol base on the east coast, there were two principal
attacks, one at 7.55 and the second about twenty-five
minutes later. Of the thirty-three PBYs there, most of
them moored out in the bay, twenty-seven had been
destroyed by the end of the attack and the remainder
put out of commission. Save for the seven PBYs which
were out on local patrol or manoeuvres when the attack
began, the Navy and Marine Corps did not get a single
plane into the air from Oahu during the action.

At just about eight o'clock twenty-five Japanese dive
bombers roared low—not more than fifty or seventy-five
feet from the ground—over the long lines of parked fighter
planes on the Army's main fighter base at Wheeler Field,
in the centre of the island. The bursting bombs, the rattle
of the enemy machine-guns, and the red ball insignia on
the wings were the first intimation of war that anyone
had at Wheeler. In a few moments the parked aircraft,
many with their fuel tanks filled, were blazing; great

clouds of oily smoke were rolling up on the still air to obscure everything and hamper the frantic efforts to pull the planes apart and get them armed. They managed to put six operable fighters into the air by 8.30 and a couple more just before the Japanese returned, in lesser strength, around nine, while another half-dozen or so got up in the final minutes of the action. But that was the extent of Wheeler's contribution to the defence. Forty-two planes were totally destroyed at Wheeler; and out of the 126 modern or fairly modern fighters on the field at the start, only forty-three were listed as in commission afterwards.

Hickam Field, like Ford Island, was a shambles within the first five minutes, and repeated attacks thereafter did a pretty thorough job. But since most of the planes there were the obsolete B-18 bombers, it did not matter so much. Of Short's twelve B-17s, as luck would have it, four were still serviceable after the attack and only four were destroyed. The Japanese had given a low priority to Bellows Field, across the island next to Kaneohe, and it was not until 8.30 that a single enemy plane made one ineffective pass at the parked aircraft of the fighter squadron which was there for gunnery practice. But although they were thus warned, the planes were without fuel or ammunition and it took time to ready them. It was not until about nine that they were taxi-ing for a take-off; and just at that moment seven Japanese appeared. Two American fighters got into the air, but were shot down as they did so. One pilot was saved, but that ended Bellows' contribution.

Meanwhile, two American air elements had flown, utterly unsuspecting, into the middle of the action. At dawn Admiral Halsey, returning from Wake Island with the *Enterprise* task force, was some two hundred miles west of Pearl. He flew off a squadron of scout bombers to perform the usual patrol ahead of the ships, but with orders to continue on in and land at Ewa. One pilot, on the extreme left wing of the patrol, was heard suddenly speaking over the voice radio circuit: "Don't shoot, this is an American plane!" and was never heard from again. Another, seeing the sky over Pearl filled with anti-aircraft bursts, wondered what crazy nonsense the Army was up to, holding anti-aircraft drills on a Sunday. When the truth dawned on him, he could not clear his machine-gun; the plane, however, managed to land. In all, seven planes of this squadron were shot down; eight of the fourteen men in them were killed and others wounded. The eleven B-17s from the mainland, though completely unarmed, had better fortune. One, trying to get into Bellows, was hit, set on fire, and destroyed just as she landed, but most of the crew were saved. Six managed to land amid the wreckage at Hickam; one landed at Wheeler, one on a golf course, and two got into the Haleiwa air-strip.

The Japanese missed only one of all our air elements—the fighter squadron at Haleiwa, about which the enemy apparently knew nothing. They were likewise unready, but the commander, Major George S. Welsh, got into the air with one wing man about 8.15 and three more pilots got up later. Major Welsh claimed four Japanese; and the others, together with the fighters which took off from Wheeler and the *Enterprise* scout bombers, got a number more. But the net result was that in the first fifteen minutes of the action the Japanese had successfully destroyed or paralyzed virtually the entire air strength of Oahu. In the same space of time they had gone far towards the accomplishment of their main objective, the destruction of the United States Pacific Fleet.

Seven of Kimmel's eight battleships were moored along the south-easterly face of Ford Island, at big concrete bollards or mooring posts set just off the shore line. *California* was at the southern end of the row, then the tanker *Neosho,* full of aviation fuel, then *Maryland* and *Oklahoma* side by side with *Oklahoma* outboard, then *Tennessee* and *West Virginia* with the latter outboard, then *Arizona* with the repair ship *Vestal* outboard of her, then *Nevada* alone. *Pennsylvania,* the eighth battleship, was in the big dry dock at the Navy Yard across the channel, together with a couple of destroyers ahead of her in the same dock. Several cruisers were in relative security in the Navy Yard slips; but the modern light cruiser *Helena* was moored at "10-10 Dock", the long quay paralleling the channel on the eastern side, with the old converted minelayer *Oglala* outboard of her. Around the north-westerly side of Ford Island there was another row of four ships lying at bollards. In order from the north end these were the light cruiser *Detroit,* the light cruiser *Raleigh,* the old battleship *Utah* converted into a target ship, and the seaplane tender *Tangier.* Most of the destroyers were anchored in nests in the broad basin of East Loch, north of Ford Island, and the submarines were in slips at their base.

Over this great fleet the forty Japanese torpedo bombers broke like a storm just before eight o'clock. They came from every direction, each pilot carefully briefed on the particular angle from which to launch his torpedo in order to get the best run and cause the maximum confusion in the defence. Taking the gunners by complete surprise, they were almost impossible to hit; in a few moments the harbour was crisscrossed by the white wakes of their missiles, and tremendous explosions were leaping up against the steel sides of the battleships. The horizontal and dive bombers were immediately behind them; and the bombs were landing even as the torpedoes went home. Every one of the five outboard battleships took one or more torpedo hits in the first few minutes, and the two inboard ships, *Maryland* and *Tennessee,* were hit by bombs. Other torpedo planes and bombers were at the same time attacking the ships moored along the north-west face of the island. The old target ship *Utah,* lying in a berth often used by the aircraft-carriers, took two torpedoes, turned over, and sank at 8.13, the first total casualty. The light cruiser *Raleigh,* lying just ahead of her, received one torpedo and later a bomb hit, and only heroic measures kept her from turning turtle.

In Battleship Row, the repair ship *Vestal,* lying alongside of *Arizona,* had afforded the latter slight protection. Two torpedoes streaked past the smaller vessel to reach the battleship,* while a heavy armour-piercing bomb found its way to *Arizona*'s forward magazine, and she blew up with a terrific detonation. The whole forward half of the ship was a total wreck, through which tremendous oil fires now poured up their flames and great billows of smoke. Just south of her *West Virginia* had taken four or five torpedo and bomb hits. Enormous rents had been torn in her plating; there was a fierce fire amidships, and she was settling now to the bottom, fortunately on an even keel. *Tennessee*, lying inboard, was not too badly damaged; but she was pinned against the bollards by the sinking *West Virginia* and was imperilled by the oil fires raging in the *Arizona* and across the water between them. South of this pair, the old *Oklahoma*, lying outboard of *Maryland*, had received four torpedo hits in the first minutes; she was soon listing extravagantly, and at 8.32 she rolled completely over and lay, like an immense whale, with her bottom and propellers showing to the now densely smoke-filled sky.

Meanwhile, a single torpedo plane, streaking in from the west, had loosed its "fish" against 10-10 Dock; passing under *Oglala*, the torpedo exploded against the bottom of *Helena*, lying inboard of the old minelayer. The light cruiser was severely damaged, but *Oglala* had her whole side stove in. Tugs dragged her away from *Helena* in time, but presently she went over, sinking on her beam ends. Across from 10-10 Dock the battleship *California*, alone at the southern end of the row, had taken two torpedoes and bomb hits; there were fires in her; the fact that her compartments had been open hindered damage control, and she was slowly settling at her moorings.

All this had been accomplished in the first half-hour

* This is uncertain. Later investigation was to throw doubt on the question of whether *Arizona* was torpedoed, but it was so reported at the time.

of the attack, and most of it in the first ten minutes. The torpedo planes, their missiles expended, faded away. There were still horizontal and dive bombers ranging unhindered over the scene.

Walter Millis

President Roosevelt to Congress: 8 December

Yesterday, 7 December 1941—a date which will live in infamy—the United States of America was suddenly and deliberately attacked by naval and air forces of the Empire of Japan.

Imperial Rescript: the 8th day of the 12th month of the 16th year of Showa

We, by the grace of heaven, Emperor of Japan, seated on the Throne of a line unbroken for ages eternal, enjoin upon ye, Our loyal and brave subjects:

We hereby declare war on the United States of America and the British Empire. The men and officers of Our Army and Navy shall do their utmost in prosecuting the war, Our public servants of various departments shall perform faithfully and diligently their appointed tasks, and all other subjects of Ours shall pursue their respective duties; the entire nation with a united will shall mobilize their total strength so that nothing will miscarry in the attainment of our war aims.

Fascists Jubilant

A night telephone call from Ribbentrop. He is over-joyed about the Japanese attack on America. He is so happy about it that I am happy with him, though I am not too sure about the final advantages of what has happened. One thing is now certain; that America will enter the conflict, and that the conflict will be so long that she will be able to release all her potential forces.

This morning I told this to the King, who had been
pleased about the event. He ended by admitting that, in
the long run, I may be right. Mussolini was happy, too.
For a long time he has favoured a definite clarification
of relations between America and the Axis.

Count Ciano

I Shall Never Look Back

All of Japan went to war singing this song. Roughly
translated, *Umi Yukaba* goes:

> Across the sea,
> Corpses in the water;
> Across the mountain,
> Corpses heaped upon the field;
> I shall die only for the Emperor,
> I shall never look back.

Tokyo

A train passes under the viaduct, and the first travellers
appear at the gates of the station. Hearing the jingling
of his bell, they flock round the newsvendor, hand over
their pennies and seize the paper. It is a very small sheet,
almost like a pamphlet. The amazing news item figures
there alone, in a few vertical lines in thick Japanese
characters. "From to-day at dawn the Imperial Army and
Navy are at war with the forces of the United States and
Great Britain in the waters of the Western Pacific."

I watch the reactions of the people who read it. They
walk on for two or three steps, then they stop suddenly
in order to read it again, bend their heads and start back.
Then they raise their faces that have once again become
expressionless, transformed into the mask of apparent
indifference. Nobody says a word to the newsvendor, none
of the readers exchange a remark with each other. . . .
I know them well enough to understand their reactions;
under their assumed impassivity they can barely control

their stupefaction and consternation. They wanted this war and yet they did not want it. They talked about it all the time, out of bravado and in imitation of their leaders, but they never really believed in it. . . . Tokyo is afraid, the Japanese are panic-stricken by their own daring.

Robert Guillain

4

DEFEAT IN THE FAR EAST

MALAYA

*On the same day that Pearl Harbor was attacked,
Japanese forces landed in Thailand and upon the north-
east coast of Malaya. Thailand ceased resistance and
allowed the passage of Japanese troops twenty-four hours
later. On 8 December 1941 began the Japanese attack
upon Hong Kong, which held out for seventeen days. In
seventy days, the Japanese were to advance the length
of the Malaya peninsula.*

PEARL HARBOR was the opening note in what became
one of the great clashes of peoples and principles.
Singapore was the full-struck chord.

George Weller, war correspondent

A Correspondent Cables to America: 7 December

Strong indications Japanese are moving up ships and
troops to launch an imminent attack with landing parties
against Thailand with immediate objectives of capturing
Bangkok. Reconnaissance by American-made Catalinas
and Hudson bombers discovered units of Japanese Navy,
including cruisers and merchant ships believed containing

troops, are now steaming down the Gulf of Siam along the Indo-China coast in the direction of Thailand. . . .

War Comes to Singapore

The war began with a bang.

Maria and I lived on the top of the highest building in Singapore, the Cathay Building, which also housed the offices of the Malayan Broadcasting Corporation and the Far Eastern headquarters of the Ministries of Information and Economic Warfare. We had gone to bed early. Suddenly, shortly after four in the morning, the first siren began to wail. Rising and falling, rising and falling, it cut across the stillness of the tropic night like some frightful oath uttered in a polite drawing-room. One after the other the sirens from different parts of the city chimed in until they formed one shrill cacophony. If it was eerie for the white people, what chill fear that sound must have struck into the breasts of hundreds of thousands of poor natives in their ramshackle houses of brick and timber! I leapt out of bed and pulled back the curtain. With complete certainty I knew that it was war. A ring of searchlights from their positions round the islands were focused straight up into the air, moving backwards and forwards, trying to spot the planes that had caused the alarm. The black-out was not at all good and all the street lights were burning. Suddenly there were bright flashes and loud explosions in the direction of the docks and the centre of the town. The anti-aircraft guns were firing. From where we watched there were no planes visible, although we could hear the drone of bombers, that low vibration that one *feels* as much as hears. Then some bombs fell down in the same quarter where the guns had been firing, not many, but they made a deeper rumbling sound quite distinct from the loud report of the guns. Then silence. The drone gradually died away. The searchlights continued their search for the raiders. The lights in the streets still shone brightly. One or two cars with dimmed lights sped through the streets. The voices

of air-raid wardens, bustling about their duties, drifted
up from below. One by one the searchlights were switched
off. A long time later the all-clear sounded.

Ian Morrison, war correspondent

*From the very beginning of the Malayan campaign,
the pattern was set: Japanese troops, trained and
equipped for jungle fighting, infiltrated, outflanked and
attacked from the rear their road-bound, ill-prepared
opponents, cutting them off or forcing them to withdraw
hurriedly to avoid that fate.*

The First Retreat

We were all so busy that we often failed to
remember—though we knew we were working against
time—that time would soon be up; but the signs had
become pretty obvious. R.A.F. Buffaloes at Alor Star had
for days been trying to chase away a Japanese plane that
came over regularly to photograph our poor old Jitra
Line: Thais on the border were becoming stricter in their
train searches; we had news that Sikh agitators had
crossed the frontier with orders to contact Sikh troops
in Malaya. Even so it came as something of a
shock—perhaps a shock of relief—when news came
through in the early morning of 8 December that a
Japanese convoy was off Kota Bahru, on the west coast,
and was being engaged by our planes and artillery. We
gave a cheer for "our artillery", knowing that it consisted
solely of four guns of our detached 21st Mountain
Battery. Plan Matador was still on (we were to advance
into Thailand and get as far as Singgora at least) and
we moved out to the railway station long before dawn.
But by ten o'clock that morning—in the meantime we
had sat passively watching Alor Star aerodrome being
bombed—the plan was altered and we were ordered into
defensive positions on the road. That night and most of
the next day we spent in one of our well-known and well-

prepared gun positions, about six miles from the frontier. 1st/14th Punjab Regiment, under Lieutenant-Colonel Fitzpatrick, were the advance guard and the four guns of 4th Mountain Battery were to support them as they fell back, gracefully and gradually we hoped, on to the Jitra Line. An ambush party, consisting mainly of Bren carriers from 1st/8th Punjab, rattled past us into Thailand during the night. It returned in the morning, reporting only partial success. Someone had committed the original military sin of firing before he got the order.

By tea-time on 9 December we had managed to make our gun position fairly comfortable, and the gunners, who were convinced that the Japanese were a most *mamouli* enemy, were quite impatient for their arrival. At five o'clock I had sudden and unexpected orders to take my Sikh section and its two guns to a position from which I could fire on a road demolition that had been made just inside Thailand. Once again we went through the motions of going out of action and proceeding up the road; but this was the last time we ever travelled it in a northward direction. By 5.30 we were in position near the 27th milestone. So much for the completeness of our preparations—not only had we never surveyed this position—we had never even seen it. We surveyed it just before dark. We were under cover of a small Chinese village, which stank with rare violence—even for a Chinese village—and contained more mosquitoes to the cubic inch of heated air than I met with in any other place in Malaya.

Soon after midnight came the sound of light machine-gun fire from the front and Lieutenant R. M. Hare of the O.P. told us to open up on the demolition. He called me to the phone to say that the first shell fired into Thailand had landed smack in the middle of the road. Jemadar Jogindar Singh, when I told him, smiled politely and asked in a slightly injured tone whether I had had any doubts about it.

For two hours or so we fired at regular intervals on

the demolition. The mosquitoes clustered upon us gratefully; a *naik* off duty snored under the muzzle of No. 1 gun; it was all very peaceful. We finished our firing task and the quiet was disturbed only by nightjars and cicadas and very infrequent small-arms fire. Suddenly a burst of light machine-gun fire came from the left and behind us; it was followed by another and another. Orders came through; we were to pull out and return to the old position; we had better hurry, the Japs were nearly round us. It was a pattern we got to know far too well in the next couple of months. Three nights later the Japanese were through the Jitra Line and we were south of Alor Star and had seen the last of the road. The sorry trek to Singapore was on and three months of preparation had been proved futile in three days.

Rawle Knox

Disaster at Sea

On 10 December two of the finest battleships in the British Navy, H.M.S. Prince of Wales *and H.M.S.* Repulse, *sailed from Singapore accompanied by four destroyers to seek and destroy enemy landing barges coming down the east coast. Admiral Phillips wore his pennant on the* Prince of Wales.

The landings carried out on the east coast of the Malay peninsula at dawn on 7 December were mostly successful except at Kota Bahru. On this day our reconnaissance planes had reported two British battleships at anchor in Singapore. At 3.15 p.m. the next day two battleships were sighted by I.165 at a point three hundred miles north of Singapore. She recognized them as the *Prince of Wales* and *Repulse*. The ships were proceeding northwards at high speed; their target was the supply line of our landings. Although they were clearly visible, they were out of torpedo range, but Commander Harada, I.165's captain, sent off a cipher message giving course and bearings. It duly reached the Malayan operational H.Q., and all submarines in the area surfaced and immediately took up the pursuit at speed.* The entire Malayan naval force, consisting of the battleships *Kongo* and *Haruna,* together with the cruiser squadron and destroyer squadron under the command of Vice-Admiral Nobutake Kondo, was not really a match for the opponents, but our ships forged ahead with all speed in the hope of forcing a night action, in which was their best chance of achieving good results. However, contact with the enemy was lost in the dark night. At 3.40 a.m. on 10 December, I.156 attacked the ships on a southerly course in a position slightly to the westward of the original sighting, but missed in the darkness. At dawn the air units, keyed up with the news from Pearl Harbor, joined in their search for the enemy.

Mochitsura Hashimoto

Reporter on *Repulse*

Wednesday, 10 December

06.30—We are putting on cover-alls, anti-flash helmets and battle helmets. Off to the beam the sky is streaked with gold. All the gun crews are at the action stations. Gallagher and I went down for breakfast of coffee, cold ham, bread and marmalade.

07.20—Back on the flag deck. We are pushing in towards shore very fast. The *Prince of Wales* is ahead; we follow; the destroyers are about a mile or a mile and a half on each side of us. We still have four of them. We

* H.M.S. *Prince of Wales* and *Repulse* were sighted by a Japanese submarine at 2 p.m., 9 December 1941, in position 7° N. latitude, 105° E. longitude, steering north. (This position was very inaccurate.)

At 3.15 a.m., 10 December, the Japanese received a report from a second submarine which indicated that the British squadron was steering south. Bad weather precluded any form of air search on 9 December.

can see the shore line and an island far ahead of us.

10.45—One twin-engined Jap is reported shadowing us. It is the same type that bombed Singapore the first night of the war. It is a type 96 Mitsubishi of the Naval Air Service.

The clouds have gone now, and the sky is a robin's-egg blue and the sun is bright yellow. Our ships plough through pea-green water, white where the hulls cleave it.

11.07—The communications loudspeaker announces: "Enemy aircraft approaching—action stations!"

I see them: one-two-three-four-five-six-seven-eight-nine. There are nine, flying line astern, one behind the other.

I would judge them about twelve thousand feet, coming straight over the *Repulse*.

11.14—And here they come.

11.15—The guns of the *Prince of Wales* just let go. At the same instant I see the flame belching from the guns of the *Wales,* ours break into a chattering, ear-splitting roar. The nine Japanese aircraft were stretched out across the bright blue, cloudless sky like star sapphires of a necklace.

I gape open-mouthed at those aircraft coming directly over us, flying so that they will pass from bow to stern over the *Repulse.* The sky is filled with black puffs from our ack-ack. They seem a discordant profanation of that beautiful sky. But the formation of Japanese planes, coming over one behind the other, is undisturbed.

Now they are directly overhead. For the first time I see the bombs coming down, materializing suddenly out of nothingness and streaming towards us like ever-enlarging tear-drops. There's a magnetic, hypnotic, limb-freezing fascination in that sight.

It never occurs to me to try and duck or run. Open-mouthed and rooted, I watch the bombs getting larger and larger. Suddenly, ten yards from me, out in the water, a huge geyser springs out of the sea, and over the side, showering water over me and my camera.

I instinctively hunch over, sort of a semi-crouch, and at the same instant there is a dull thud. The whole ship shudders. Pieces of paint fall from the deck over the flag deck.

11.17—"Fire on the boat deck. Fire below!" That just came over the loud-speakers. There are fountains of water all around the ship. Some are near misses. Most of the bombs are hitting the water ten to thirty yards off the port side. Beautiful fountains of thick white at the base and then tapering up into fine spray.

That first bomb was a direct hit. Someone on the flag deck says, "Fire in marines' mess and hangar."

That bomb struck the catapult deck, penetrated, exploded underneath. The bomb hit twenty yards astern of my position on the flat deck. A number of men [fifty] were killed.

11.45—. . . The torpedo-carrying bombers are coming in. We are putting up a beautiful barrage, a wall of fire. But the bombers come on, in a long glide, from all angles, not simultaneously but alternately. Some come head-on, some astern and from all positions on both sides of the ship. They level out.

About three hundred yards distant from the ship and a hundred yards above the water they drop their torpedoes.

The torpedoes seem small, dropping flat into the water, sending up splashes, then streaking towards us. Those bombers are so close you can almost see the colour of the pilot's eyes. The bombers are machine-gunning our decks as they come in.

11.51 1/2—Captain Tennant is sending a message to the *Wales*: "Have you sustained any damage?"

The answer comes back: "We are out of control. Steering gear is gone."

The decks of the *Repulse* are littered with empty shell-cases. Upon the faces of the sailors there's a mixture of incredulity and a sort of sensuous pleasure, but I don't detect fear. There's an ecstatic happiness, but strangely, I don't see anything approaching hate for the attackers. For the British this is a contest. The facial expression is interpreted by an officer. He turned to me and says,

"Plucky blokes, those Japs. That was as beautiful an attack as ever I expect to see."

Cecil Brown, war correspondent

The End

A new wave of planes appeared at 12.20 p.m. The end was near, though we did not know it. *Prince of Wales* lay about ten cables astern of our port side. She was helpless. Not only was her steering-gear destroyed, but also her screws by that first torpedo. Unlike the German *Bismarck* caught by the Navy in the Atlantic, which lost only her steering-gear and was able to keep moving in a circle, *Prince of Wales* was a hulk.

All the aircraft made for her. I do not know how many there were in this last attack, but it was afterwards estimated that there were between fifty and eighty Japanese torpedo-bombers in operation during the entire action. *Prince of Wales* fought desperately to beat off the determined killers who attacked her like a pack of dogs on a wounded buck. *Repulse* and the destroyers formed a rough circle around her, to add our fire-power. All ships fired with the intention of protecting *Prince of Wales,* and in doing so each neglected her own defences.

It was difficult to make out her outline through the smoke and flame from all her guns except the 14-inchers. I saw one plane drop a torpedo. It fell nose-heavy into the sea and churned up a thin wake as it drove straight at the immobile *Prince of Wales*. It exploded against her bows. A couple of seconds later another hit her—and another.

I gazed at her turning slowly over on her port side, her stern going under, and dots of men jumping into the sea, and was thrown against the bulkhead by a tremendous shock as *Repulse* was hit by a torpedo on her port side.

O. D. Gallagher, war correspondent

The torpedo strikes the ship about twenty yards astern

of my position. It feels as though the ship has crashed into dock. I am thrown four feet across the deck but I keep my feet. Almost immediately, it seems, the ship lists.

The command roars out of the loudspeaker, "Blow up your life belts!"

I take down mine from the shelf. It is a blue-serge affair with a rubber bladder inside. I tie one of the cords around my waist and start to bring another cord up around the neck. Just as I start to tie it the command comes, "All possible men to starboard."

Captain Tennant's voice is coming over the ship's loudspeaker, a cool voice: "All hands on deck. Prepare to abandon ship." There is a pause for just an instant, then: "God be with you."

There is no alarm, no confusion, no panic. We on the flag deck move towards a companionway leading to the quarter deck. Abrahams, the Admiralty photographer, Gallagher and I are together. The coolness of everyone is incredible. There is no pushing, but no pausing either. One youngster seems in a great hurry. He tries to edge his way into the line at the top of the companionway to get down faster to the quarter deck.

A young sub-lieutenant taps him on the shoulder and says quietly, "Now, now, we are all going the same way, too."

The youngster immediately gets hold of himself.

The *Repulse* is going down.

The torpedo-smashed *Prince of Wales,* still a half to three-quarters of a mile ahead, is low in the water, half shrouded in smoke, a destroyer by her side.

Japanese bombers are still winging around like vultures, still attacking the *Wales.* A few of those shot down are bright splotches of burning orange on the blue South China Sea.

Men are tossing overboard rafts, lifebelts, benches, pieces of wood, anything that will float. Standing at the edge of the ship, I see one man (Midshipman Peter Gillis, an eighteen-year-old Australian from Sydney) dive from the air defence control tower at the top of the main mast.

He dives a hundred and seventy feet and starts to swim away.

Men are jumping into the sea from the four or five defence control towers that segment the main mast like a series of ledges. One man misses his distance, dives, hits the side of the *Repulse,* breaks every bone in his body and crumples into the sea like a sack of wet cement. Another misses his direction and dives from one of the towers straight down the smokestack.

Men are running all along the deck of the ship to get further astern. The ship is lower in the water at the stern and their jump therefore will be shorter. Twelve Royal Marines run back too far, jump into the water and are sucked into the propeller.

The screws of the *Repulse* are still turning. There are five or six hundred heads bobbing in the water. The men are being swept astern because the *Repulse* is still making way and there's a strong tide here, too.

**Captain Tennant on the bridge turns to the navigating officer: "It looks a bit different from this angle, doesn't it, pilot?"

The navigating officer nods, but says nothing. The group of officers on the bridge look at each other, and at the skipper.

"Well, gentlemen," Captain Tennant says quietly, "you had better get out of it now."

"Aren't you coming with us, sir?" two or three eagerly demand simultaneously.

The Captain smiles, shakes his head negatively, then says impatiently, "Off you go now. There's not much time." They are all hanging on to something, one leg braced to keep an even keel as the ship heels over more and more.

"But, Captain," the lieutenant commander says, "you must come with us. You've done all you could for this

---

** Cecil Brown wrote the passage between double asterisks from the accounts of eye-witness survivors.

ship. More than most men could."

Captain Tennant does not budge. The men are getting restive. Almost by pre-arrangement they all move towards their skipper. They push him forcibly through the narrow doorway and on to the deck. The *Repulse* is almost on her beam-ends. Captain Tennant will go no farther. The officers and men of the bridge seize Captain Tennant and push him over the side. Then they jump into the sea.**

The jump is about twenty feet. The water is warm; it is not water, but thick oil. My first action is to look at my stop watch. It is smashed at 12.35, one hour and twenty minutes after the first Japanese bomb came through twelve thousand feet to crash into the catapult deck of the *Repulse*.

It doesn't occur to me to swim away from the ship until I see others striking out. Then I realize how difficult it is. The oil soaks into my clothes, weighting them and I think under-water demons are tugging at me, trying to drag me down. The airless lifebelt, absorbing oil too, tightens and tautens the preserver cords around my neck. I say to myself, "I'm going to choke to death, I'm going to choke to death."

The oil burns in my eyes as though someone is jabbing hot pokers into the eyes. That oil in the eyes is the worst thing. I've swallowed a bit of oil already, and it's beginning to sicken me.

Fifty feet from the ship, hardly swimming at all now, I see the bow of the *Repulse* swing straight into the air like a church steeple. Its red under-plates stand out as stark and as gruesome as the blood on the faces of the men around me. Then the tug and draw of the suction of thirty-two thousand tons of steel sliding to the bottom hits me. Something powerful, almost irresistible, snaps at my feet. It feels as though someone were trying to pull my legs out by the hip sockets. But I am more fortunate than some others. They are closer to the ship. They are sucked back.

When the *Repulse* goes down it sends over a huge wave,

a wave of oil. I happen to have my mouth open and I take aboard considerable oil. That makes me terribly sick at the stomach.

After being picked up by one of the escorting destroyers:

Down there in the wardroom I am told the sequence of attacks on the *Prince of Wales*.

The attack was similar to our own. High-level bombers and torpedo-carrying bombers. With four torpedoes in the *Wales,* Admiral Phillips said, "Tell the *Express* (which was then alongside the *Wales*) to signal to Singapore for tugs to tow us home."

It was obvious the Admiral hadn't yet made up his mind that the ship was going to sink.

I ask a lieutenant-commander from the *Wales* about Admiral Phillips and Captain Leach.

They were last seen standing on the bridge of the *Prince of Wales*.

"The Admiral and the Captain stood there together," the officer says. "They would not go. As we started away, Captain Leach waved, and called out, 'Good-bye. Thank you. Good luck. God bless you'."

Then the water rose up to meet them, meeting and then covering them.

Cecil Brown

I still remember the chill sense of calamity which was caused by the loss of these two ships. It was worse than calamity. It was calamity that had the premonitions of further calamity. No details were available that evening although most people had visions of Japanese suicide squads flying their loaded planes straight into the ships. For the first time we had an inkling of what the true balance of factors was in this Pacific war. We saw before us, still vaguely perhaps, that long dark tunnel through which we should have to pass before we emerged in the sunlight on the far side. Blown clean away at one fell swoop was one of the main pillars on which our sense of security rested.

Ian Morrison

On the same day that the Prince of Wales *and* Repulse *went down, the Japanese took Kota Bahru airfield, the most advanced striking base which the Allies possessed. Within a week they were within a very few miles of Penang, and the loss of the island was the first of many shocks to come in the land battle.*

Penang Bombed: 12 December

At least six hundred people were killed in this raid, and an equal number wounded. The correspondents in Singapore were allowed to say that the casualties numbered seventy. Penang was the first city to demonstrate the depths of Chinese courage and Malay stoicism. The Asiatics had refused to take cover, and were machine-gunned in the streets. The hospitals were filled with terribly wounded people; they were still bringing them in two days afterwards. Here sat a wrinkled old man, his body curled like a sea shell around his grandchild, the only living member of his son's family of eight. On Saturday they found an old woman, wounded and with both her legs broken. When they brought her to the hospital grounds and laid her on the bare floor—there were not nearly enough cots—she piped up, "I'm not going to die yet. I'm going to live to see the Japs beaten."

George Weller

Disposing of the Dead

It was horrible. We had to work with gas masks and stick bayonets into the bodies and pitch them into a truck. We didn't bury them but just poured some kerosene over them and charred the bodies a bit.

A volunteer

Doubt: 13 December

Raffles Hotel still has dancing every night, but there are not as many dancers.

A good deal of the apathy about war has gone. In any event, it is true that the certainty that war would not come to Singapore has disappeared.

Cecil Brown

Realization: 18 December

The Japanese troops are now fourteen miles from Penang. This news came as a terrific shock to everyone in Singapore, and, as I understand it, throughout Malaya. People can hardly believe the Japs now have Alor Star and Sungei Patani. It was the first news they had that the Japanese had penetrated more than seventy-five miles from the Thai border. Up to now the people of Malaya thought that the Japs were being held almost at the frontier; instead they are well within Malaya and are about to take Penang.

. . . . The usual official communique came out this evening. It said, "We have successfully disengaged the enemy and are south of the River Krain."

I stared at that phrase—"successfully disengaged the enemy". It made no sense to me and I mulled over it for minutes. Then it suddenly occurred to me that someone had coined a beautiful phrase of defeatist optimism. I rolled it around on my tongue—*successfully disengaged the enemy*.

It also meant to me that the British were south of Penang, since the River Krain is south of that island.
. . .

. . . . Refugees are streaming into Singapore, and since the British refuse to admit the Penang débâcle, the people fear the worst. You can almost see morale collapsing like a punctured tyre.

Cecil Brown

The Invaders

The Japanese not only outfought us in Malaya—they out-thought us too. In everything they showed that they had devoted considerable care and study to the special requirements of a campaign taking place in the tropical jungle of the Malayan peninsula.

Thus they wore the lightest of uniforms, a singlet, cotton shorts, rubber-soled shoes. There was no uniformity about either the colour or the form of their dress. Both dress and equipment were as light as they could be, and all our commanders agreed that their cross-country capacity was remarkable. There was no uniformity about the headgear. Various types were worn, steel helmets, cotton khaki caps, slouch hats taken from prisoners or our own dead. Often they wore Malay sarongs. Two prisoners captured near Batu Pahat were disguised as Chinese coolies. This adoption of native dress troubled our troops, since the country through which the war was being fought was fairly thickly populated and our men were never able to distinguish between friend and foe. On my first trip to the front I heard innumerable "fifth-column" stories. The British Tommy began to think that the entire native population was fighting against him. He could never be quite certain that the young Malay lolling on the far side of the road or the Tamil coolie just disappearing into a rubber plantation was not a Japanese in disguise.

The Asiatic appearance of the enemy was also an enormous advantage to him. It enabled him to masquerade as a native of the country. The British troops would not have been able to distinguish between Chinese, Japanese and Malays if they had been wearing their respective national dresses, let alone when they were all wearing sarongs.

In the matter of food also the Japanese were at an advantage. Being rice-eaters, they were able to live off the country, eating the same food as the Malays and the Chinese used to eat. The British troops were dependent upon elaborate catering arrangements. The Japanese soldier would set off through the jungle carrying a bottle of water and a large ball of rice, with some preserved seaweed and a few pickles to make the rice palatable. Those were his rations for three or four days.

Nearly all the Japanese infantry were armed with tommy-guns or other light automatic weapons. They were ideal for this close-range jungle fighting. Our men were armed chiefly with rifles and the percentage of automatic weapons was small. There were several bayonet engagements, a form of warfare for which the enemy seemed to have a marked distaste. Many of our officers continued to swear by the rifle right up to the end of the campaign, and there are sound arguments on both sides in the rifle-versus-tommy-gun controversy. But it always seemed to me that the rifle's chief use is as an accurate long-range weapon, and in Malay there was rarely an extended field of fire. The advanced Japanese units would carry perhaps six or eight drums of ammunition with them and further supplies would be brought up in boxes on the carriers of push-bikes.

After the tommy-gun the next most popular weapon of the enemy was a light 2-inch mortar. Again, it was the weapon ideally suited to jungle warfare. It was very mobile and was easily transported and operated by two men. It was very accurate. The shell burst with a very loud report. There was also a 4-inch mortar which was seen mounted on armoured carriers. Except for the 2-inch mortar, Japanese artillery, until the siege of Singapore, played a comparatively small part in the fighting.

Hand-grenades were another weapon, extremely practicable in close fighting, of which the enemy made extensive use. Cases were reported in which Japanese climbed up trees and then tried to lob them down on to our vehicles.

Their local knowledge was excellent. They had good maps with them, and their guides were mostly former Japanese residents of Malaya whose job it had been to gain a detailed knowledge of the terrain.

They were fond of arboreal tactics and snipers would often climb up trees to shoot at our outposts. One of our casualties was shot in the foot while standing in a trench three feet deep. A British officer who went after a Japanese sniper reported to be concealed in a tree told me that he felt as if he was walking up to game at home.

One of the most conspicuous features of the campaign was the great use which the Japanese made of bicycles. They may have brought some with them from Japan, but most were simply commandeered from natives in the villages, possibly being paid for in the notes which the Japanese Army brought with them. (These notes were the same size, colour, and design as the British notes but said, "The Japanese Government promises to pay the bearer on demand" the sum of ten dollars, fifty cents, or whatever the denomination was. These notes must have been printed long in advance of the outbreak of war, still further evidence of the care and thoroughness with which the Japanese planned their campaign in the Pacific. In the Philippines, in the Netherlands East Indies, in Burma, the Japanese Army brought their own specially printed notes with them.) Bicycles still further increased the mobility of the Japanese and enabled their forward troops to progress at great speed.

They made full use of the numerous rivers and "crocodile-infested" streams up-country, sometimes using collapsible rubber boats, sometimes native craft commandeered or bought from the local inhabitants, sometimes native rafts made of bamboo poles lashed together with rattan. The Chinese sampans, capable of carrying forty men and their equipment, proved ideal for entering the mangrove swamps owing to their shallow draught. The first landings at Kota Bahru were made from specially constructed iron barges, brought overland from Singora. At a later date these barges were taken overland to the Straits of Johore and used in landings on the island.

It will be seen that the highest degree of mobility was the keynote of the enemy's equipment. The British forces were nothing like so mobile. One only had to see the

British soldier on his way to the front, seemingly borne down with heavy boots, tin helmet, gas-mask, heavy pack, canvas webbing, rifle and bayonet, to sense that he lacked a certain freedom of movement. He had also been trained to be very dependent on his vehicular transport and this complicated, if it did not impede, movement. One used to see British troops seemingly immobilized by their own transport.

In their tactics the Japanese practised an extreme devolution of command. Small groups of men, even single individuals, would be told to make their way as best they could to a point on the map a number of miles ahead. It would be up to them to get there. They would set off through the jungle, quietly picking their way, sometimes lying concealed for hours. Arrived at the given point behind our lines they would re-form. Contact with their forces in the rear would be maintained by portable wireless apparatus. If they came up against one of our outposts they would attack it from the front, but, if the opposition were severe, would make no attempt to press home the frontal attack. Instead, they would creep round and attack it either from the flank or from the rear. Similarly, if our troops advanced, the enemy would simply melt into the jungle on each side and again attack from the flank. Such were the tactics employed by the Japanese not only against sections but against whole brigades and divisions. The landings on the west coast which later caused us so much trouble, when sometimes one or two thousand men would slip ashore under cover of darkness, were simply attempts to outflank our positions on a much larger scale.

These tactics were made possible by several things—by the Japanese superiority in numbers; by the fact that the terrain in Malaya favoured the attacker at every turn and hindered the defender; by the remarkable cross-country capacity of the Japanese infantryman who was the spearhead of the attack; by the enemy's superior local knowledge.

Ian Morrison

The Defenders: An Officer Speaks

It's like this. Before the war we would be working from a map to conduct our manoeuvres. Our colonel or the brigadier would say, "Now this is thick jungle here and this is mangrove swamp. We can rule this out. In this sector all we have to concern ourselves with is the main road."

Thus we based out strategy on that type of operation. We kept to the roads everywhere. Why, I went through a mangrove swamp the other day and nowhere did I go down in the mud over my ankles. Anyhow, you can walk on the roots in almost any swamp and in that way avoid sinking down.

Japanese Propaganda

Not only did the Japanese drop bombs on Malaya; they also dropped leaflets by the thousand, in every language spoken in the peninsula, English, Malay, Chinese, Hindustani, Urdu, Gurmukhi. The leaflets were usually remarkable as much for the fatuity of their contents as for the incorrectness of the idiom in which they were couched. From a Japanese aircraft, flying so high that it was invisible to the naked eye, they would flutter down out of the sky on Singapore or on the towns up-country. I remember one in English purporting to be a newspaper extra and carrying a spurious Lisbon date-line, which declared that the United States had opened separate peace negotiations with Japan. Another, addressed to the officers and men of the British Army, asked, "Why do you submit to the intolerable torture of malarial mosquitoes merely to pamper the British aristocrat? Do not dedicate your lives merely to fatten the British high-hat." One addressed to the Indian troops would show a British officer sheltering in the rear while the Indians fought the enemy. One in Malay would contain a crude drawing of a fat white man with a whisky-glass in his hand treading a Malay underfoot, or a map of the Malayan peninsula with the Rising Sun flags all round it and the Union Jack flying only in the middle of the peninsula. One addressed to the Australians showed a blonde floozy tossing restlessly on her bed and crying out, "Oh, Johnny, come back to me. I am so lonely without you." One dropped on Singapore on Christmas Day had a drawing of what looked like several cavemen brandishing torches, with the legend underneath in Chinese and Malay—"Burn all the white devils in the sacred white flame of victory." Bedrock in crudity was reached with a leaflet containing a reprint of a letter taken from the body of a dead Australian, written by his wife in Australia and giving him all the news about home and children. Pamphlets of this nature simply made the few white men who saw them feel that they were pitted against a brutal and barbaric foe. A pamphlet of another type, however, had a certain effect on the Asiatic population. One which fell on Singapore simply advised the native population to evacuate the city on a certain date. Fearing a terrific blitz on the date mentioned, a certain number of natives did evacuate, causing, if they were labourers or men engaged on essential services, still further complications in the problem of native labour. The day in question passed quite uneventfully, nor was the scale of Japanese air attacks noticeably intensified during the days following. Occasionally the natives received advance information whether there was going to be a raid that day or not, and the British staff at aerodromes would always prepare for a raid if they noticed any unusual movement on the part of the native inhabitants.

Ian Morrison

Japanese supremacy in the air was as obvious as their other advantages.

. . . . For the most part the night marches were our sorest trial. They were for us the reality of the Japanese superiority in the air. While the planes wheeled overhead we could not move without risk. We moved by night. We fought by day. In our impotence we watched the Japanese airmen searching for their target, coming closer to make doubly sure, then diving to the attack. There was a rattle of small-arms fire and somewhere behind the pump-pump of a Bofors, but always, it seemed, the planes soared away unharmed. Then one morning a squadron of British bombers skimmed low over the rubber trees and every man sprang up to cheer. False hopes! Within the week they had vanished from the fighting areas, and were not seen there any more.

Lieutenant C. A. R. Smallwood

Unless additional aircraft are supplied to the British forces in Malaya, Singapore stands in grave danger from the land advance. The wishful thinking and almost country-wide conviction among the military that the Japanese would back down as well as the underestimation of the Japanese strength plus the suddenness of the Japanese attack are responsible for the present situation.

There is throughout Singapore great criticism of the amazing unwillingness of the high command to inform the people what is going on. This method of treating Asiatics as well as Europeans as children who are unable to stand bad news is inevitably causing internal repercussions.

Cecil Brown

On 12 January 1942 Kuala Lumpur, second city of the peninsula, fell, but as the British and Commonwealth forces were inexorably driven southwards down the length of the Malay Peninsula their resistance became more effective in some places. The advancing Japanese did not always have things their own way.

Penang radio used to announce that "Kuala Lumpur will be bombed tomorrow at eleven in the morning and five in the afternoon". It usually was.

The Fall of Kuala Lumpur

On the outskirts of the city there were two or three
high columns of black smoke—they had been a feature
of Kuala Lumpur for several days past—as some
remaining stocks of rubber were destroyed. We visited
one such fire. The latex was burning fiercely, giving out
such heat that one could not go within fifty yards, sending
an enormous mushroom of inky smoke straight up into
the air. The manager of this estate, an Australian who
had been in Malaya for many years, had everything
packed up in his car and was just about to leave for the
south. The stocks of rice from the godown were being
distributed to the Indian and Chinese labourers. Two
Indian clerks were keeping a tally. It was quite orderly.
Each labourer would have enough rice to keep him for
at least two months. In the processing plant next door
to the godown all the machinery had been smashed up.

. . . . The scene that met one's eyes in the city was
fantastic. Civil authority had broken down. The European
officials and residents had all evacuated. The white police
officers had gone and most of the Indian and Malay
constables had returned to their homes in the surrounding
villages. There was looting in progress such as I have
never seen before. Most of the big foreign department
stores had already been whittled clean since the white
personnel had gone. There was now a general sack of
all shops and premises going on.

. . . . Radios, rolls of cloth, tins of preserved foods,
furniture, telephones, carpets, golf-clubs, there was every
conceivable object being fiercely fought for and taken
away. One man had even brought an ox-cart into town
and was loading it up in the main street outside
Whiteaways. The most striking sight I saw was a young
Tamil coolie, naked except for a green loincloth, who
had had tremendous luck. He had found a long cylindrical
tin, three inches in diameter and a foot long, well wrapped
up. What could it contain? Obviously a tin like this could
only contain some rare and luxurious Western delicacy.

He sat on the kerbstone turning the tin round in his hands. He wished that he could read that Western language so that he might know what the tin contained. Should he open it now or should he wait until he got home? Curiosity got the better of him and he decided to open the tin. Carefully he peeled off the paper and took off the lid. Three white Slazenger tennis-balls rolled slowly out, bounced on the pavement and then trickled into the gutter, where they soon lost their speckless whiteness.

. . . . The only thing that was not being looted was booze. Several days previously the army had collected as much of the liquor in Kuala Lumpur as it could find. Tens of thousands of bottles and cases were amassed. When the time came for a move south, Local Defence Volunteers laid into the cases of gin and whisky and other intoxicants with sledge-hammers and destroyed them. It was a wise precaution.

. . . . Meanwhile the milling crowd of looters in the streets seemed to be becoming larger. Men were coming in from miles around to see what they could bag. Others were coming in for second and third trips. Only in some areas did the Chinese shopkeepers, with that toughness of fibre which is the secret of their country's greatness, arm themselves with long wooden staves and band together to protect their property from the ravages of would-be despoilers. Such were the last hours of the largest city on the Malayan mainland.

Ian Morrison

Fighting Back

It's difficult to find much optimism in these steady withdrawals. But it *is* noteworthy that British resistance shows signs of stiffening. This is due to the British forces becoming more concentrated, and to their increasing ability to fight the kind of jungle guerrilla warfare that the Japanese have found successful.

This does not mean that the Japanese drive to Singapore is being stopped. And the speed of the Japanese

advance has decreased in the past few weeks. To many
people here, it still seems rapid because the Japanese are
about two hundred miles nearer to Singapore than they
were when they crossed the Thai border into Malaya a
month ago.

Cecil Brown

Australians in Ambush

He* resolved, in this opening engagement, to try and
lead the Japanese into a trap. He chose a bridge on the
main road a few miles north of Gemas. The bridge was
prepared for demolition and a small group of men, upon
whom would devolve the task of blowing it up, concealed
themselves in the jungle near the bridge. One company
took up positions in the jungle on each side of the road,
and behind them were strung out the rest of the battalion.
The scheme was to let the Japanese through and then
fall upon them from each side of the road. The men took
up their positions and were given four days' rations. Only
two days' rations would have sufficed, for the Japanese
appeared very much earlier than we thought.

They cannot have expected anything at all. They came
marching along the road about four in the afternoon of
15 January in small groups, many of them wheeling
bicycles. Several companies came over the bridge and
walked down the road blissfully unaware that keen eyes
were watching them from out of the jungle on each side.
The officer in charge of blowing up the bridge decided
at last that he had let enough Japanese over. He waited
until there were as many actually on the bridge as he
thought there were likely to be at any one moment and
then released the fuse. There was a tremendous explosion.
The Japanese on the bridge were blown sky-high. Bridge,
bodies and bicycles went soaring up. The explosion was

* Major-General Gordon Bennett, commanding the Australians
in Malaya (Ed.)

the signal for the battalion to fall upon the Japanese, which they did with loud yells. Rifles barked, tommy-guns sputtered, many of the Australians dashed in with their bayonets. Nearly all the Japanese who were on the hither side of the bridge were killed. Later it was estimated that between eight hundred and a thousand of the enemy were killed, while the Australians suffered less than a hundred killed and wounded. The Australians then fell back south of Segamat.

It was a triumphant beginning. It set all the Australians cock-a-hoop. It had a tonic effect on all the British forces. But more was still to come.

Foiled in their attempt to come straight down the main road, the Japanese did what they always did and tried to come round the side. They switched their main push from Gemas to the coast. Bennett astutely foresaw what the probable Japanese strategy would be and took appropriate measures.

Our line along the south bank of the Muar river was originally held by 45 Indian Brigade. It was a recently-formed unit, the men were raw and untrained, and they had only been in the country a few days. When the Japanese attacked in the Muar river sector two days later, the Indians failed to hold them. The fighting was severe and several of the senior white officers of the brigade were killed. There was great confusion. When the 45th finally extricated themselves from the mess, they were sent back to Singapore and played little further part in the fighting. In an effort to stabilize the situation in the Muar sector, Bennett had to divert, first the 19th Battalion, and then the 29th, in the direction of the coast. The Australian anti-tank gunners went with them and took up a position nine miles south of Muar on the coast road. Bennett suspected that the Japanese might try to use their tanks down this coast road. He read the enemy's intentions correctly.

The 19th Battalion established contact with the enemy south of Muar late on the afternoon of 17 January. Japanese units had filtered through the jungle. At dawn they launched an attack with tanks down the main road. They appear to have used only ten tanks, all of the medium type. Tank-traps had been constructed and two anti-tank guns, well concealed with thick foliage, were trained down the road, the first some distance ahead of the other. A point was chosen where the road ran through a cutting with banks on each side so that any tanks would have difficulty in turning there and would not be able to escape into the rubber plantations on each side. The tanks came rumbling down the road at dawn, each flying the pennant of the Rising Sun. The first gun allowed six tanks to pass down the road so that they could be dealt with by the gun in the rear, and it was actually the rear gun that was the first to go into action. The Australian gunners, tense with expectancy, waited until the leading tank was only fifty yards away. Then, with loud shouts of "Whacko!" they let the Japanese have everything they'd got. The rear gun had a perfect field of fire. Five tanks were picked off, one after the other. They tried to turn round but could not do so in the cutting. Several caught fire and the ammunition inside them began to explode. The sixth tank was screened by the others and the gun could not sight it effectively, so one of the Australians picked up two hand-grenades, ran along the top of the cutting and threw them under the sixth tank, putting it out of action. Most of the Japanese crews were killed inside the tanks. A few scrambled out but were promptly picked off by rifle-fire. Meanwhile the forward gun, farther up the road, had let loose against the four remaining tanks, which were also close behind each other. They too were picked off, one after the other. In this second engagement a remarkable incident is reported to have occurred. I give it for what it is worth, although I was never able to obtain proper confirmation. A foreign officer in uniform was reported by two of the Australian gunners to have clambered out of one of the rearmost tanks, seized a bicycle that was affixed to the rear of the tank, and pedalled madly off up the road. If it was indeed a foreign officer, he could only have been one of the

German military experts who had been advising the Japanese.

Ian Morrison

By 30 January the Malay Peninsula was lost. Less than two hundred survivors of the Argyll and Sutherland Highlanders marched across the Causeway on to Singapore Island with their pipers playing. They were the last; behind them the Causeway was blown, and on the following day the British Commander-in-Chief broadcast to the island:

"The battle of Malay has come to an end and the battle of Singapore is started. For more than two months our troops have fought the enemy on the mainland. The enemy has had the advantage of great air superiority and considerable freedom of movement by sea.

"Our task has been both to impose losses on the enemy and to gain time to enable forces of the Allies to be concentrated for this struggle in the Far East.

"To-day we stand beleaguered in our island fortress until help can come, as assuredly it will come. This we are determined to do. In carrying out this task we want the active help of every man and woman in the fortress.

"There is work for all to do. Any enemy who sets foot in the fortress must be dealt with immediately. The enemy within our gates must be ruthlessly weeded out. There must be no more loose talk and rumour-mongering. Our duty is clear. With firm resolve and fixed determination we shall win through."

It's a bit late in the day for Percival to call on "every man and woman" of the seven hundred thousand natives. Their will to fight is gone.

Cecil Brown

Air attacks on the island grew in intensity. The outnumbered and dwindling defenders took heavy toll of the bombers, but they could not stop them. Below them, the city lay almost defenceless.

Fighters over Singapore

"We sailed right through the formation from one side to the other, shooting at everything in sight. Then when I came out the other side I saw two fighters coming at me—little chubby fellows with great big radial engines in front and painted bright green all over. I thought 'All right, you ——s!' and I started climbing for all I was worth. They couldn't keep up with me at all. I got well above them and then turned and dived on the nearest one. I got real close before I let him have it, and honest, you never saw anything like it. His machine just seemed to explode, with pieces flying off and smoke pouring out. He whipped up sort of, right in front of me, and then spun over sideways. The last I saw of him he was just a ball of fire going down. I gave the other one a burst, ammunition then so I dived away and headed for home. . . ."

. . . . There was a Chinese businessman in Singapore who had a standing offer of a bottle of champagne for every Jap plane destroyed, so that evening Red and Denny, accompanied by some of the others, drove into town to collect the two bottles they had earned by their victories.

Arthur G. Donahue

The Opposition is Very Strong

The British interception of the Japanese pilots talking to each other over their radio telephones is very good.

One Japanese pilot over Singapore called his base and shouted frantically, "The opposition is very strong—the opposition is very strong!"

"What is very strong," his base called, "the air opposition or the anti-aircraft?"

"My observer is dying," the pilot shouted.

Then there was a pause.

"He is dead. May I return now? The opposition is very strong," the pilot kept insisting. "My observer is dead—may I return now—may I return now?"

"Continue with your mission," he was told.

"I must return now—the opposition is too strong."

"Yes, return now," he finally was told.

There was another Japanese bomber in a flight of twenty-seven over Singapore. The aircraft fire was considerable and the British intercepted one pilot talking to his wing commander: "I think I should release my bombs now," he said.

"No, not yet," the commander told him.

The firing continued very heavily and he called his squadron leader again nervously: "I think I should release my bombs now."

He was told to await orders, but he kept pestering and finally was told: "All right, you can release your bombs and return to your base. But remember," the squadron leader said, "you have another mission this afternoon."

Cecil Brown

Air-Raid Precautions

They are not building any air-raid shelters underground in Singapore and the safest shelters appear to be the concrete sewers, a foot wide and three feet deep, which line all the streets. People are being urged to use them. An A.R.P. warden said, "Personally, if I were caught in the open I would just put my pride in my pocket and dive into a sewer. It is recommended, however, that those jumping in the sewers use respirators because of the stink."

On Orchard Road, one of the main shopping districts, there is one deep trench which has been improved by the British, who have put wooden boards across the top and covered it over with sandbags.

The idea is a good one but when it rains the water in the trench reaches the wooden top. A person thus has the choice of jumping into the water and keeping his nose pressed against the boards to keep from drowning or sitting outside and dodging the bomb splinters.

Cecil Brown

On 8-9 February the Japanese secured footholds on the island itself.

The Japs have crossed the Straits of Johore and landed on Singapore Island. It happened late Saturday night and it was not officially announced until this morning—thirty-six hours afterwards. I can just imagine what a shock it must have been to the people to find out that the enemy had been on the island for thirty-six hours.

The other day General Percival said, "We intend to hold Singapore. Everyone must realize that it's a common fight for military and civilians alike."

And the *Sydney Telegraph* editorial comments bitterly to-day: "So, when Singapore is in deadly danger, the civilian is expected to fight! With what? What has trained him? A month ago the brass hats in Singapore would have turned away in horror at the thought of inviting civilians to fight."

Cecil Brown

Last Stand

On the night of 8 February we heard a tremendous bombardment going on over in the west of the island, and later learned that the Japs had got ashore there and were making progress eastwards. This was about ten miles to our left rear; no enemy activity appeared on our sector, but we intensified our harrassing fire.

Next day we were ordered to withdraw to a perimeter round Singapore city, to conform to the Australians on our left, who were being hard pressed. Some of our guns were able to pull their trails round and support the troops on our left, but the close country made observation almost impossible. No attack or landing took place on our front; we had worked unceasingly on our gun positions and we felt desperately disappointed at having to leave them.

In the Singapore perimeter we held the central sector in the north and west of the suburbs. The gun area was necessarily very congested and batteries had to fit in where they could, in between buildings, on car parks und playing-fields, etc., all huddled together. Divisional H.Q. was between them and the forward posts. Here we fought the last bitter battle for Singapore. The Japs pressed us mainly from the west up the Bukit Timar road and from the north towards the reservoirs and Thompson Village.

We had F.O.Os with the infantry and were continuously firing tasks, but observation was very difficult, our wireless did not work and our lines were cut repeatedly. We constantly put down divisional artillery concentrations on both Bukit Timar villages and the main roads through them; later we knew from the numerous Jap graves in these places how effective our fire had been; but it was always at night that the Japs managed to infiltrate through our positions in the jungle country and in the morning the situation had invariably deteriorated. Enemy aircraft were over continuously; they had given up high-level attack now and were dive-bombing instead. Many were shot down by the L.A.A. gunners, but more came. Medium and heavy artillery now joined in and especially bombarded our congested gun area. They even had an observation balloon up some miles to the northward, which we presumed was directing the fire; but it was of course an impossible target—in any case our ammunition was dwindling fast. One's mind felt deadened and one could not believe this was really the end. Vain rumours spread of vast British reinforcements of aircraft and of landings behind the Japs. The sticky heat and frequent torrential rainstorms increased one's physical exhaustion. Already atrocity stories were beginning to come in.

Lieutenant-Colonel S. E. Skey

Thomson Road was now a veritable deathtrap, for transport from the north, west and east was converging on this main Singapore artery, and movement on the choked highway was slow and tedious. Enemy artillery was shelling many targets, snipers were harassing the drivers, and every now and then the enemy planes unloosed their loads of horror. The screams of the wounded and dying, the roar of burning trucks and cars, the deafening explosions of shells and bombs and the sickening whine and thud of small-arms bullets was something to instil fear into the stoutest heart.

On a little side road, nearly in the centre of the carnage, was a Tommy private, with a Vickers, mounted for ack-ack, pouring fire from a red-hot barrel at every plane that passed. Right in the centre of the road he stayed and carried on, no camouflage and no fear, and his answer to all and sundry was, "The bloody ——s will never think of looking for me in the open, and I want to see a bloody plane brought down."

Surrender

An invitation to our Command to surrender was dropped on 11 February by an aeroplane. The leaflets were signed by Yamashita and began: "I advise immediate surrender of the British forces at Singapore, from the standpoint of *bushido,* to the Japanese Army and Navy forces, which have already dominated Malaya, annihilated the British Fleet in the Far East, and acquired complete control of the China Sea and the Pacific and Indian Oceans, as well as southwestern Asia."

Ian Morrison

This demand was ignored, and the fighting continued. Three days later it was obvious that further resistance was hopeless, and General Percival sent a white flag to the Japanese.

The unceasing blitz continued throughout the night and next morning, 15 February. Company areas received a heavy battering, but few shells fell in the immediate vicinity of the palace itself, which was undamaged. The shelling was very accurate and obviously targets were selected deliberately, notably 8 Divisional H.Q. in Tanglin Barracks and the Cathay Building in the city. A map taken from a captured Japanese officer showed in detail the dispositions of the defending troops on the island and, interestingly enough, a plan of their own attack from the north-west. The only error in positions shown was that of Brigade H.Q. which had, however, only moved some hours previously. Espionage was then very thorough, and though the enemy had not yet broken through the perimeter his artillery and aerial successes could not be checked, and he was content to shell and bomb the city into submission. It became known during the afternoon that a cessation of hostilities would be asked for at 3.30 p.m. This was inevitable, as conditions in the city were worsening, and, adding to the general confusion, there was a breakdown of all essential services. The appalling number of native casualties was estimated at thirty-five thousand.

Consequently, while the defending army never for one moment expected to see the raising of the white flag, this sacrifice of innocent human beings could not go on. Shells became fewer, the noise of the battle gradually subsided, and at six o'clock all was quiet, except the drone of watchful planes overhead and a few stray enemy shells. Orders to cease fire at 8.30 p.m. came from headquarters, and the Malayan campaign of seventy weary days' duration came to an end.

A strange quiet settled over the Battalion positions. The men could not but feel thankful for the relief from the bombs and shells and the continuous strain of the past five weeks, but to the many who had never entertained the idea of capitulation it came as a staggering and sorrowful blow. It was difficult to realize that they were beaten and were prisoners of war. They were prepared to fight on in the streets, but they had no choice. They felt, at least, the consolation of a job done to the utmost of their ability, and had to be satisfied with that.

The personal message of the G.O.C. A.I.F., Malaya, Major-General Gordon Bennett, was accepted with appreciation. It was as follows: "The G.O.C. A.I.F., Malaya, wishes to thank all ranks for their fine fighting and excellent co-operation in the war in Malaya. You have maintained the highest traditions of the A.I.F. and have done your tasks nobly. You can at least march out with pride in your achievement."

Finally, Lieutenant-General Percival's last message came to hand: "It has been necessary to give up the struggle but I want the true reason explained to all ranks. The forward troops continue to hold their ground, but the essentials of war have run short. In a few days we shall have neither food nor petrol. Many types of ammunition are short and the water supply, on which the vast population and many of the fighting forces are dependent, threatens to fail. . . . This has been brought about by being driven off our dumps by hostile air and artillery action. Without these sinews of war we cannot fight on. I thank all ranks for their efforts throughout the campaign."

The Opening Battle

Prime Minister Curtin issued a statement to-day describing the fall of Singapore as the opening battle of Australia.

"I tell this nation that, as things stand to-day, brains and brawn are better than even bets or beer."

Cecil Brown

JAVA—THE PHILIPPINES

While the British were being pitchforked out of Malaya, the Japanese swept through the Netherlands East Indies. Having first secured southern Sumatra, they turned on Java, where British, Dutch and some American units concentrated after the fall of Singapore. The last remaining Allied naval force in these waters was destroyed

*in the Java Sea at the end of February, and on 8 March
the outmatched land forces in Java surrendered to the
Japanese.*

*Meanwhile, the Americans were heavily set upon in the
the Philippines. The Japanese landed on Luzon twenty-
four hours after Malaya had been invaded, while their
major attack—setting between eighty and a hundred
thousand men ashore—came on 22 December 1941. It
was preceded by violent attacks from the air, during which
Manila and the nearby naval base at Cavite were savagely
bombed. American resistance was fierce.*

JAVA: LANDING PLANES

A few minutes later twelve P-40 Es, the Kittyhawks,
came in. This is a huge field at Daly Waters—in many
respects a perfect field. There are no barriers and visibility
is excellent on all sides. We stood beside our bombers,
watching the Kittyhawks circle to follow their leader
down. The leader made a perfect landing, the next one
bounced but got down. The next one seemed to be coming
down too low, short of the aerodrome, and heading for
a field. He came down in the field and hit a ditch. The
next one did the same—down on the field and half turned
over. The following Kittyhawk did the same. Lieutenant
Rose was shouting and screaming, "What the hell's the
matter with them? They've got all the field in the world
here to land on and they are coming down in the grass
and weeds."

The others came in all right, until the final one of the
twelve. He made five attempts to get down but when four
or five feet off the ground he decided he couldn't make
it, put on the gas, and zoomed up and away again for
another circle. Five times he did that.

"You can just imagine," Lieutenant Rose said, "what
that poor kid in there is going through."

A sergeant mechanic with us said, "The only way we'll
get him down is shoot him down."

I remarked to some of the airmen standing by that
if a pilot couldn't make a simple landing in a strange and
good field, how could he fight in combat, when the enemy
is on his tail.

"These boys are going to be slaughtered out here,"
one pilot said.

He finally came down on the aerodrome, and unlike
the three others, did not crack up. These pilots were
youngsters just out of flying school, with insufficient
experience. There's no help for that, I suppose. Men, even
untrained, are needed desperately if Java is to be saved.

Cecil Brown

THE PHILIPPINES

Bombs on Manila: 8 December

We hadn't long to wait after Pearl Harbor.

The next day I stood on the balcony of the *Herald*
building and saw the first enemy planes cut down through
the skies like great aerial bolos.

Fifty-four Japanese sky monsters, flashing silver in the
bright noonday, were flying in two magnificently formed
Vs.

Above the scream of the sirens the church bells
solemnly announced the noon hour.

Unprotected and unprepared, Manila lay under the
enemy planes—a city of ancient nunneries and chromium-
fronted night clubs, or skyscrapers towering over *nipa*
shacks, of antiquity and modernity, of East and West.

I heard the *Herald* staff clattering out of the building
into Muralla Calle, where citizens in the customary
spotless white were being herded by the police under the
moss-covered old Spanish wall. Women clustered under
the acacia-trees in the park. I found myself grinning—a
few of them had opened their umbrellas for additional
protection!

Half-a-dozen bearded Fathers came out of the College

of San Juan de Letran next door, looked up and saw the planes, and, gathering up their white robes, rushed back into the building.

Colonel Carlos P. Romulo

The Defenders

We hopped a truck, threw our guns and ammunition aboard, and raced to the Cavite docks just as the Japs unloaded their first stick of bombs over Nichols Field across the bay below Manila. I had watched the merciless bombing of Chinese cities, but they were nothing like this. These Japs were using a new technique. They flew out of the clouds, with the sun at their tails, in two formations of twenty-seven planes each. They hummed along like a swarm of bees, high and flying straight.

Approaching the target, the squadron leader flipped sideways, then dived. The others followed quickly. After the longest minute I ever lived through, the leader let go of the first stick of bombs. They looked like silvery eggs glistening in the sun as they were detached in a bunch from beneath the plane, then scattered out over a wide area. Then came a strange rattle of machine-guns from the plane. They hadn't done this over Chapei. There in China they had just unloaded their bombs, climbed back again, and come in for another run. But this time they were firing machine-guns from the planes—strafing.

On they came, until fifty-four planes had unloaded their bombs and strafed the ground. Then they climbed back up to an open sky to rendezvous high. Off they flew, over Manila.

When the bombs hit Nichols Field, great showers of earth and debris shot skyward. As a boy I remember throwing handfuls of dust into the sky. This was the way it looked now, except that the clouds of dust we saw contained sticks and bricks and human bodies and pieces of machinery. No sooner had the dust clouds descended than great puffs of smoke followed; then flames leaped above the tree-tops. We couldn't see the Army flying-field, because it was too far away, but the bursting bombs, smoke and flames were plainly visible as we raced along in the truck to the docks. The earth quaked, and a roar of hot air puffed into our faces. Then came the crackling of flames and the deep rumble of falling debris.

. . . . I glanced skyward. The Japs were coming back towards us, still flying high. The anti-aircraft fire had stopped. Our planes were skimming the tree-tops now. Suddenly they shot upward, one ahead of the other in a single file.

"Here it comes, boys!"

"Yeah. This is it!"

Our planes kept climbing, straight for the bellies of those big twin-engined jobs. They still hadn't spotted our planes. They thought they had complete mastery of the skies, and they roared along like migrating ducks chased by a handful of sparrows.

Our fighters were now within range of the bombers and climbing fast. The leading plane now had the leading Jap bomber in his gun sight. There was a burst of fire and tracer bullets from the nose of the American fighter as he flew straight for the bomber. For a second it looked as if they would crash in mid-air. A tiny trickle of blue smoke trailed from the leading bomber. He wavered a little, then slanted earthwards, his wings whining like a crying baby.

"Got him!" someone cried, and we shouted and danced like little boys, clapping our hands and hugging each other.

The leader of our fighters zoomed up and over the Jap bombers, flipped back, and dived down towards them again. At the same time our second fighter came within range of the second squadron of twenty-seven Jap bombers. He opened up with guns in his wings and nose, giving the Japs everything he had. Another bomber trailed bluish smoke, then seemed to stop in mid-air and spin earthwards. Just then there was a terrific explosion as the first Jap bomber hit the earth and burst into flames. This was followed by another crash and a burst of flames as the second bomber buried itself in the ground.

By this time all eight of our fighters had made a run at the Japs, flying between their formations, over them and circling back behind them, attacking the planes in the rear of the formation.

"Now you're cookin' with gas!" the gun captain yelled, as if the American fliers could hear him.

The Japs didn't fly over Nichols Field as they had before. This time they headed straight for the sea and the cloud bank which had moved farther out over the water.

The Americans followed them all the way. A third bomber crashed in flames shortly after the second. A fourth and fifth went down soon after the others, with the American fighters still climbing beneath them and diving back in a wide circle to gun the bombers trailing the formation. Unescorted by fighter planes, the bombers were easy targets. It was like shooting bottles lined up on a fence. They would crack, then fall to explode as they bounded on the earth.

The sixth plane was shot out of the formation before the Japs split up to fly in three directions from about twenty miles south-east of Manila. The sixth big bomber didn't spin and crash like the others but descended in a wide circle, turning back across the bay towards us. He seemed to be heading straight for Cavite on a wide circle across the tree-tops and the bay.

"He's coming at us!" I cried.

"Yeah. Get ready," the gun captain ordered.

Every man lifted his rifle or tommy-gun to his shoulder and waited. The .50-calibre machine-gun on the truck was lowered so that its muzzle was trained on the big bomber as he came nearer, flying more than a thousand yards away from us and coming in fast on a wide circle. He was wobbling, almost out of control. Our fighters must have hit the controls, and the pilot seemed to be trying to pull her out. Her engines would idle, then they would cough and roar again as the pilot gunned her, trying to keep from crashing. Now the Jap had cleared the trees lining the shore, and he was approaching Cavite with the wind whistling through his wings and his motor groaning. The Jap was less than five hundred yards away now, low over the water and within easy range of us.

"When he comes in, let him have it!" the gunner ordered.

"Here he comes!"

The bomber's engines roared over the water, and the big plane seemed to settle on an even keel, its wings ceased wobbling, and he began to climb slowly.

"O.K., boys!" the gunner yelled. "Fire!"

The tracers hit right in the nose and ploughed back through the fuselage and tail as the plane passed through the driving bullets. It was now less than four hundred yards away, flying straight over the water, so close that I could see the faces of the men at the controls as they grinned in defiance at us.

The plane lunged upwards, stalled, then flipped its tail up as the nose went straight down. There was a geyser of water, a hiss of steam as the hot motors caught fire and the detonators set the bomb load off. There was a hell of an explosion. A second later, and bits of wreckage splashed on the dock at our feet, and the plane disappeared from the surface, leaving a burning pool of oil and fuel where she went down.

William Martin Camp, U.S.M.C.

Cavite Abandoned

Finally came the order to advance. Truck motors roared and carbon monoxide fumes lay heavy beneath the smoke-clouds. The trucks started with a jerk as the wheels began to roll. There was no more talking. Everyone looked back and saw the dying embers and the ghostly shadows and the rising smoke. It was like a graveyard, deathly quiet, deserted and silent except for the last consuming flames which crackled like the inferno of Hell.

Thus began the retirement from Cavite at 1.30 a.m.

on the morning of 11 December. A very small force under a fighting Marine officer of the fleet was remaining behind: they would man a few A.A. batteries to prevent the Japs from knowing we were evacuating the yard. They were to leave in small boats after we were well under way.

"That's stupid," someone said. "We ain't foolin' the Japs. Why, they know every move we've made so far. Ten to one they know we're leavin' right now. We'll be lucky if we ain't bombed along the road."

The road to Manila was once a broad four-laned highway of concrete pan macadam, hard and smooth, but the dust from fallen buildings and great clouds of dirt had descended upon it in a thin layer which was stirred up as we rolled along in the heavy convoy. The road was crowded with refugees loaded in automobiles, *carabao*-drawn carts, *carranatas,* push-carts with heavy wooden wheels, wagons and all kinds of vehicles from the primitive farm carts to modern limousines. Those who lived in Manila were swarming to get out of the city, and country people were streaming into it, hoping to find safety there from the bombs.

In the light of the fires I could see on every face that drawn, terrified look, the same expression I recalled on the faces of the Chinese who had streamed into the International Settlement of Shanghai when the Japs bombed their homes and destroyed their towns. In every vehicle were the same things—blankets, chairs, boxes. Bundles of clothing and cooking utensils were tied up in sheets and blankets. Some of the wealthier families had mattresses piled upon the tops of their cars, with favourite chairs or tables or bicycles lashed to the rear. In the carts and wagons of the poor were chairs, tables, copper kettles, oil stoves, blankets and bundles of clothing. The poor were taking everything they owned, but the rich were leaving all but a few treasures behind.

William Martin Camp

Manila, Open City: 27 December

In order to spare the metropolitan area from possible ravages of attack either by air or ground, Manila is hereby declared an open city with the characteristics of a military objective. In order that no excuse may be given for a possible mistake, the American High Commissioner, the Commonwealth Government, and all combatant military installations will be withdrawn from its environs as rapidly as possible.

General MacArthur

In the New Year General MacArthur's forces were pinned down in the fortress island of Corregidor off Manila and in the Bataan peninsula. There they held out for several months.

Retreat to Corregidor: 1 January 1942

We drove through a city dark except for its burning areas. The port area was still in flames. Not a civilian showed himself against that back-drop of fire. The flames were hot on my face as I stumbled wearily up the gang-plank of the old steamer *Hyde*.

Even the boat was dark. An officer called our names in the dark. I answered mine and, slumping to the deck, and with my musette bag for a pillow, was instantly asleep.

I woke once in mid-channel. Captain John Christiansen, lying beside me, asked what was the matter. I told him I was cold. When I awoke again I discovered the sun was up and that the blanket he had given me was his only one.

The *Hyde* was against the dock of Corregidor. I looked at that hunk of rock surrounded by water. My first thought was, "What a hole!" My second was, "We'll be trapped here!"

To the east was Cavite, still in flames. To the west

was the jungle peninsula of Bataan, where our boys were making their last fight.

Still numb from sleep on the deck of the old steamer, I hooked my musette strap over my shoulder. With weariness riding my shoulders I stumbled down the gangplank on to the gritty soil of Corregidor.

At that very moment just twelve miles behind me Japanese soldiers were goose-stepping into Manila.

. . . . At 6.30 in the morning that New Year's Day I walked into the Malinta Tunnel on Corregidor.

The smell of the place hit me like a blow in the face. There was the stench of sweat and dirty clothes, the coppery smell of blood and disinfectant, coming from the lateral where the hospital was situated, and over all, the heavy stink of creosote hanging like a blanket in the air that moved sluggishly when it moved at all.

It had been taken for granted that in the event of war all the inhabitants of Corregidor would take shelter in the tunnel and its cluster of branching laterals sunk into the solid stone of the "Rock".

As many as five thousand people gathered there during raids. Those who could not get in were unprotected. I think the population of Corregidor at this time was about nine thousand—a number that would shrink rapidly in the death-dealing months to come.

I stood there gaping, bewildered and alarmed by the bedlam going on about me. This was the final refuge of a fortress we had all assumed had been prepared and impregnable for years.

Now that disaster was upon us, soldiers were rushing about belatedly installing beds and desks and sewage drains and electric lights.

The tunnel was wide enough to permit two ambulances to drive side by side down its length. Its stone arch was damp. Everywhere was the graveyard smell of wet rock—where it wasn't overwhelmed by sharper and even less pleasant odours.

Soldiers were sleeping along the sides of the tunnel, on camp-beds and ammunition-cases or curled up on the cement floor. Their boots were in one another's faces. Ambulances rolled within a few inches of their heads. The bombs that fell night and day shook the furthermost stone laterals of the tunnel.

Nobody paid any attention to me. I wandered in and out of the laterals carrying my luggage. These cave-like places were the offices for Ordnance, Quartermaster, Anti-aircraft, Harbour Defence, Finance, Signal Corps, and U.S.A.F.F.E. headquarters. The hospital was the largest and the best-organized lateral in the tunnel. From it jutted perhaps a dozen smaller laterals. These were for the women, the President and High Commissioner, the doctors and officer patients, the operating ward, the medical ward, the dental ward and other wards, the laboratory, X-ray department, and the hospital mess. In this mess, President Quezon, his family, and Cabinet, Commissioner Sayre, and his staff took their meals.

Colonel Romulo

Retreat to Bataan

I looked at the road ahead, and all I could see was a line of Filipino children standing by the road, holding their little brown fingers up in a V-sign. Their faces were wreathed in smiles.

I looked down. A little fellow was running along beside me.

"Hi, Marine!" he said, smiling up at me.

"Hello there, sonny."

"How are you to-day, Marine?"

"Fine. How're you?"

"I'm fine. Say, Marine, you are not leavin' us here all alone, are you? You're not running away, are you?"

I squeezed his hand. He was about ten years old. His smile was only a half-smile, half eager, half afraid.

"No, sonny. Not running away. Just retiring to prepared positions. That's all."

. . . . That's the way it was. *To the rear! To the rear!*

From Lingayen to the tar-covered Olongapo Road, then to Abucay, farther down Bataan. Infantry, artillery, cavalry, and machine-gun units tried to hold them back, but they just kept coming, all the way, head on, at point-blank range. There was nothing to stop them. They came in by the hundreds, the thousands. Their blood ran down the hills, seeped into the earth until it was sticky, then ran over the surface like water, down the valleys into the streams, and down the streams into the sea. Bodies cascaded down the hills like waterfalls, rolling and tumbling and lying still. Others followed, and the command was always:

"To the rear . . . to the rear. . . ."

The Filipino Scouts held them off for the first eleven days and eleven nights after the Lingayen invasion. It was continuous attacking, retreating to new positions, stopping long enough to slaughter a few hundred more, then being driven back by the sheer force of overwhelming numbers. There weren't enough guns to stop them.

"They're mad! They're crazy. Why, if one of our officers sent men to their deaths like that, he would be court-martialled and shot by firing-squads," said the colonel from Spokane.

"It's mass suicide, that's what it is, sir. Mass suicide."

"Just keep firing, men. Keep firing. We'll go to the rear after this wave. . . . Keep firing. . . ."

This was the retirement to Bataan. Wainwright's forces from the north just made it in time. So did the forces coming back up over the bridge at San Fernando Pampanga. The last convoy crossed the bridge. Then came the South Corps. The last man across the bridge stopped just long enough to dynamite it.

William Martin Camp

Persuasion

The first night I found myself looking forward to sleeping in the open air. I curled up in my borrowed blanket on the bank of the creek and prepared to enjoy the beauty of the stars and the symphony of running water and cicadas.

"Here's where I get my first night's sleep since Pearl Harbor," I said drowsily to Colonel Lauro Hernandez, a former classmate of mine, who stretched out near by.

I thought some meaning was hidden in his silence. I knew there was when a few minutes later all round us in the darkness a thousand enemy guns seemed to open fire. I nearly jumped out of my blanket.

"Take it easy," said Lauro; "it's just the fire-cracker gag."

I settled back on the ground. I hadn't recognized the Japanese firecracker trick, although we heard plenty about it. It was one of the many stunts the enemy were using in their attempt to break down the morale of the boys in the lines. Their planes circled overhead all night long scattering bombs hit and miss over Bataan. Their pistol-shots rang all night in the forest. They had a device for hurling long strings of firecrackers over the trees and on to our front lines. They hoped the boy in the fox-hole, hearing them, would think he was surrounded and shoot back, thereby making himself a target for the enemy.

I listened, my body tense. The cicadas had stopped humming. Then I heard a drawn-out human sigh. It was like the last intake of a man that is dying. Only it sounded inhuman and monstrous, because it came from everywhere and nowhere; as if the trees were in anguish. Then silence—then groans from the forests, and later, a scream.

The sounds were nerve-wracking. But I was on a river bank surrounded by men I knew, who were listening with me. I was not alone, weak with hunger and sleeplessness, in a fox-hole in the dead of night. Lauro spoke to me again in a whisper. He explained that these sounds were being broadcast from Japanese sounds trucks on the very front of their lines.

Out of the night came a woman's voice, sweet and persuasive. In sentimental words it announced the dedication of a programme to "the brave and gallant defenders of Bataan". Songs followed, quavering through the forest. They were selected to arouse nostalgia to breaking-point in a boy facing death and longing for home. *Home, Sweet Home, Old Folks at Home*—this was the kind of song the Japanese broadcast in the dead of night, alternating heartbreak with horror.

Colonel Romulo

The Tokyo radio gave us the business. They called upon us for immediate surrender.

"Dear friends . . . Lay down your arms . . . it is useless to resist . . . You are completely encircled . . . You will get no assistance . . . What dishonour is there in following the example of the defenders of Hong Kong, Singapore and the Netherlands East Indies, in the acceptance of an honourable defeat?"

That's what the Japanese radio broadcast. Not long afterwards, the Japanese bombers flew over. They dropped no bombs that day. Instead, they dropped shiny tin cans which floated down from the skies and popped as they hit the earth. Inside were notes addressed to the commanding general of the forces of Americans and Filipinos.

"Your Excellency. Your duty has been performed. Accept our sincere advice and save the lives of those officers and men under your command. Surrender. Make an honourable surrender. There is no dishonour in an honourable defeat."

William Martin Camp

Death in a Fox-hole

I lay there for about half an hour when Oakley grabbed his stomach and began groaning.

"Try what I did," I told him. "It'll make you feel better."

He crawled to the end of the hole and squatted there, grunting and groaning with pain. There are two kinds of dysentery in the Orient, one a mild form, which we

called the "Yangtse rapids", and another which is more
serious and requires a doctor's treatment.

"I've had the 'rapids' for a week," Oakley groaned.
"Now this. . . ."

He rolled over, writhing in pain.

"We gotta get him out of here," Witherspoon said to
me. "He's got to go to hospital. He'll die if we don't get
him out of here."

It was about ten o'clock in the morning, and the sun
was high. We had been there since about ten o'clock the
night before. Somewhere ahead of us were the Jap snipers.
I was trying to decide which was worse, having him killed
by the snipers or die of the awful cramps which were
causing him to roll his eyes and froth at the mouth.

At last I decided it was worth a try. I stood up and
started to climb out of the hole, so Witherspoon could
help him up to me, and we could both drag him back.
If we could cross that narrow strip of open space which
lay between our fox-hole and the trees behind we would
be safe. From there on we could carry him back in a
stretcher made of our shirts and a couple of saplings.

I had no sooner raised my head about the earth than
a sudden burst of machine-gun fire splashed in the dust
around me. I dropped back down, and Witherspoon shook
his head.

"No use," he said. "We can't make it."

Oakley was clawing the earth now, and his finger-tips
were bleeding. If I hadn't known what it was, I might
have thought it was sunstroke or epilepsy. He was chewing
his tongue, and the saliva which ran down his chin was
pink with blood. His eyeballs were turned back in his
head with only a little bit of the pupils showing.

"God! We've got to do something!" Witherspoon cried,
his face ashen with fright. "We can't let him die like this!"

I dropped down and crawled over to where he lay.
I took his head in my hands and tried to prise his jaws
apart to release his tongue.

"Gimme something. Quick!" I said.

Witherspoon looked around, but there was nothing we

could use to put in his mouth to prevent him eating his tongue.

"Here!" Witherspoon said, handing me a bayonet. "Try this."

"No! He'll kill himself with that. What if he falls on it or rolls over! It'll kill him."

But there was nothing else to do, so I pulled his jaws apart and Witherspoon placed the tip of the bayonet between his teeth. I released his jaws gently until his teeth touched the cold steel, and they began grinding against it. He was twitching convulsively, and with each breath his cries were becoming weaker and weaker until they were no more than a whisper. I held his head in my lap, while Witherspoon stroked his stomach, pressing down hard with downward strokes. Whatever it was inside him, it had to come out.

We did this for about an hour. The pain seemed to go away, and he stopped gritting his teeth against the tip of the bayonet.

"He's coming along all right now," I said. "He'll be over it in a minute."

"God! What is this?" Witherspoon exclaimed, looking at the back of his trousers. "It's blood!"

I put his head down and crawled towards his feet. His trousers were soaked with blood, and it was running down, seeping into the ground. I ripped off his trousers to his knees. They were soaked with it. There was an odour like rotted flesh, the same odour which hovered over Bataan day and night from the thousands of dead which lay in the sun.

"Haemorrhages," I said. "He's bleeding from behind."

"He'll bleed to death."

We rolled him over on his stomach and parted his legs. I placed my hand over him to try to stop the blood, but it came through my fingers. I tried stopping him up with the slimy dirt, but it was useless. The blood forced the mud poultice away.

He died a few minutes later without opening his eyes again. Since we couldn't move out of the hole we dug the side in until his body was covered with the fresh earth.

William Martin Camp

This Is It!

That night the flares of the Sakdalista and the Ganaps* lit up Bataan like a birthday cake. The Japs couldn't have given us a more positive warning. Those flares, lighting up prospective targets and bombing routes, were as infallible as a barometer at sea. At Cavite, in Manila, and in northern Bataan they forecast the next day's offensives without fail. Burning now in the hills behind Mariveles naval base, near the hospital up the zig-zag at Cabcaben, along the beaches near our embattlements, and in the trees near field headquarters locations, they were ample warning of what was to come at dawn. Time to prepare, time to double the watch, time to check equipment and rush arms and ammunition to fill up the gaps.

"This is it, guys! This is it!" everyone was saying.

"Yeah, it's it, all right."

It was strange to note the varied effect those lights had upon some of the men around me. To some it meant a relief from the constant strain of expectancy; to others it only increased their anxiety and filled them with awe and fear, for you never knew where one would pop up next. It might be right behind you, in the trees above you, or at some distant, difficult pinnacle. It never failed to produce psychological fear and foreboding. I had a weird premonition which I could not shake as I watched them burn fiercely at every vital installation, including those which had been known only to a few. A chill on my neck and at the roots of my hair came over me, and the more I thought of it, the more convinced I became that this was really "it". Just what "it" meant I didn't or couldn't imagine.

William Martin Camp

* Filipino Fifth Column (Ed.)

Bombardment

All that day it continued with increased fury, from the air, from Jap shore batteries across the bay, and from ships anchored off-shore beyond the range of our artillery. Several Jap destroyers had slipped up in the night, blacked out and in the dark of the moon, and had measured the distance to us so that their ship batteries could open up at daylight. They were softening us up for an invasion, and there was nothing we could do about it except to hope they would be withdrawn as the fourteenth day passed and the fifteen-day limit of the Jap general's threat had expired.

That night, 6 April, we heard of the general's order to his Filipino and American forces to renew the attack, all along the line in every sector.

"The reserves have arrived," said the Marine who relieved me at midnight.

"What about us?" I asked eagerly.

The Marine shrugged and shook his head. "We hold on," he said.

There wasn't much to hold on to by this time. The Jap destroyers had kept up a steady fire, lobbing their shells all around our positions, on the rocks of the beach in front of us and in the hills behind us.

As darkness came on, they ceased firing and began playing beams of their searchlights against the shore, sweeping up and down, surveying the situation. Just before midnight they had fired a few star shells which descended over our heads, lighting Bataan with a weird, artificial, white glow. Twice our anti-aircraft batteries exploded the star shells, and we were safe in the darkness once more. But the Jap destroyers had found us and were probably moving in closer under cover of darkness for a renewed assault at dawn.

William Martin Camp

On 9 April 1942 Bataan surrendered. On 6 May

General Wainwright finally lowered his flag on Corregidor, and the fighting in the Philippines was left to the Resistance. As soon as the position had become hopeless, General MacArthur had been evacuated to Australia to take command of the Allied forces gathering there.

MacArthur Leaves Corregidor: 11 March

Corregidor rises abruptly from the water's edge where Bulkely's P.T. stood by. All boarded promptly except the General, who stopped and turned slowly to look back. What a transformation had taken place in that normally beautiful spot. Its vivid green foliage was gone with its trees, its shrubs, its flowers, all bruised and torn by the hail of relentless and devastating bombardment. That warped and twisted face of scorched rock seemed to reflect the writhings of a tortured body. It had become a black mass of destruction. Up on Topside the heavy guns still rent the air with their red blasts and deep roars. They were commanded by Paul Bunker, MacArthur's classmate at West Point, a famous all-American back in the team MacArthur had managed. He and many others of those thousands were old, old friends, bound by ties of deepest comradeship. What thoughts must have crowded his mind as he looked his farewell. And then I saw him slowly raise his cap in salute, there in the twilight, as he glanced up through the smoky haze with its smell of death and stench of destruction thick in the night air. And it seemed to me that I could see a sudden convulsive twitch in the muscles of his jaw, a sudden whitening in the bronze of his face. I said to the man next to me, "What's his chance of getting through?" "About one in five," was the reply. And then the General's quiet voice as he stepped aboard the boat: "You may cast off, Buck, when you are ready." And then they moved off into the night.

American eye-witness

The Fall

Down below we can hear the great thunder. The bombs have loosened the ceiling in some of the tunnels, and they have caved in at some places, cutting off any possible escape. We have heard that some of our boys are trapped in the tunnels farther along, but there is no confirmation of it. Everyone has turned to and is preparing his own little shelter, just in case we have to duck behind a rock in the tunnels and stop them as they come through the entrances.

Three times during the afternoon the Japs tried to make a landing, but we have repulsed them. They haven't learned yet how to take advantage of air support in attacking a stronghold and gaining a foothold. We didn't know it until to-day. But we have learned how effective is their bombing and strafing, and we know that if they tried it once they would be swarming all over the Rock.

Funny how long it takes a Jap to catch on. But they do catch on, and there's no denying the fact. It is sundown now, and the transports have all moved in a little closer. They are gunwale to gunwale now, or so we hear from the topside.

Word has been passed that we've made our last radio contact with the States. It happened about four o'clock this afternoon. No one knows what the last message was, but soon after it was sent a well-placed bomb blew the works all to hell, and the operators with it.

Time is short. Witherspoon and Weaver and I are lying on our backs. There is a little light coming in from a hole in the ceiling where a bomb crashed through. The last rays of the red sun are shining over Mariveles: although we can't see the lonely mountain silhouetted against the sunset, we know that's the way it was yesterday, the day before, and the day before. And that's the way it will be to-morrow and the next day and the next day. Hereafter, it will remind all who view it of the blood that was spilled here.

Everyone is in high spirits. That old Marine Corps

spirit. Even as they brought around the last of the mule-meat everyone ate it and there was plenty of grumbling. As long as there's plenty of belly-aching, men will not lose heart.

The Army officer who plays the violin is still alive. We heard him a few minutes ago. He sang the "Shepherd" song we all love.

William Martin Camp

Intrinsically it is but a barren, war-worn rock, hallowed, as so many other places, by death and disaster. Yet it symbolizes within itself that priceless, deathless thing, the honour of a nation. Until we lift our flag from its dust, we stand unredeemed before mankind. Until we claim again the ghastly remnants of its last gaunt garrison, we can but stand humble supplicants before Almighty God.

General MacArthur

BURMA

Once the Japanese had control of Thailand, it was obvious that they must soon attack Burma and open for themselves a way into India.

The people of the country were quite unprepared for invasion, and, as the British suffered defeat after defeat and the Japanese swept forward, they were stunned at the collapse of a Power they had always thought, if they thought about it at all, invincible and part of nature. The vast majority had no feeling that the war was their business; they wished only to avoid it. A small minority, mostly soldiers and officials, were actively loyal; about the same number, nationalist politicians, the relics of the old rebels of 1924, students, and some political *pongyis* (Buddhist priests) were actively hostile. These elements were rendered more formidable by the leadership of Japanese-trained Burmans, imported with the invading army, and by the flocking to their standards of numbers of dacoits and bad characters attracted by the prospect of loot.

Lieutenant-General William Slim

On 16 January 1942 the Japanese advance began, through Tenasserim and into Lower Burma. The British 17 Division was forced to retreat with heavy losses.

The army commander, however, as I was afraid he would, insisted on a continuance of his forward defence policy and, to start with, a strong defence of the very unsuitable Moulmein position. I perfectly well realized that great pressure must have been put upon him by the Governor of Burma to hold this politically important town, and that its loss would have a bad effect upon civilian morale. But that really was a very short-sighted view compared to the much more devastating effect of decisive military defeat.

Now the result of this appreciation of mine, and its rejection by the army commander, formed a major difference of opinion between us which widened and deepened as the days went by, and as it became more and more clear to me that the tactics imposed on me might lead to the loss of my whole division, on which the defence of Rangoon at that time almost solely depended. I quite understood the army commander's objections to my plan. He was being pressed strongly by General Wavell to fight as far forward as possible "to gain time"; and he was also constantly pressed politically by the Governor that I should hold on to "bits of Burma". Dreadful bottlenecks like Moulmein, from which withdrawal had to be made over a wide stretch of water by river steamer, had to be held as long as possible because otherwise it might be bad for the morale of the civil population. Kawkareik, with a river obstacle and ferry behind it, was just as bad.

 . . . . The Japanese intentions were now fairly clear. As expected, their main forces were advancing directly on to Moulmein from the east via Kawkareik. In addition they had diverted a regiment, equivalent to a British brigade, as a northern flanking force in the direction of Paan on the Salween river. From the south they had followed up their Tavoy success by a minor advance along the coast and another advance by a small force through the Three Pagodas Pass. They were closing on Moulmein from all directions, therefore, and the force advancing on Paan was directly threatening our line of withdrawal. These continued to be the stock Japanese tactics throughout the fighting in 1942, 1943 and the first part of 1944. Such tactics were extremely difficult to counter from our point of view, and we did not do so with any real effect until our air supply had been built up in 1944 to such proportions that the troops outflanked could stand fast and fight on in the knowledge that their food and ammunition would arrive by air.

. . . . On Sunday, 25 January, the army commander arrived up from Rangoon and we had a good look round and a long talk on the situation. It was quite obvious that the morale of the troops was poor. In the first place they felt keenly their lack of training in jungle war, their lack of artillery and air support, and their inability to move where they wanted owing to our acute lack of transport. The Indian troops had absolutely no confidence in the Burmese and the Burmese had no confidence in themselves as regular soldiers. They suffered the same depression as did our troops earlier at Dunkirk, Crete and Singapore, in seeing hostile aircraft continually in the air and very few of our own. The sick rate was also very high. I spent nearly all my time in morale-raising. On the 26th I spent the whole day going round brigades and units. Up at Moulmein things seemed fairly quiet; but two days later, on Friday the 30th, the Japanese attack developed after a good deal of preliminary reconnaissance and probing.

By this time my signallers had managed to run me up an excellent telephone line, by means of which I was in constant verbal communication with Roger Ekin, who had been appointed to command the Moulmein defences.

Eventually, after some severe fighting, the defences were breached and the brigade fought its way down to the quays and embarked on the waiting steamers. The Indian mountain battery did magnificently to get all their guns away, but the final withdrawal was a nightmare with the steamers shelled and machine-gunned all the way across the Gulf of Martaban, and we were extremely lucky not to have more casualties than we did. The Japanese pressed their assault without regard for losses and suffered fairly heavily. Actually this extremely difficult operation was very creditable to the commanders and troops concerned; had there been the slightest panic or confusion the operation would have resulted in complete disaster.

. . . . By the capture of Moulmein the Japanese had advanced a big step towards the complete occupation of Burma, and had gained yet another airfield within striking distance of Rangoon.

Major-General Smyth, G.O.C. 17 Division

The Division fought a last, bitter delaying action on the Sittang river, but was pushed back towards Rangoon. The capital was now doomed. Thus, in the last week of February, ended the first phase of the Japanese invasion.

Rangoon: The First Invasion

Pilots of the meagre Allied air force, who constantly and effectively assailed the advancing Japanese, were unwelcome guests at the Mingalodon Golf Club.

We were present at the fall of the *Burra Sahib*'s last bastion in Rangoon, this club. While our member was engaged in "avoiding as much of the unpleasantness of war as possible" (which apparently entailed living exactly as he had done before the Japanese came to Burma), the club was invaded by a group of some twenty boisterous young roughnecks who shouted with laughter, drank up all the club's refreshing iced beer, and smoked as many of the club's cigarettes as they could afford to buy. They slept on beds and benches all over the cool, big lounge where the *Burra Sahib* and his ladies used to drink their *chota-pegs* on Saturday afternoons after golf and on Sundays before eating throat-blistering curry which sent them to sleep.

They showed no respect whatsoever for the strait-laced conventions ruling the club. They stripped off their shirts and lay on the sacred lawn in front of the club-house sunning themselves. They actually had long talks with the Burmese waiters, learning about Burma and the customs of its people. An unheard-of thing, this fraternizing with the "boys" whose job it was to wait on their *Burra Sahib*.

Then the club hit back. The managing member, Sidney Bush, a dear old man somewhat flustered by the war, was told not to serve the club's iced beer to the young roughnecks; nor the club's cigarettes. "After all, the members' needs must be considered first. If we sell our stocks to all these young fellows there'll be nothing left for the members."

O. D. Gallagher

The Last Days

With few exceptions the normal civilian population had gone, including the fire-brigade and all municipal employees. The empty streets were patrolled by troops carrying tommy-guns and rifles. The only other inhabitants were criminals, criminal lunatics, lunatics and lepers.

They had been released from the gaols and institutions on the order of an officer of the Indian Civil Service. He had misread an order sent to him regarding their disposal. The convicts numbered some five thousand. At night they made Rangoon a city of the damned. They prowled the deserted streets in search of loot. When they were seen looting they were shot by the soldiers. Numerous fires burned. Some were houses (many in neglected slum areas) set alight by their owners before they, too, evacuated. Other fires were laid by the looters, gone

amuck, unbalanced by their sudden, unexpected freedom.
Yet others were laid by fifth-columnists.

The senior civil servant who had given the criminals,
lunatics and lepers their freedom committed suicide.
Another did the same soon afterwards.

Lepers and lunatics wandered aimlessly about in search
of food, some sharing pickings of the refuse-heap with
the many mongrel dogs. An occasional Buddhist monk
walked the street going about his business protected from
assault by the long saffron robes of his faith.

Down at the docks all was chaos. Burmese looters were
rummaging about and had found some medical supplies
in cases. On examining these they judged them to be of
no use except for the bottles. They tossed them away
on the concrete wharves and watched them explode.

An A.V.G. ground-crew man, who went to the docks
to see what there was that might be useful for the unit,
saw them at it. "They were having a great time," he said.
"They were tickled pink by the explosions."

O. D. Gallagher

*Rangoon fell to the Japanese on 9 March. The British
forces in the city escaped only through the lack of
imagination of a Japanese commander, who removed a
road-block at the critical moment. The battered defenders,
reinforced by Chinese troops but now cut off from the
outside world, retreated north, concentrated and turned
to face their enemies once more. General William Slim
was appointed to lead the troops in the field, under
General Alexander as Army Commander.*

General Slim Arrives

A day at Mandalay while we waited for an aircraft
gave us an opportunity to look round. We saw a number
of units and details that had been withdrawn for various
reasons from the fighting to reform or to be used as
reinforcements. Gunners who had lost their guns—the
most pathetic people in the world—staffs of broken-up

formations and evacuated camps, a hotchpotch of bits and pieces, odd groups and individuals. The British looked worried, the Indians puzzled, and the Burmese sulky. I had a suspicion that, unless someone very quickly took hold pretty tightly, a rot might set in behind the front.

. . . . There was, however, one bright gleam on the otherwise murky scene—the Chinese. At Christmas 1941, Generalissimo Chiang Kai-Shek had generously offered the Chinese 5 and 6 Armies to co-operate in the defence of Burma. General Wavell had accepted at once 93 Division of 6 Army, the most readily available, and moved it into the Shan States; 49 Division of the same Army was to be brought through Lashio to the Salween at Takaw. The third division, the 55th, which was scattered and not as ready as the others, was to concentrate at Wanting, there to equip and train. At the end of January, when arrangements for their maintenance had been hurriedly made, the Generalissimo, at Hutton's request, agreed that 5 Army should take over the Toungoo area. This Army consisted of 22, 96 and 200 Divisions, and was considered the best equipped and trained force in China. During February the Chinese troops, much hampered by lack of transport, moved forward into Burma.

. . . . A Chinese "Army" corresponded to a European Corps and consisted usually of two or three divisions. The division itself was not only much smaller than its British or American equivalent, having a strength of from seven to nine thousand, but only two-thirds of the men were armed; the other third replaced the absent animal or motor transport and acted as carriers. As a result the rifle power of a Chinese division at full strength rarely exceeded three thousand, with a couple of hundred light machine-guns, thirty or forty medium machine-guns, and a few 3-inch mortars. There were no artillery units except a very occasional anti-tank gun of small calibre, no medical services, meagre signals, a staff car or two, half a dozen trucks, and a couple of hundred shaggy, ill-kept

ponies. Nevertheless the Chinese soldier was tough, brave
and experienced—after all, he had already been fighting
on his own without help for years. He was the veteran
among the Allies, and could claim up to this time that
he had held back the Japanese more successfully than
any of the others. Indeed, he registered his arrival in the
forward areas by several minor but marked successes
against enemy detachments.

General Slim

The Chinese Arrive in Burma

A junior Chinese officer and four men walked into the
Pyinmana Club the second night they were there. There
was no one about as most of the population had fled since
a light Japanese bombing a week or two before. Naturally
enough, the Chinese helped themselves to a drink.
Whisky, brandy, gin, and all the rest were on the shelves,
but the abstemious Chinese took two bottles of ginger-ale
and four of soda-water. The Indian butler left in charge
of the club walked in, saw the party in progress, and ran
for help.

He returned with a senior Chinese officer who
immediately made the revellers pay for their ginger-ale
and soda. The careful Indian butler examined the till
and declared that it lacked one rupee. In the search the
senior officer found a silver rupee in the pocket of one
of the soldiers. He gave this to the butler and drew his
Mauser pistol. . . .

"Oh, please don't shoot him," begged the Indian, on
his knees. "Perhaps it is not my rupee."

And the senior officer returned his pistol to its holster;
instead he drew his sword. Before you could say "an-
tidisestablishmentarianism" he had lopped a piece off the
top of the soldier's ear. Everyone spoke of the Chinese
troops in Burma up to this date as the best-behaved troops
they had seen.

O. D. Gallagher

In Burma as elsewhere, Japanese air superiority was almost complete.

Now great wedges of silver bombers droned across the sky and one after another the cities of Burma spurted with flame and vanished in roaring holocausts. Prome, Meiktila, Mandalay, Thazi, Pyinmana, Maymyo, Lashio, Taung-gyi, largely wooden towns, all of them crumbled and burned. The Japanese used pattern bombing, coming over in faultless formation, giving themselves a leisurely dummy run or two, and then letting all their bombs go in one shattering crump. They were very accurate. We always said they had in each formation only one leader capable of aiming and all took the time from him. It was certainly effective, but I personally preferred it to the methods of the Italians and the French when they also had no air opposition. They had cruised round, dropping a few sticks at a time, and keeping one in suspense. With the Japanese it was all over quickly; you had either had it, or were alive till next time. Whatever the method, it was effective enough with the civil population. The police, hospital staffs, air-raid precaution units, public services, railways, collapsed. Labour vanished into the jungle; towns were evacuated. Only a few devoted British, Anglo-Burmans and Burmese carried nobly on.

. . . . One raid occurred as divisional commanders and others were assembled at Corps Headquarters for a conference. Some of us were just finishing breakfast when the alarm went. In a group we walked towards the slit trenches, I still carrying a cup of tea. Looking up, we could see the usual tight wedge of twenty or thirty bombers coming straight over. The mess servants and others saw them too and began to run for shelter. I had been insistent on stopping people running at these times as it had led to panic, so continuing our move at a slow and dignified pace, I called out to them to stop running and walk. I remember shouting in Hindustani, "There's plenty of time. Don't hurry!"—a remark that almost qualified for the Famous Last Words series. At that instant we heard the unmistakable scream of bombs actually falling. With one accord two or three generals and half a dozen other senior officers, abandoning dignity, plunged for the nearest trench. Scott, being no mean athlete, arrived first, took a leap and landed with shattering impact on a couple of Indian sweepers already crouching out of sight. I followed, a cup of tea and all; the rest piled in on top, and the whole salvo of bombs went off in one devastating bang.

Poor Scott, crushed under our combined weight, feeling warm liquid dripping over him, was convinced that I had been blown into the trench and was now bleeding to death all over him. His struggles to come to my assistance were heroic, but almost fatal to the wretched bottom layer of sweepers. We hauled ourselves and them out, and, slightly shamefacedly, returned to our conference.

General Slim

On 24 March the rot set in once again. The Chinese forces in eastern Burma were attacked and driven out of Toungoo by the Japanese. Now the long retreat began for the last time; the British up the Irrawaddy and Chindwin and the Chinese between the Sittang and Salween. Time after time fierce battles were fought as the Japanese tried to cut off the withdrawing armies, who attacked desperately to hold them back and secure the line of escape.

The April Retreat: Battle for the Oilfields

North of the Pin Chaung at the old Corps Headquarters location, the enemy had reappeared in greater strength and re-established their block. This time in addition to Price and his Frontier Force Gurkhas, there were available some West Yorkshires and a few tanks coming up from the south. A concerted attack again cleared the road, inflicting heavy casualties, the Japanese leaving many bodies in our uniforms. Transport then moved over the ford again, but numbers of vehicles had been lost by air attack during the enforced halt. More enemy appeared south of the cleared block, about a thousand of them being shelled by our artillery with effect, but again they established a block, this time near the ford. The situation was not encouraging and I was greatly relieved to hear that the 113th Regiment of the Chinese 38 Division was just arriving at Kyaukpadaung. I dashed off in my jeep to meet their commander and give him his orders.

Apart from the Guerrilla Battalion that had so reluctantly come to us at Taungdwingyi, this was the first time I had had Chinese troops under me. I found the Regimental Commander in the upstairs room of one of the few houses still standing in Kyaukpadaung village. He was a slight but tough-looking little Chinaman, with a real poker face, a pair of field-glasses and a huge Mauser pistol. We were introduced by the British liaison officer with the regiment, who spoke perfect Chinese. We shook hands, and got down to business with a map. As I described the situation the Chinese colonel struck me as intelligent and quick to grasp what I wanted. This was to bring his regiment, in lorries which I had ready, down to the Pin Chaung at once, and then send back the transport to fetch the next regiment as quickly as possible. I explained that it was my intention to attack with those two regiments, or, if possible, with the whole division, across the Pin Chaung early on the 18th in co-operation with a breakout by 1 Burma Division. Having explained all this fully I asked him, through the interpreter, if he understood. He replied that he did.

"Then let's get moving," I said cheerfully. The translation of this remark brought a flow of Chinese. He could not, he said, budge from Kyaukpadaung until he had the orders of General Sun, his divisional Commander.

"But," I explained, "General Sun has been placed under my orders. If he were here I should tell him to do what I have told you to do, and he would do it. Isn't that right?"

"Yes," agreed my Regimental Commander readily.

"All right, then let's get going."

"But I cannot move until I get the orders of General Sun."

And so it went on for an hour and a half, at the end of which I could cheerfully have shot the colonel with his own pistol. At last, just when I was feeling desperate, he suddenly smiled and said, "All right, I will do it!"

Why he changed his mind I do not know. I suspect some of the Chinese of various ranks who had flowed in and out of the room through our interview must have brought a message from Sun, telling him to do whatever I wanted. Once he got moving, I had no complaints about my Chinaman. Indeed, within the next few days I got to like him very much.

. . . . Meanwhile the Burma Division had begun in real earnest the Battle of the Oilfields. And a brutal battle it was.

At 6.30 in the morning the Burma Division attacked. Progress was made, under cover of artillery, but the guns were running short of shells. Then some Burman troops faltered. In spite of this, a by-pass road was cleared, and a good deal of transport got down almost to the Pin Chaung itself, only to be held up by Japanese on the south bank. The British and Indian troops of the Division fought doggedly over low ridge after ridge, the Japanese defending each one to the last man. A detachment of the Inniskillings struggled through to the Pin Chaung and enthusiastically greeted the troops it found there, believing them to be Chinese. They were Japanese, who lured the Irishmen into an ambush. The tanks made a last attack on the road block, but it was defended by several anti-tank guns and the tanks, bogged in the soft sand, became sitting targets. The attack, like that of the Chinese from the other side, petered to a standstill.

More Japanese were coming in from the east and were reported on the river. The situation was grave. At half-past four in the afternoon, Scott reported on the radio that his men were exhausted from want of water and continuous marching and fighting. He could hold that night, he thought, but if he waited until morning his men, still without water, would be so weakened they would have little or no offensive power to renew the attack. He asked permission to destroy his guns and transport and fight his way out that night. Scott was the last man to paint an unduly dark picture. I knew his men were almost at the end of their strength and in a desperate position. I could not help wishing that he had not been so close a friend. I thought of his wife and of his boys. There were lots of other wives, too, in England, India and Burma whose hearts would be under that black cloud a couple of miles away. Stupid to remember that now! Better get it out of my head.

I thought for a moment, sitting there with the headphones on, in the van with the operator crouching beside me, his eyes anxiously on my face. Then I told Scott he must hang on. I had ordered a Chinese attack again with all available tanks and artillery for the next morning. If Burma Division attacked then we ought to break through, and save our precious guns and transport. I was afraid too that if our men came out in driblets as they would in the dark, mixed up with Japanese, the Chinese and indeed our own soldiers would fail to recognize them and their losses would be heavy. Scott took it as I knew he would. He said, "All right, we'll hang on and we'll do our best in the morning, but, for God's sake, Bill, make those Chinese attack."

I stepped out of the van feeling about as depressed as a man could. There, standing in a little half-circle waiting for me, were a couple of my own staff, an officer or two from the Tank Brigade, Sun, and the Chinese liaison officers. They stood there silent and looked at me. All commanders know that look. They see it in the eyes of their staffs and their men when things are really bad, when even the most confident staff officer and the toughest soldier want holding up, and they turn where they *should* turn for support—to their commander. And sometimes he does not know what to say. He feels very much alone.

"Well, gentlemen," I said, putting on what I hoped was a confident, cheerful expression, "it might be worse!"

One of the group, in a sepulchral voice, replied with a single word:

"How?"

I could cheerfully have murdered him, but instead I had to keep my temper.

"Oh," I said, grinning, "it might be raining!"

Two hours later, it was—hard. As I crept under a truck for shelter I thought of that fellow and wished I *had* murdered him.

Throughout the night, as we sat inside a circle of leaguered tanks just above the Pin Chaung, we could hear and see the crump and flash of Japanese shells and mortar bombs flailing Scott's wretched men. His guns did not reply. They were down to about twenty rounds per gun now and he was keeping those for the morning. Time and again the Japanese put in infantry attacks, attempting to infiltrate under cover of darkness and shelling. These attacks, one after the other, were beaten off, but certain of the Burma troops panicked, abandoned their positions, throwing extra strain on the British and Indians.

The day began for me before dawn with a severe blow. The Chinese attack across the Pin Chaung to take Twingon, a village about a mile south of the ford, which I had hoped would start soon after daylight, could not be got ready in time. After a good deal of talk it was promised for 12.30 as the earliest possible hour. I was then faced with the problem of either telling Scott to hold his attack, which was due to go in at seven o'clock, or to let it go as arranged. I decided to let it go, rather than keep his men and transport sitting cramped and waterless under artillery, mortar and air attack.

At seven o'clock the Burma Division resumed the attack, but a reinforced Japanese defence held it after it had made some progress. Meanwhile on the north bank, while still urging the Chinese to hurry their preparations, we had managed to scrape up a small British force which attacked and during the morning actually got a squadron of tanks and some of the West Yorkshire Regiment across the Chaung. This small success might have been expanded had not one of those infuriating mishaps so common in battle occurred. An officer some distance in rear received a report that strong enemy forces were advancing to cut off the transport assembled about Gwegyo. Without realizing the situation forward, or still less, that the threatening forces advancing on him were not Japanese but Chinese, he ordered back the tanks and accompanying infantry to deal with this new, but imaginary, danger.

Burma Division was once more halted in a tight perimeter and was being heavily shelled. The heat was intense, there was still no water, the troops were exhausted and they had suffered heavy casualties, their wounded, of course, being still with them. At this stage, the Burma battalions, in spite of the efforts of their officers, really disintegrated. 1 Burma Brigade reported that the bulk of their troops were no longer reliable; even 13 Brigade said that some of theirs were shaky. It was hardly to be wondered at; their ordeal had been terribly severe.

The Chinese attack, promised for 12.30, had now been postponed to 14.00 hours. Just before that time it was again put back to 16.00 hours. We managed, however, to get it off at 15.00 instead.

Unhappily before that time communication with Scott had ceased and his last desperate effort to break out could not be co-ordinated with the Chinese attack. His squadron of tanks had found and cleared a rough track, leading east, down to the Pin Chaung, over which it was hoped vehicles could move. Scott himself formed up the column, guns in front, wounded in ambulances and trucks next, followed by such vehicles as had survived the bombardment. With a spearhead of tanks and infantry, the column lurched down the narrow, uneven path, through the low hillocks. But the trail turned to sand; the leading ambulances were bogged and the column stopped. As many wounded as possible were piled on the tanks, and Scott gave the order to abandon vehicles and fight a way out on foot, across the Pin Chaung. This his men did, some in formed bodies, some in small groups, and on the other side they met the Chinese. At the sight of the water in the Chaung the mules which had come out with them went mad and the men flung themselves face downwards into it. The haggard, red-eyed British, Indian and Burmese soldiers who staggered up the bank were a terrible sight, but every man I saw was still carrying his rifle. The two brigades of the Division had reached Yenangyaung at a strength of not more than one; there they had lost in killed and wounded twenty per cent of that small number, with a considerable portion of their guns, mortars and vehicles. None of these losses, in either men or equipment, could be replaced. After its ordeal, the Division would be of no fighting value until it had rested, and, as best it could, reorganized. We collected it that night about Gwegyo.

When the Chinese did attack they went in splendidly. They were thrilled at the tank and artillery support they were getting and showed real dash. They took Twingon, rescuing some two hundred of our prisoners and wounded. Next day, 19 April, 38 Division attacked again and with tanks penetrated into Yenangyaung itself, repulsing a Japanese counter-attack. The fighting was severe and the Chinese acquitted themselves well, inflicting heavy losses, vouched for by our own officers. Sun now expected a really heavy Japanese attack at dawn on the 21st. I discussed this with him and agreed that he should come out of the town, back to the Pin Chaung. His Division had done well and I did not want it frittered away in a house-to-house dogfight for the shell of Yenangyaung. In spite of the stories I had heard from American sources of Chinese unwillingness to fight, I had remembered how enthusiastic officers, who had served with our own Chinese Hong Kong regiment, had been about their men, and I had expected the Chinese soldier to be tough and brave. I was, I confess, surprised at how he responded to the stimulus of proper tank and artillery support, and at the aggressive spirit he had shown. I had never expected, either, to get a Chinese general of the calibre of Sun.

As I talked this over with Davies, my chief of staff and my mainstay in these difficult times, we thought we saw a chance of striking back at 33 Japanese Division. True, our 1 Burma Division, never really a division in either establishment or equipment, was at the moment incapable of action, but it was definitely recovering in the peace of Mount Popa, where we had sent it. In a week or two we might hope to have it back in the field at a strength of, say, a brigade. If we could get 17 Division, still in Taungdwingyi, we might, with the Chinese 38 Division and anything else we could scrape up, try a counter-stroke. We were always building up our house of cards, Davies and I, and seeing it fall down—but we went on. So we renewed our attempts to persuade Burma Army to let us take 17 Division from Taungdwingyi. Meanwhile 38 Division and, as usual, 7 Armoured Brigade covered 1 Burma Division as it lay gasping but not dying.

A number of our badly wounded had of necessity been left in the ambulances when the Burma Division had finally broken out. A young gunner officer volunteered to go back to discover their fate. Under cover of darkness, he did so. The ambulances were still standing on the track but every man in them had had his throat cut or been bayoneted to death.

General Slim

Mandalay Falls

Mandalay was full of dumps, stores and camps of every kind—almost all of them deserted. A few officers and men of the administrative services and departments remained, but there had been a general and not very creditable exodus. We were to find more and more that demoralization behind the line was spreading. From now on, while the fighting troops, knowing that their object—to get out intact to India—was at last clear, actually improved in morale and fighting power, the amorphous mass of non-fighting units on the line of communication deteriorated rapidly. In its withdrawal the Corps was from now on preceded by an undisciplined mob of fugitives intent only on escape. No longer in organized units, without any supply arrangements, having deserted their officers, they banded together in gangs, looting, robbing and not infrequently murdering the unfortunate villagers on their route. They were almost entirely Indians and very few belonged to combatant units of the Army. Most of them were soldiers only in name, but their cowardice and their conduct brought disrepute on the real Indian soldiers who followed. It was not to be wondered that as we retreated we found villages burnt and abandoned and such inhabitants as were not in hiding frightened and unfriendly.

It was impossible to guard all the stores lying unattended in Mandalay. On one dump we did, however, put a small guard—that of special octane petrol for our tanks. We were growing greatly anxious about their fuel supply and the find was a godsend, but, when the tanks arrived next day to refill they found nothing but twisted and blackened drums. A senior staff officer, alleged to be from Burma Army, had appeared, and ordered it to be destroyed, and so, with the help of the guard, it was. In the growing confusion mistakes of this kind were almost inevitable, but none the less damaging.

Numbers of 5 Army Chinese were collected in Mandalay and attempts were being made to get them away to the north by train. At the same time I was anxious to rescue some of the more important items such as rifles, Bren guns, ammunition, medical stores and boots, without which we could not continue to fight. With this object two or three small trains were being loaded under the direction of a few stout-hearted British and Anglo-Burmese railway officials who set a magnificent example of devotion to duty. My Chinese of 38 Division came one afternoon and told me that a certain Chinese general had discovered these trains and was coming that

night with his troops to seize them and to escape north.
I was in a quandary. I had not enough troops to guard
them against the numbers who would appear, nor did
I want a fight with our allies. I sent warning to our railway
friends and asked them to steam the engines ten miles
up the line. In due course the Chinese arrived, piled
themselves in, on, and all over the wagons. The General
ordered the trains to start. He was then told there were
no engines, as on my orders they had been taken away.
There was nothing for my Chinese friend to do but to
call off his men and think of some other way of stealing
a train. Eventually he succeeded in doing so and got away,
but it was not one of my trains. I met him frequently
afterwards in India. We never mentioned trains, but I
noticed that he regarded me with an increased respect.

The Corps, with the exception of 63 Brigade that still
held the approaches to the Ava Bridge on the south bank,
was now all safely over the Irrawaddy. There had been
an anxious moment with the tanks. I found a line of them
halted on the south side of the bridge with officers in
consultation. A Stuart tank weighs some thirteen tons and
a notice warned us that the roadway running across the
bridge on brackets each side of the railway had a
maximum capacity of six tons. I asked who had built
the bridge and was shown a tablet with the name of a
well-known British engineering firm. My experience has
been that any permanent bridge built by British engineers
will almost certainly have a safety factor of one hundred
per cent, and I ordered the tanks to cross, one by one.
I confess I watched nervously to see if the roadway sagged
under the first as it made a gingerly passage, but all was
well. Good old British engineers! At last even the Chinese
C.-in-C. agreed that all his men were over, and so 63
Brigade was withdrawn across the bridge. With a
resounding thump it was blown at 23.59 hours on 30
April, and its centre spans fell neatly into the river—a
sad sight, and a signal that we had lost Burma.

General Slim

The physical condition, morale, and spirit of the British Army was at a low ebb. Three months of bitter campaigning and worse hardship had enfeebled the whole Imperial Army and exacted a heavy toll in fighting fitness. Moreover, the average soldier in the Imperial Army no longer wanted to fight in Burma. The Indians were anxious to get back to their native land, and the British wanted to clear out of that forsaken country. This was obvious from their oft-repeated greetings of "See you in India", but it was more apparent from hundred of bitter comments that increased in violence as the days wore on. Though the high British authorities had delayed the Chinese from originally coming into Burma, a typical comment heard on the retreat past Mandalay was: "If the Chinese want the goddam country, give it to them."

But it is doubtful if the Chinese, at least their Army, at that particular time, wanted anything to do with Burma. They were just as fed up with Burma as their British comrades-in-arms. In addition, they were handicapped by being less familiar with Burma than the British.

Jack Belden, American journalist

The End of the Road: India, mid-May

The men of Burma Corps, when they reached Imphal, were physically and mentally very near the end of their strength. They had endured casualties, hardships, hunger, sickness and, above all, the heartbreaking frustration of retreat to a degree that few armies have suffered and yet held together as armies. They were, even at the last, as I had proved, ready if called upon to turn and fight again, but they had been buoyed up by the thought that once over the border into India, not only would other troops interpose between them and the enemy to give them relief from the strain they had supported so long, but that welcome and rest would await them.

. . . . As the wasted units marched wearily into Imphal, through the sheets of monsoon rain, they were directed into areas of jungle on the steep hillsides and told to

bivouac there. It seemed to them that no preparations
at all had been made for their reception. They had arrived
with nothing but the soaked, worn and filthy clothing they
stood up in; they had no blankets, no waterproof sheets,
no tentage. Nor did they find any awaiting them. On those
dripping, gloomy hillsides there was no shelter but the
trees, little if any clothing or blankets, no adequate water
or medical arrangements. As Taffy Davies, indefatigable
in labouring to ease the sufferings of our troops, wryly
said. "The slogan in India seems to be, 'Isn't that Burma
Army annihilated yet?'."

General Slim

*While the British walked the long nine hundred miles
back to India, the Chinese under their tough, hard-bitten
leader General "Vinegar Joe" Stilwell, found their own
way out. In mid-April those Chinese troops not already
involved in their first defeat had been completely shattered
by a new Japanese attack. Henceforth their military value
was slight.*

Stilwell

He already had something of a reputation for shortness
of temper and for distrust of most of the rest of the world.
I must admit he surprised me a little, when, at our first
meeting, he said, "Well, general, I must tell you that my
motto in all dealings is 'buyer beware'," but he never,
as far as I was concerned, lived up to that old horse-
trader's motto. He was over sixty, but he was tough,
mentally and physically; he could be as obstinate as a
whole team of mules; he could be, and frequently was,
downright rude to people whom, often for no good reason,
he did not like. But when he said he would do a thing
he did it. True, you had to get him to *say* that he would,
quite clearly and definitely—and that was not always
easy—but once he had, you knew he would keep to his
word. He had a habit, which I found very disarming, of
arguing most tenaciously against some proposal and then

suddenly looking at you over the top of his glasses with the shadow of a grin, and saying, "Now tell me what you want me to do and I'll do it!" He was two people; one when he had an audience, and a quite different person when talking to you alone. I think it amused him to keep up in public the "Vinegar Joe, Tough Guy" attitude, especially in front of his staff. Americans, whether they liked him or not—and he had more enemies among Americans than among British—were all scared of him. He had courage to an extent few people have, and determination, which, as he usually concentrated it along narrow lines, had a dynamic force. He was not a great soldier in the highest sense, but he was a real leader in the field; no one else I know could have made his Chinese do what they did. He was, undoubtedly, the most colourful character in south-east Asia—and I liked him.

General Slim

The Disintegration of Dynamite Chen

At the time of the Japanese attack Dynamite Chen had his division strung out in great depth, on an extremely narrow front, along the Lashio road leading from Mawchi through Bawlake. His units in general were echeloned on the road. In brief, Chen had committed two grave errors: he had echeloned in depth to an unbelievable extent so that not one of his units formed an adequate defence force; and he had formed such a narrow front that the Japanese could envelop any one of his units at will. American staff officers on the spot warned him of his dangerous position and tried to get him to change his dispositions, but Chen was so slow in moving that the corrections came too late. General Stilwell personally ordered Chen to get busy. If he had obeyed promptly and fought with determination, his division might conceivably have held on.

In the middle of April the Japanese struck these dispositions with the speed and force of a thunderbolt. Moving slightly off the road, the Japanese enveloped

Chen's battalions on both flanks. When the Chinese division commander sought to attack these enveloping columns by bringing up his rear units, he found his rear echelons in turn enveloped by the enemy. The Japanese thrust quick striking forces between Chen's companies and battalions; between the battalions and the regiments; and finally interposed themselves between his regiments and the division command.

Just what happened after that is not exactly clear. Chinese units were cut off from one another. Innumerable Japanese infiltrated between them. With a mass of road blocks woven around them, the Chinese troops were thrown into indescribable confusion. The soldiers, who had been confined so strictly to a narrow valley by their commander, now fled to the hills. Liaison between different units was lost and finally the division disintegrated.

Suddenly one morning the whole of 55 Division disappeared. It disappeared as completely as if a hole had opened in the earth and swallowed all the soldiers.

What had happened to the division, how all the soldiers could so completely vanish from the face of the earth, was a complete mystery to everyone. General Stilwell, talking to me shortly afterwards, said, "There's not a trace of them. It's the damnedest thing I ever heard of."

For two days not a single soldier of the 55th was heard from or seen. When finally a few stragglers staggered into 6 Army headquarters, they could not tell what had happened. The only thing certain was that a great yawning gap had been opened in the lines.

Through this hole the Japanese now poured a motor column with the speed of an express train. During the first days of the battle the enemy had moved at a rate of ten miles a day; this rate soon increased to twenty-five miles a day, and finally to forty and fifty miles on a tortuous road in very rugged terrain northwest of the Salween valley, which should have been simple to defend.

Jack Belden

The Road North

There was no known highway leading to the north. Numerous reconnaissance parties sent out in all directions had finally discovered a cart track following close along the railway and through a dry bamboo forest. This track had been explored for fifty miles in a jeep by Major Frank Merrill, who reported that it might be passable for trucks and sedans, but beyond that fifty miles was unknown territory. On the morning of 2 May, amid circumstances of uncertainty, with the Japanese seeking to cut us off, Stilwell put his Chinese divisions and his American staff officers on that road, on that rutted cart track in that burning, arid, desolate country, and we struck northward, following the railway, moving without information of the enemy and driving towards an undetermined goal.

. . . . A growing mass of Chinese soldiery ahead of us crowded between the thickets and blocked passage; artillery bogged down in hollows and stuck in dried-up sandy washes; soldiers grunted and strained to pull them out; huge trucks loaded with forty and fifty soldiers, clinging to the framework of the sides, to mudguards and radiator bonnets, caught in the thickets and branches of dead trees overhanging the cart track; traffic halted, went forward, came to a standstill again.

We went so slowly that at nine o'clock we had not gone five miles. We had got down many times to help stuck guns extricate themselves and to unsnarl trucks tangled up with the thickets. We began to be disturbed by our slow pace and we despaired of ever getting by the Chinese column. Finally Merrill spied an opening in the thickets and rushed through it across the fields, thereby getting ahead of the Chinese. I followed swiftly and on coming to the upper end of the opening halted my jeep across the face of the leading Chinese truck so that Stilwell could come up and get by.

. . . Again Colonel Williams ran after Stilwell, saying, "The men can't stand this sun, general. They're not in condition yet. We've got to march only early in the morning and late in the afternoon."

"We also have to average at the very least fourteen miles a day, and so far we've done less than five and it's almost eleven o'clock," said the general.

In about half an hour, however, by a small sandy, gravel beach, the general called a noonday halt. As officers and young enlisted men came up one by one and flopped on the sand with their arms stretched out at full length in an attitude of extreme fatigue, the general . . . looked at me and remarked: "When I was their age, if I couldn't do this before breakfast, I would have been ashamed."

He began to divest himself of his pants and his shirt, and, with his campaign hat still on his head to protect him from the noonday sun, went into the stream, sat down, and bathed. Others soon roused themselves, lay in the stream, and tried to suck water back into their pores. The girls, now quieter than before, but still more lively than the men, dug small holes in the sand, placed leaves in the bottom of them, and when the water seeped through the sand as through a filter they scooped it up and drank. There seemed to be a trick in this, for when Jones and I tried it, our water always remained muddy and full of sand, never clearing like that of the girls.

Jack Belden

General Stilwell and his men reached India at about the same time as General Slim.

As well as the retreating armies, many thousands of refugees were struggling away through the jungle. Twenty thousand reached India between May and July. Thousands more trickled in throughout the summer and autumn. By the end of November all those still alive had come in.

Survival of the fittest was the order of the day. At the few hastily-erected camps along the road only those with energy enough to fight their way near the cookhouse were fed. The nights, even in May, were bitterly cold, and about sixty miles of the road were over four thousand feet above sea-level. When the rains started the plight of these people, with no more clothing than the flimsy rags they clutched about them, defies description. Every day dozens gave up the struggle and died where they fell by the roadside.

None who witnessed them can ever forget the innumerable scenes of individual tragedy. There were two children not more than eight years old, with abdomens grossly distended and the limbs of skeletons, trying to awaken a mother who had passed beyond human aid; there was a little girl of four or five having to be forcibly separated from her dead father, and an old woman who dropped exhausted by the roadside while her husband, reduced to a mere automaton with only the will to live, staggered on.

Some carried small bundles, and it was pathetic to see how they clung to the last to things that represented home—a brass flower-vase, a pair of ornate candle-sticks, and in one case an ancient gramophone.

British Nursing Sister

Starvation

Each morning about dawn people started wandering into camp, some of them having spent the night a few hundred yards away, unaware of the camp close by. Others would wander up from the refugee camp and demand a second issue of food. We were so short of food and there were so many people that it was only possible to feed them once. Our war cry was "Keep them hungry, keep them moving". We did not want people to get that comfortable feeling under their belts because it made them relax and deprived them of the necessary urge to get out of the jungle as quickly as possible. The new arrivals in camp had to wait until the food was cooked, which was seldom before half past-eight. In the meantime, we would take a walk round the camp and tell people to get a move on.

. . . . For the first three days we fed the refugees on Tagung Hka stew. We had no rice to spare, or any other food that we had brought from India, but our stew contained plenty of nutriment. Many Hindus who, under normal conditions, would have found beef loathsome to their taste, now, poor things, in their extremity hungrily ate this nourishing stew. We had refugees of every caste, and for very religiously-minded people who were really hungry and were still not prepared to eat meat, we kept a stew made principally of plantain.

. . . . It was also necessary to make the refugees fight both physically and mentally for their life. When no drugs were available this was done by shouting and insulting them until they got angry. If this did not work they were slapped all over and their legs and arms rubbed. When their faces showed signs of flushing they were shown a cup of glucose D and water. This they were allowed to sniff but not drink for a little while. Then they were given a few drops at a time. All this time things were said to the refugees which were calculated to arouse their emotions. After they had drunk two ounces of glucose and water they were given nothing more until they started to react. It usually took twenty minutes before they would start to gurk and belch. When this happened we knew they would live and not die. They were then allowed another two ounces of glucose and water. Half an hour later they would be put in a position where they could see everyone eating and drinking tea. They were given nothing until all the others had finished. Then they were given a small cup of tea with lots of milk, sugar and salt in it. The refugees were now ready to be carried for about four miles, where they would again be given a small amount of glucose water. On reaching a camp for the night they were given only tea, milk, salt and glucose or sugar. By this time their kidneys had started to work and the refugees wanted to urinate. If this did not happen they were given very strong tea, which generally did the trick. In the morning the refugees were made to watch the coolies eat, but were kept hungry and longing for food. They were then given half a biscuit softened in a hot cup of Marmite or tea. The refugees would then be carried to a permanent camp where they would be kept for a week. For the first few days they were given mainly tea, milk, sugar, salt, Marmite and biscuit. Then they were introduced to germinated gram and onions, garlic and rice. In a week or so these people were fit enough to be carried over the next pass, and after a day's rest went on to India.

The main thing to remember about refugees is that their morale must be kept up. Their desire to fight for their life must be continually stimulated. They must never be allowed to stop seeing the flag still flying or to feel they have no further responsibility towards themselves or their families.

A. R. Tainsh, supply and transport officer

POSTSCRIPT

I claim we got a hell of a beating. We got run out of Burma, and it is humiliating as hell. I think we should find out what caused it and go back and retake it.

General Stilwell, May 1942

5

RUSSIA, 1942
THE LAST TRIUMPHS
OF GERMANY

THE WINTER RETREAT

Throughout the winter of 1941-42 the Russian forces, better equipped for and more accustomed to the frightful conditions, continued to hammer at the Germans, who fell back along almost the whole of their vast front.

The Barn

The next ten days were concentrated hell as the Russians hammered ceaselessly at Gridino in an effort to break our defensive line and clear the way to Rzhev and Smolensk. The whole of the Central Army Group's front was called upon to repel the Red steam-roller offensive, but the Gridino corner of the defensive bulge round Rzhev was the nearest point to Moscow of the whole front and took a tremendous pounding. Major Klostermann's outlook was bounded by the shrinking, disintegrating village. And my field of vision extended only from the dressing station to the big Kolchoze barn, forty yards behind the house. That Kolchoze barn became our main concern.

On 8 January, the Russians captured it again and every man able to hold a weapon—stretcher-bearers, wounded men, Heinrich and myself—ran out into the bitter cold to engage them in fierce hand-to-hand fighting. The small infantry gun was used at point-blank range against the massive barn. We were inevitably being overwhelmed by weight of numbers when Klostermann staged a counter-attack with some of his men and the Reds were thrown out. A renewed Russian attack during the night petered out in the face of concentrated fire from small-arms and our heavy 21 cm. mortars. Towards morning, the Reds retaliated from a safe distance by plastering us with artillery shell-fire.

The Russian artillery fire stopped at about 5 a.m. and we heard a screaming mob coming towards us from the east again. Their high-pitched *"Oorair! Oorair!"* came across the snow to us. On they came towards the barn, yelling and screaming at the top of their voices. A flare picked them out—a close-packed body of charging men. From our holes in the snow and our wooden barricades behind the dressing station we fired our automatics and rifles into the advancing mass. They went down by the dozen, but the men behind trod the bodies into the snow. They took the Kolchoze barn again, but this time we fired grenades into the barn, where the Russians were still kicking up an infernal din. Some of the Reds charged out of the barn right into the muzzles of our guns. Confused hand-to-hand fighting developed, but suddenly the mass of Russians in the barn took to their heels and fled into the darkness.

Cautiously some of our men entered the barn. There were dead and wounded Russians littering the floor, victims of the grenades. But in a corner were two Russians singing raucously, quite oblivious of what was going on around them. Then it dawned on us—the Russians were blind drunk! From the less seriously wounded we gathered that the commissars, becoming desperate at the Red Army's inability to break through our lines in night attacks, had issued their troops with generous rations of alcohol, and when all the men were thoroughly drunk, had launched the attack.

And then something even more grotesque came to our notice. Two old women were cowering against the wall—in their muffled state we had taken them for men. They and about fifty more old men and women, civilians from the Russian-held villages, had been forced to run in front of the Red Troops when they charged our positions. All but the two old women of this human shield had been shot down by us and trampled underfoot by the troops behind. But they had served the diabolical Russian purpose—fifty useless civilians had perished instead of fifty soldiers. We went outside and, lying in the snow, was the evidence; defenceless, unarmed civilians bore testimony in death. Three were wounded but still alive. They were carried into the dressing station along with our own thirty wounded. Eight of our men were dead.

Our village was shrinking round us as house after house was burnt down or destroyed by artillery fire. Never-ending alarms kept us on edge day and night. Next day, 10 January, we were bombed by the Luftwaffe and nine of our men were killed. We cursed our own airmen for their stupidity and their accuracy. Then a patrol of twelve men was surprised by the Russians and practically annihilated; two badly wounded men staggered back. Two more Russian attacks were hurled back; in one of them, one of our own mortars was misdirected in the confusion and eight of our soldiers were severely wounded as a result. The Reds brought their terrifying "Stalin-organ" into the fight and plastered the village with mortar shells. While the "Stalin-organ" was playing its devilish tune, every man in the battalion lay flat wherever he was and prayed that none of the shells from that battery of destruction was inscribed with his name. Fortunately after Gridino had been plastered thoroughly the "organ" was moved to another sector to repeat its tune.

Heinrich Haape

The Major

A second blow fell almost immediately. The commander of the division's anti-tank battalion shot himself. He had been a friend of mine. He was a much-decorated soldier of the first World War; during the second he had gained further military distinction in France, Greece and Russia. In ten years of war I met very few men who were genuinely quite without fear. He was one of them. He loved danger. He was dauntless. He was also an excellent strategist and tireless in striving for the welfare of his men. Through some odd coincidence it had come to light that he had allowed some friends in Bucharest to lend him Roumanian money and had repaid the amounts in Germany in German money. This was a currency offence. From the legal point of view the soldier was considered to be German territory wherever he might be. An offence of this kind seemed rather ridiculous in circumstances as they were then. Presumably it could have been settled without fuss by some disciplinary action which the divisional commander could have devised as principal judicial administrator. But there was another matter as well. For months a lieutenant on my friend's staff had been taking notes of the major's remarks about the régime. These the lieutenant had sent to one of the Party's offices in Germany and they came back to the division by way of circuitous official channels for "opinion and report". . . . The major faced degradation and removal to a punitive unit as a private, second class. He was a man of forty-five who had led a blameless life. He shot himself. Military honours for his funeral were refused and the regulations even forbade the chaplain to speak at the graveside. However, owing to the general's magnanimity, permission for a dignified burial was given.

Peter Bamm, German medical officer

Spring: German Winter Clothing arrives

The difference between new and old hands at this game of making war in the snow was further accentuated on 25 March, when there was a three-hour thaw at midday. Then it became cold again and by evening a blizzard was raging across the wide snowfields. For the newcomers the brief thaw was of little consequence, but on us it made a great impression—it was the first sign of the approach of a new spring.

And the next day our winter clothing arrived! Huge quantities of fur coats, woollens, fur-lined boots, thick overcoats—all of it collected from the civilians in Germany after a moving appeal to the nation by Goebbels in December. He had told the people at home that we were equipped with warm clothing—we had plenty of it—but it was impossible to have too much in a Russian winter. So the good folk in Germany had sacrificed their fur coats, warm boots, jerseys, overcoats, anything that looked vaguely as if it would keep out the Russian cold, little knowing that we should all have frozen to death had we not been able to shoot the enemy down and pillage their dead bodies to warm our own. The patriotic pile of clothing looked rather ridiculous as it lay in the command-post stable the day after the first thaw of spring.

Heinrich Haape

In September 1941 Leningrad, the second city of Russia, had been invested by the Germans. From then until the spring of 1943, Leningrad was more or less closely blockaded. A lifeline could be kept open across the frozen waters of Lake Ladoga during the winter, but with the thaw, this road across the ice disappeared.

Flight into Leningrad: Spring 1942

All my life I shall preserve the memory of that evening towards the end of April 1942, when our plane, escorted by fighters, flew very low over Lake Ladoga and beneath us, on the ice, which was cracked and fissured, with surging tides of water in between, stretched the road, the only road, which throughout the winter had linked Leningrad with the rest of the country. The people of Leningrad called it The Road of Life. It had already been torn to shreds—virtually obliterated—and in places was a mere flood of water. The plane flew straight towards the misty, crimson, diffuse globe of the sun, which caught the tops of the pine and firs along the entire length of the lakeshore behind us in the tender glow of spring.

A. Fadeyev

Fighting in the Suburbs

When the Germans approached Kolpino the workers of the Izhorsky plant took a vow not to yield either the factory or the town; the Germans would have to force a passage over their dead bones. In the result the front came right up to Kolpino itself. The town and the factory were subjected to systematic assault from the air and to an artillery bombardment which went on without pause day and night. Several generations of Izhorsky people, from infants at the breast to the most ancient men and women, were represented among those killed by bomb or shell fragments. But Kolpino remained in the hands of the Izhorsky workers, and the factory, in spite of everything, went on producing.

Much of Kolpino is ruins. When I was with Lieutenant-Colonel Shubin at the artillery observation post, the enemy's field guns were methodically, remorselessly and senselessly pounding the little wooden houses and huts. Our forward line was a few kilometres in front of us, almost on the edge of the town; the firing there was particularly heavy. But the peacetime ways of the town had not altogether ceased. Women did their washing at the pond. Two girls at the crossroads chatted and laughed. An old woman in a black dress walked slowly along the road, carrying in her arms a grandchild a few months old. The infant slept.

Snipers

Lieutenant Gorbatenko . . . told us about a singular duel in which he engaged for a whole day with an enemy sniper. Having taken up his position at night, towards dawn Lieutenant Gorbatenko detected a faint stir behind a bush on the edge of the enemy trench ahead. With this position as his proximate target Gorbatenko fired. A few seconds later a soldier's spade was thrust up above the enemy trench and waved from side to side. His opponent was signaling a miss. Gorbatenko kept quiet and waited a long time in the hope that his opponent would show himself. But nothing at all stirred in the enemy trench. Gorbatenko, whose position was well camouflaged, moved cautiously to obtain a closer view, but he had scarcely shifted his head when a shot rang out from the enemy trench and a bullet whistled past his ear, singeing his hair. Gorbatenko dived back into his trench, hung out his own spade and waved it from side to side, in his turn showing that he hadn't been hit.

In this way, changing their positions and spying on each other's faintest movement, they stuck to their duel for a good many hours, each of them signaling with his spade on every occasion that the other's shot had missed.

In the end Gorbatenko killed his man: he caught him out. After one of the enemy sniper's shots he made no attempt to signal with the spade, but kept still, feigning death. A little later his opponent decided to make certain and began to peer over the trench. Still Gorbatenko gave no sign of life. As he had reckoned in advance, the other abandoned all caution in a short time and hung boldly over the trench, so Gorbatenko dispatched him without difficulty.

Leningrad Landscape

The sight of somebody—man, woman or child—

dragging a child's sledge on which lay a dead body wrapped up in a blanket or a bit of canvas became a daily commonplace of the winter Leningrad landscape. The spectacle of somebody dying of hunger in a snow-covered street was by no means rare. Pedestrians passed by, removed their caps and muttered a word or two in sympathy, or sometimes did not even stop, since there was no help they could offer.

The Widow

In one of the bays of the shop a group of women were standing at enormous milling machines, milling mines, scattering sparks in all directions. There were stacks of mines, still hot from the moulds, on the floor near them. I stopped next to one of the women. Her face was visible only in profile. A dark kerchief was drawn low over her brow and I could not guess her age. Her hands protected by huge gauntlets, she picked up a mine from the heap and then, using the whole weight of her body, held it against the rapidly revolving wheel of the machine. A sheaf of sparks flew round her. This was the preliminary process of rough milling before the mines reached the lathes for turning. Without paying any attention to me she picked up mine after mine and pressed them with all the force of her body against the wheel. It was plain that to do this involved a very considerable physical strain, for the woman's whole body quivered with the effort.

This was a man's work, and heavy work at that. I wanted to see the woman's face and I remained where I was until she turned towards me. She seemed to me a woman of about forty. Her face had a strange beauty. Delicate and stern of feature, it was the face of a saint.

"Is it hard work?" I asked.

"Yes, at first it was very hard," she said, picking up a mine and holding it against the revolving wheel, making the sparks fly once more.

"Where is your husband?" I asked after a brief interval, during which she put the mine down and picked up another.

"He died last winter."

Blockade Jelly

When I entered the room my cousin, who had a friend with her, a woman as emaciated as herself, was having her dinner. Because of the increased rations for the First of May, their dinner, judged by Leningrad standards, might have been called luxurious. It included even beer and vodka prepared from dried orange rind. Among the dishes was the famous Leningrad-blockade jelly—a jelly made from carpenter's glue. Here was the reverse process: you cooked the glue, removed all the bone scum—or, rather, the scum of what had once been bone—and added gelatine to the rest. Then you let it cool.

This jelly was absolutely tasteless and its nutritive value was dubious, but it was a stay and comfort for many people in Leningrad.

The White Nights

Over Leningrad descended the white nights. You could stand for hours on the Troitsky Bridge when on a white night the moon rose over the Summer Garden, and below, along the Neva, motionless and beautiful in the lilac mist, rose the great colonnades of the Bourse, the Winter Palace, the Admiralty.

And day and night the windows of Leningrad's dwellings were flung wide open. The sounds of wireless music or of gramophone records descended into the street. Wandering along a quiet shady street you would hear, from somewhere inside a wide-flung window, a girl carefully attacking her piano exercises and from time to time the severe voice of the piano teacher. And it was comforting, walking at night along the Neva, to see between the wings of the Kazan Cathedral the huge silver fish of a barrage balloon faintly stirring on its rigging and capable at a moment's notice of rising to the sky.

But there were few air-raid alarms during those summer months. The Leningrad airmen protected their own city and air battles took place some way from its approaches. Sometimes a single plane broke through the defences on the outskirts and dropped its bombs. The artillery bombardment of the city was by now of a stealthy, thieving character only. Suddenly on a clear sunny day or during a beautiful white night the distant sound of a big gun would be heard and a shell would scream overhead and burst somewhere near the Griboyedov canal or Uritsky Square. A second, a third—now here, now there—and the thief would make off.

A. Fadeyev

With the departure of all Germany's hopes of a quick end to the war in the East, the official German attitude to the Russian people suffered a radical change for the worse.

Russian Volunteers

During their leave most of our men had been deeply shocked; the discontent all over Germany had left them perplexed and worried. A number had been detailed to accompany trains to Germany as medical orderlies. These trains carried Russians—both men and women—who had been enrolled . . . on a purely voluntary basis for service in the war industries. The men had been greatly disturbed by the complete lack of consideration with which these civilians had been treated on the journey. We still felt that we were on friendly terms with the Russians. The men, ignorant of the fact that these workers were heading straight for slavery, put down what they had witnessed to shortcomings in organization.

There was no longer any rhyme or reason in these things. The party was ceremoniously proclaiming the liberation of the Russian people from Soviet enslavement and going through the farce of setting up a Ukrainian puppet government in Kiev which was allowed to do little more than draft its own constitution. Hundreds of thousands of Russians were already fighting in the German Army and were displaying the same bravery that they had shown when they had been in the Red Army only a short while before. They were fighting for the deliverance of their country from the system of the Soviets. Simultaneously, hundreds of thousands of prisoners-of-war who would have been just as willing to take up the struggle against communism were left to starve in prison camps in the Ukraine. This too our people had learned from accounts given to them by escort troops whom they had come across occasionally on leave trains.

Peter Bamm

The Slavs are to work for us. In so far as we do not need them, they may die. They should not receive the benefits of the German public health system. We do not care about their fertility. They may practice abortion and use contraceptives; the more the better. We do not want them educated; it is enough if they can count up to one hundred. Such stooges will be the more useful to us. Religion we leave to them as a diversion. As to food, they will not get any more than is absolutely necessary. We are the masters; we come first.

Martin Bormann, Chief of the Nazi Party

The winter campaign in Russia is nearing its close. The outstanding bravery and self-sacrificing effort of our troops on the Eastern Front have achieved a great defensive success. The enemy suffered very severe losses in men and material. . . . As soon as weather and terrain conditions are favourable the superior German command and German forces must take the initiative once again to force the enemy to do our bidding.

Adolf Hitler, 5 April 1942

THE LAST TRIUMPHS

The main German offensive on the Eastern Front for 1942 was directed towards the south-east, in order to overrun the Caucasian oilfields. The first objective was to neutralize the Crimea, so securing the right flank of the main thrust. Then one army crossed the Don and thrust far down between the Black Sea and the Caspian, while another advanced east upon Stalingrad to control the Volga and protect the left flank of the main penetration.

The capture of Stalingrad will close the isthmus between the Don and the Volga, as well as the river itself: fast mobile units will also advance down the Volga to block the river at Astrakhan. . . .

Adolf Hitler, 2 July 1942

"The Russians are Finished"

Halder: "The Russians have assembled a million troops in the Saratov area and a further half-million east of the Caucasus. The Soviet High Command will go over to the offensive, when the German forces reach the Volga. Stalin will launch an attack in this area, exactly similar to the one he launched against Denikin during the Russian revolution."

He added: "The Russians are producing fifteen hundred tanks per month, against a German figure of six hundred. I am warning you that a crisis is coming, and for sure."

Hitler: "Spare me this idiotic nonsense. The Russians are finished. In four weeks' time they will collapse."

The Road to the Crimea

When one sees one of the roads along which reinforcements go forward to the front, the time-worn phrase "an army worming its way along" describes the

scene perfectly. Every man, every horse, every vehicle
had its being twice over. Once in the control office of
any command and once out here in the mud. At
headquarters everything is neat and tidy; out here chaos
is complete. Units become separated by many miles. No
one can do anything to stop a new unit slipping from the
left or right into a small gap between the marching
columns. The "road" is little more than a track—over
which the light Russian peasant carts just manage to
travel—hurriedly reinforced with gravel and a few broken
stones. Stones are at a premium in the steppe. In a matter
of hours an army's reinforcements grind a peasant track
like that out of existence. This one had the added
inconvenience of a ditch on either side which made it
practically impossible to avoid an obstruction by cutting
out into the fields.

This is the sort of thing that would happen: The back
wheel of some horsedrawn vehicle in the mile-long column
slips into a deep shell crater concealed by a puddle of
water. The wheel breaks. The shaft rises in the air. The
horses, wrenched upwards, shy and kick over the traces.
One of the leads parts. The vehicle behind tries to
overtake on the left but is unable to drive quite clear of
the deep ruts. The right-hand back wheel of the second
vehicle catches in the left-hand back wheel of the first.
The horses rear and start kicking in all directions. There
is no going forwards or backwards. An ammunition lorry
returning empty from the front tries to pass the hopeless
tangle on the narrow strip of roadway that remains.
Shouts—"We must get through!" It slowly subsides into
the ditch and sticks fast. It is a private van converted
to army use and is quite incapable of getting out on its
own.

Now there is an impassable obstruction on the roads,
on the army's supply route! Everyone becomes infected
with uncontrollable fury. Everyone shouts at everyone
else. Sweating, swearing, mud-spattered men start laying
into sweating, shivering, mud-caked horses that are
already frothing at the mouth. All at once the fury passes.

Someone lights a cheroot. Someone take the initiative.
The horses are unhitched. The lorry is dragged out
backwards from the ditch by horses harnessed to a
swingletree attached to a rope. The vehicle with a broken
wheel is emptied of its load. There is general laughter
if a pale blue eiderdown or a few live geese come to light
in the process. The men step into the pool of water which
runs over the tops of their boots. They seize hold of the
muddy wheel, and shouting "Heave! Heave!", manhandle
the empty vehicle to the side. The horses are re-harnessed
to the second wagon and it sets off once more. The lorry
passes them, backfiring as it goes, on its way to the
ammunition depot in the rear.

This scene is repeated a hundred times a day with
monotonous regularity. But by each evening there has
been a progression of twelve, six, occasionally only three
miles. At one point a few fascines of intertwined gorse
have been laid across the ditch. The whole crawling mass
has meandered twenty yards on to the open field to by-
pass a dud bomb which lies unexploded in the middle
of the road. To left and right the fields are strewn with
a weird assortment of stoves, milking stools, bedsteads,
wireless-sets, munition boxes, lamps. It is like the
aftermath of a flood. Every few hundred yards is a
broken-down vehicle; or a dead horse with swollen belly;
or a corpse. Crows rise with a heavy flapping of wings.
Tattered grey clouds chase without pause high above the
living and the dead.

Peter Bamm

Sevastopol

The colossal battle for Sevastopol lasted a full month.

On the morning of 7 June, as dawn turned the eastern
sky to gold and swept the shadows from the valleys, our
artillery opened up in its full fury by way of a prelude
to the infantry assault. Simultaneously the squadrons of
the Luftwaffe hurtled down on to their allotted targets.

The scene before us was indescribable, since it was unique in modern warfare for the leader of an army to command a view of his entire battlefield. To the north-west the eye could range from the woodlands that hid the fierce battles of LIV Corps' left wing from view right over to the heights south of the Belbek valley, for which we were to fight so bitterly. Looking due west, one could see the heights of Gaytany, and behind them, in the far distance, the shimmer of Severnaya Bay where it joined the Black Sea. Even the spurs of the Khersones peninsula, on which we were to find vestiges of Hellenic culture, were visible in clear weather. To the southwest there towered the menacing heights of Zapun and the rugged cliffs of the coastal range. At night, within the wide circumference of the fortress, one saw the flashes of enemy gunfire, and by day the clouds of rock and dust cast up by the bursts of our heavy shells and the bombs dropped by German aircraft. It was indeed a fantastic setting for such a gigantic spectacle!

. . . . The second phase of the offensive, lasting up to 17 June, was marked on both fronts by a bitter struggle for every foot of ground, every pill-box and every trench. Time and again the Russians tried to win back what they had lost by launching violent counter-attacks. In their big strong-points, and in the smaller pill-boxes too, they often fought till the last man and the last round. While the main burden of these battles was borne by the infantry and engineers, the advanced observation posts of our artillery still deserve special mention, since it was chiefly they who had to direct the fire which made it possible to take individual strong-points and pill-boxes. They, together with the assault guns, were the infantry's best helpmates.

On 13 June the valiant 16th Infantry Regiment of 22 Division, led by Colonel von Choltitz, succeeded in taking Fort Stalin, before which its attack had come to a standstill the previous winter. The spirit of our infantry was typified by one wounded man of this regiment who, pointing to his smashed arm and bandaged head, was heard to cry: "I can take this lot now we've got the Stalin!"

. . . . 22 Division gained control along its whole front of the cliffs overlooking Severnaya Bay. There was extremely hard fighting for the railway tunnel on the boundary between 22 and 50 Divisions, out of which the enemy launched a strong counter-attack with a brigade that had recently arrived by cruiser. The tunnel was finally captured by shelling its entrance. Not only hundreds of troops came out but an even greater number of civilians, including women and children. Particular difficulty was experienced in winkling the enemy out of his last hideouts on the northern shore of the bay, where deep galleries for storing supplies and ammunition had been driven into the sheer wall of rock. These had been equipped for defence by the addition of steel doors. Since the occupants, under pressure from their commissars, showed no sign of surrendering, we had to try to blow the doors open. As our engineers approached the first of them, there was an explosion inside the casemate and a large slab of cliff came tumbling down, burying not only the enemy within but also our own squad of engineers. The commissar in command had blown the casemate and its occupants sky-high. In the end a second lieutenant from an assault battery, who had brought up his gun along the coastal road regardless of enemy shelling from the southern shore, managed to force the other casemates to open up after he had fired on their embrasures at point-blank range. Crowds of completely worn-out soldiers and civilians emerged, their commissars having committed suicide.

General von Manstein, G.O.C. 11 Army

Inside Sevastopol: An Underground Factory

At last, through a long dark tunnel, I reached typical Sevastopol, underground. The noise was incredible. The Admiralty was a monastery compared with this. The vast cellar was subdivided by heavy metal screens where hundreds of lathes hummed and rattled, turning out grenades. A tractor motor was roaring. It was generating electricity, but was puffing and smoking like a bad old samovar. When the motor stopped, the lights went out; immediately every worker lit a cigarette, and the cave glowed with hundreds of faint lights. It has been agreed among them that only when work was held up by a failure of current should there be smoking. On the same table a cook and a compositor worked side by side, the one peeling potatoes, the other setting up the front page of a newspaper. The potatoes lay among the type.

The machines worked twenty-four hours daily, their noise not stopping a moment. With the tobacco smoke mingled the smells of the kitchen, gas, and stale air.

The whole front was relying on this factory for its grenades.

Boris Voyetekhov

The Docks

Into the shoving, swirling crowd the infantrymen from the ship moved with vigour, pushing away from the gangways old men and women who were waiting to be evacuated, till they had formed a line and had answered their roll call. They were going straight to the front.

The crew, who rarely slept, so constant was the crowd of people and the mass of cases in their quarters, unloaded the cargo themselves, working the noisy derricks quickly but efficiently. Soon the quay was crowded with new aeroplane engines, boxes of shells, bombs, freshly-painted machine-guns, mobile artillery, flasks of oil and acids, spare parts for tank caterpillars, sacks of flour, salt, canned meat, and much more besides.

The pile grew between the ship and the waiting evacuees and wounded. I remember two voices among all this confusion, one a woman's crying, "Where is my aspidistra?", the other that of a tall, gaunt Red Army man who was quietly passing through the crowd with a child's toy rifle in his hand, phlegmatically shouting, "Whose rifle? Whose rifle?" As I listened, the voices were drowned by the clamour of people coming aboard the destroyer.

The crew had just finished unloading the munitions from deep holds and now began to take on the thousands of pieces of evacuees' luggage. No restriction had been put on what could be transported. Even plants were allowed. Only in this way could the stubborn reluctance of the people of Sevastopol to leave their beloved city be broken down. That is why now, on abandoning their homes, these people were taking with them every object which reminded them of their childhood, youth, or old age, of their joys and woes, anything that in unknown cities or villages could bring back to these southern people memories of their life beside the sea. The Navy understood this, and with solicitude sailors carried up the gangway ancient models of sailing ships, knick-knacks, family portraits framed in lifebelts, old seascapes, deck chairs, ornamental tables and screens which for decades had stood unmoved in front parlours.

Amid these tears, the hurtling of shells, the skirmishes with the fire and the business of loading, the commissar of the destroyer was approached by a small, pale-faced man who took out a notebook and in his toneless voice asked, "How many meetings did you hold during the trip? Did you read any articles aloud?" The commissar looked coldly at this intruder and said abruptly, "We had a meeting to discuss the liquidation of fools like you. It was a very successful meeting, too. Aren't you ashamed to ask such questions when there isn't a man you can see here who has slept for the last ten days or eaten except at night on the journey back? Get away."

The little man fidgeted where he stood for a moment and then went away. I saw neither shame nor regret in his dim fish-like eyes.

Divers

The commissar was insatiable. He knew that before Sevastopol the Germans had massed fourteen divisions with a huge force of aircraft and that these were now being hurled at the city in their third offensive. Wiping

sweat from his brow and drinking yet more water, he
carefully thumbed sunk ships' papers and bills of lading,
asking persistently, "Where are those six aeroplane
engines? Why haven't I had those cases of dry bread?
Where are the bandages, the cotton-wool, and drugs? What
are you doing there on the bottom? Playing chess with
the dead?"

"Just that," replied the chief diver, "and you had better
come and take a hand down below; then you will be
satisfied that it is impossible to get up those motors. They
are covered with piles of dead horses and cavalrymen
in the hold. Drugs"—he hesitated—"I can't go there."

"Why not?"

"I have been a diver for thirty years. During that time
I have seen things that drove people who were working
next to me mad, or else they would come up grey-haired,
but to go into that cabin where, if I open the door, dead
bodies of children rush towards me—no, I can't and I
won't."

"Well," said the commissar, "that means you are letting
living children die for the lack of food and bandages."

The discussions ended as always with the divers going
straight back to their cutters and down below.

The Battle of the Loudspeakers

The loudspeakers fell silent. Each side made use of
this form of propaganda, and when night fell a regular
radio duel began. Actually it was more of a scramble
than a duel—a scrambling fight among announcers,
drivers and gunners. Heavily-armoured radio vans would
dash wildly from valley to valley trying to avoid the
gunfire that would be directed at them as they gave their
positions away by their sound. The announcers would
compete not only in volume but in the presentation of
their material. Each talked the enemy's language—we,
German and Roumanian; they, Russian. The announcers
came to know each other well during the siege and loudly
reproached each other for professional faults, for bad

grammar, poor jokes, traces of drunkenness in their voices, and other technical shortcomings. These exchanges of personalities were highly popular in the trenches, and every time the quips and the cracks of our announcer were heard, roars of laughter would be audible from the German trenches.

The Last Assault

At this moment something remarkable happened in the enemy trenches, the like of which had never happened before on the Sevastopol front. It was solemn religious chanting that reached our ears from the enemy lines, a great chorus that surged across the bitter, stony ground. The gramophone was stopped and everybody listened. It was the Roumanians, praying for victory, despairingly, as they faced the sun on the Crimean hills.

Boris Voyetekhov

After our experience of Soviet methods to date we were bound to assume that the enemy would make a last stand behind Sevastopol's perimeter defences and finally in the city itself. An order from Stalin had been repeatedly wirelessed to the defenders to hold out to the last man and the last round, and we knew that every member of the civil population capable of bearing arms had been mustered.

And so 1 July began with a massed bombardment of the perimeter fortifications and the enemy's strong-points in the interior of the city. Before long our reconnaissance aircraft reported that no further serious resistance need be anticipated. The shelling was stopped and the divisions moved in. It seemed probable that the enemy had pulled the bulk of his forces out to the west the previous night.

But the struggle was still not over. Although the Soviet Coast Army had given up the city, it had only done so in order to offer further resistance from behind the defences which sealed off the Khersones peninsula—either in pursuance of Stalin's backs-to-the-wall order or else in the hope of still getting part of the army evacuated by Red Fleet vessels at night from the deep inlets west of Sevastopol. As it turned out, only very few of the top commanders and commissars were fetched away by motor-torpedo boat, one of them being the army commander, General Petrov. When his successor tried to escape in the same way he was intercepted by our Italian E-boat.

Thus the final battles on the Khersones peninsula lasted up till 4 July. While 72 Division captured the armour-plated fort of "Maxim Gorki II", which was defended by several thousand men, the other divisions gradually pushed the enemy back towards the extreme tip of the peninsula. The Russians made repeated attempts to break through to the east by night, presumably in the hope of joining up with the partisans in the Yaila Mountains. Whole masses of them rushed at our lines, their arms linked to prevent anyone from hanging back. At their head, urging them on, there were often women and girls of the Communist Youth, themselves bearing arms. Inevitably the losses which sallies of this kind entailed were extraordinarily high.

In the end the remnants of the Coast Army sought refuge in big caverns on the shore of the Khersones peninsula, where they waited in vain to be evacuated. When they surrendered on 4 July, thirty thousand men emerged from this small tip of land alone.

In all, the number of prisoners taken in the fortress was over ninety thousand, and the enemy's losses in killed amounted to many times our own. The amount of booty captured was so vast that it could not immediately be calculated. A naturally strong fortress, reinforced and consolidated in every conceivable way and defended by a whole army, had fallen. The army was annihilated and the entire Crimea now in German hands. At just the right time from the operational point of view, 11 Army had become free for use in the big German offensive on the southern wing of the Eastern Front.

General von Manstein

The Fallen City

We had been surprised to find no civilian casualties until Sergeant Kienzle discovered them in the vaults of the cathedral. I made my way there with a few medical orderlies. Old women, young women, children and old men lay next to each other on piles of straw. Their wounds have been well cared for surgically, but the dressings consisted of the barest emergency bandages. Probably the Russians had had no proper bandaging material left.

In one corner a priest belonging to the Russian Orthodox Church was kneeling on the straw. In his raised hand he bore a crucifix. The feeble light of the candle hardly reached to the ceiling of the vault but it sparkled on the jewels with which the crucifix was adorned. He was murmuring a prayer. Before him an old woman was dying, one of the bony, arthritic hands clawing the air. Her fellow sufferers repeated the prayers in unison. A deep rattling sound came from the old woman's throat and then she died. The priest got up; the old woman's hand remained poised in mid-air.

When I got back to our quarters which were situated at the edge of the town above the Khersones peninsula, Rombach was already waiting for me. I wanted to tell him what I had just seen but I didn't get a chance. He only said, "Come with me."

We drove a mile southwards out of the town. Among the vineyards on the southern slopes of Sevastopol—not far from the spot where Iphigenia had looked over the waters of the Propontis towards Hellas—the Russians had abandoned their wounded.

They lay scattered in their thousands between the vines. For days they had had nothing to eat and for forty-eight hours nothing to drink. For the most part they had received no surgical attention. Hour after hour the sun blazed down on them. Over the hills there passed a wind of sighs. The misery of these men who had been crushed by war did not cry out to heaven; it merely stirred gently like a light breeze across the hills. Down in the valley one could see several wire enclosures into which thirty thousand uninjured prisoners had been crowded together to await their fate. Now and then a shot rang out.

. . . . The miserable little trickle of warm and dirty water was nothing like enough to prevent the danger of hundreds of men dying from thirst. The wounded began to gain fresh hope but we couldn't provide sufficient *voda* or water as quickly as all that.

Every hour or so I went among them to pick out those in most urgent need of surgical attention. As I went through the tents they turned towards me with raised hands and the words: *"Voda, Gospodin! Voda!"* swirled in my wake like the rushing of a ship's backwater.

Sometimes in my dreams I still hear that cry: *"Voda, Gospodin! Voda!"*

Then they began to die.

We tried and tried to think of a way out. In the meantime down in the Severnaya Bay, about two and a half miles away, a few of the larger wells had been restored to working order and we decided to bring all the walking wounded there. This would reduce the number of those whom we still had to supply to about twelve hundred.

Only a small proportion of the total number of wounded had as yet been accommodated in the tents. The majority still lay out in the open. We had selected a number of lightly injured Russians to assist us as supervisors, and in order to distinguish them they wore a gauze bandage around their left arm. We sent these men through the vineyards to tell everybody who could walk to collect together and to march down to the wells. The prisoners, totally apathetic, didn't stir. Thereupon the supervisors tore the vine-props from the ground and started jumping about among the men cudgelling and beating them. That at last brought all those who still had them on to their legs. We stood by and watched. To have interfered with the brutality of this procedure would have been pure sentimentality, for it saved a host of seriously injured men from death by thirst.

With dragging gait, supporting themselves on sticks or leaning against each other, surrounded by myriads of flies, they shuffled towards the wells. A long, heart-rending procession, they trailed through Iphigenia's landscape under the dazzling Crimean sun.

They would quench their thirst. They would gain a little strength. But it would only help them to keep on along the dreary route into the realm of the barbarians. And of that realm we were the frontier.

Fortitude without justice is the tool of the wicked. Saint Ambrose said so fifteen hundred years ago.

Peter Bamm

The main thrust of the Germans under von Kleist to the south-east continued with extraordinary momentum into the heart of the Caucasian oilfields, which the Russians had destroyed. One railway, winding down the shores of the Caspian Sea, enabled the Russians to send reinforcements southwards which could meet head on and combat the German advance, which, so incredibly far from its firm base, was losing momentum.

Into the Caucasus

Late each evening we would radio the approximate positions of our subordinate units to the Army Headquarters. This Headquarters in turn would radio the information back to Supreme Headquarters during the night. Halder and his colleagues—the "Boesemüller squad", as they were nicknamed after the famous book about the first World War—reported to Hitler at about 11.00 hours on the next morning, and issued orders immediately after this conference. These orders could not arrive at the front line until late afternoon, by which time the situation was completely altered, the divisions having moved perhaps fifty or a hundred miles in the meantime!

Our advance drove further and further south. The seriousness of our manoeuvres could be judged by the Russian reaction. While Tukhachevski, the Russian Commander-in-Chief, had a narrow escape from 29 Mechanized, the Russians scraped together what tanks they could muster. They were defeated in a fierce tank battle near Chertkovo by my 23 Panzer on 12 July, and on 14 July a large Russian force was trapped near the important railway centre of Millerovo.

For somebody who has never lived in such an atmosphere, watching the disintegration of an enemy army from its rear, it is hard to imagine the details: surrendering units, individual and massed refugees, broken-down vehicles, retreating enemy columns, streams of prisoners with and without guards, attacks of enemy aircraft. It is an indescribable turmoil.

. . . . As Rostov-on-Don fell to the German forces the southern part of the Russian front appeared to disintegrate. The Russians, pouring back from the Rostov area, were constantly pressing in upon my units, while from the east the Caucasian Cavalry Corps, bolstered with strong tank formations, tried to relieve the situation for the defeated and retreating troops.

The mission of protecting von Kleist's eastern flank meant advancing southward with complete disregard for our flanks and lines of communication. While my 3 Panzer Division, in the lead, cut the railway leading from Stalingrad to the Black Sea in the neighbourhood of Proletarskaya, winning a bridgehead over the Manych in a dramatic and bitter night battle against N.K.W.P. troops and forces from Krasnodar Officers' School, 23 Panzer Division dealt a decisive defeat to the Caucasian Cavalry Corps, knocking out sixty-eight tanks, mostly heavy types, in one hour, and capturing the chief-of-staff of the formation.

Our eastern flank was meanwhile being covered in a very nominal fashion by a mobile regiment of grenadiers (armoured infantry), and the lines of communication, although often cut for a period by the Russians who were streaming eastward, were maintained by the establishment of a convoy system, with independent tank companies protecting and escorting supplies over stretches. In fact, XL Panzer Corps fought in three directions at once in an eccentric battle, the main effort being made southwards.

. . . . The heat of the Kuban steppe was stifling. We were glad to approach the Caucasus mountains and breathe cooler air. By this time my corps had spent over a month behind the Soviet lines. Rumours of disagreements at Supreme Headquarters on account of the eccentricity of the manoeuvres—southward toward the Caucasus and north-eastward against Stalingrad—did not worry us at this time, but difficulties with fuel supply were already being felt.

. . . . There was bitter street fighting in Piatigorsk, with N.K.W.P. troops, *women* signal formations and the Krasnodar Officers' School participating on the Russian side.

The tank regiment of 3 Panzer could participate in this murderous struggle only with advance parties. The regimental commander, Baron von Liebenstein, Guderian's former Chief of Staff, was immobilized through lack of fuel on the outskirts of Pushkin's town when, like a highwayman, he "took over" a couple of Russian columns, thus providing us with fuel and well-manufactured American Lease-Lend trucks.

At this time (9 August) the troops of XL Panzer Corps were covering about three hundred miles in depth. This situation was not due to tactical measures. A similar situation had arisen during 1941 south of Moscow. Leadership had ceased to mean taking measures appropriate to the tactical situation, but merely restricting them to whatever fuel the supply would permit.

When we remonstrated we were informed by those in the highest quarters that "We could not expect you to rush forward like this, could we?" As a matter of fact, Hitler had been warned by his experts that the available fuel supply of six thousand cubic metres would suffice either for the Stalingrad *or* the Caucasus operation. But quite illogically he expected his subordinates to go on "with fanatical energy," if without fuel, in both directions!

. . . . The guide book issued by our general staff stated that the many rivers streaming down from the mountains and crossing our path would be dry in summer time. The opposite was the case, since the snowy summits melting under the August sun sent down plenty of water. Bridging equipment soon became scarce, especially under the successful bombing attacks by the Russian Air Force. We asked for more aerial protection than could be given by the few fighters which were available. The answer was always: "In a fortnight or so Stalingrad will be taken. Then you can get plenty of aerial cover."

General Baron Leo Geyr von Schweppenburg, G.O.C.
XL Panzer Corps

Farthest South

It was now the middle of August. Our operations were being slowed down by two factors, the lack of fuel and the growing strength of the Russian Air Force, the fastest and first reserves to appear in strength. The Air Force did much to delay us and thus saved the situation for the Russians.

A few days earlier we had still hoped to rush the passes over the Caucasus and thus reach the Turkish border. We wanted to do this by combining mountaineer battalions with Panzers, although this was an unusual group of task forces. In a single night my Chief of Staff had worked out special orders for this sort of co-operation with the help of the staff of a Bavarian mountaineer battalion. Unfortunately the idea had to be dropped.

. . . . XL German Panzer Corps had covered during its great raid, mostly in rear of the Southern Russian front, almost a thousand miles between the end of June and 8 August. It reached the Grozny oilfields but was unable to capture them.

Hitler's preliminary objective, the Baku oilfields, also remained unconquered and intact.

.... The most decisive factor during these weeks, from our point of view, was the growing stream of American Lease-Lend supply to the Russians, which our air reconnaissance saw and our intelligence reported upon. Only this could sustain the tottering giant in his hour of weakness.

General von Schweppenburg

As the Germans reached the fullest extent of their conquests, Russia's demands on her allies to open a "Second Front" in the West, to relieve pressure on her, became insistent.

Second Front Now!

The talk I had to-day with Oumansky was typical of the present nervousness and also of the desire on the part of official Russians to do some propaganda among Allied correspondents.

Oumansky said, "I am afraid resentment against the Allies, against England in particular, is going to rise very rapidly, as things go on deteriorating at our front. And, mind you, the Germans have already started the old stunt they practised so successfully in France. Their leaflets keep saying: 'Russians, where are your Allies?' or else: 'The Hungarians and Roumanians are better Allies to us than the British are to you.' And in these leaflets are contained peace offers to the Russians—in terms you can imagine.

"It has no effect on our troops yet; most of them believe that the Germans are doing it just *because* they are scared of the Second Front, and that they are in a hurry to make peace with us, so as to be able to turn against England. But it may have a very bad effect after a while; it will not create defeatism, but certainly strong anti-British sentiment. For remember, this country has a traditional distrust of England, dating back to the time of Palmerston and Disraeli. . . ."

Feeling against the Allies continues to be quite bad. In a tramcar to-day there was an old woman—fairly well educated, judging by her way of speech—who was saying, "Never trust the English. You young people know nothing about it, but I am old enough to remember how Lord Beaconsfield, otherwise D'Isra-eli" (she pronounced the four-syllable name viciously) "let us down over Turkey in 1878."

Alexander Werth, war correspondent

The Russian Soldier

What we soldiers are interested in above all else are three things: a wash, food and sleep. Nothing else matters much. We don't sing songs—only sometimes, usually under compulsion. Perhaps they do in the rear; but we frontliners aren't interested in songs. It isn't what you people in Moscow imagine. We aren't interested in women either—not much. Oh yes, there *are* girls at the front—girls serving in canteens, and typists, and all that. But they won't look at anything below the rank of lieutenant-colonel—not they!

Sometimes we get staff officers arriving at our local headquarters, and when they are offered to sleep on the floor, among the lice, they say, "Oh no, really; I'll be quite comfortable sitting up in this chair, really quite comfortable!" It makes us snigger every time we see them sitting there pretending to sleep, and scared stiff of the lice getting into their spick-and-span uniform! Oh, I know, these people also do their job; I suppose it's just the old antagonism between the front and the rear. It's always existed; you can't help it. Take, for instance, our general. Some of us went to see him about an important matter. A young and pretty blonde came out: "No," she said, "you can't go straight in; the General is still resting." (You never say of a superior he's sleeping; you must always say "resting".) "You will have to wait till I announce you." "And who are you, miss?" we said. "I'm the typist," she said. The General was, of course, sleeping comfortably in a real bed.

The Germans fight very ferociously, and I suppose this winter they'll be much better equipped than last winter. They've learned their lesson. Recently, it's true, I watched through a periscope in the front line the fellows on the hill opposite. I could see them putting up their collars, and stamping their feet, and generally looking distinctly cold; but then they were Hungarians, as many of them are at Voronezh; and I don't suppose the Germans will bother much about *their* winter equipment.

Our one aim now is to get to Germany, to give them what's coming to them. Last year we still used to give cigarettes to some miserable shivering Fritzes—but not now.

Russian private soldier

6

RESISTANCE

The Europe which the Third Reich brought under its heel between 1939 and 1941 did not submit tamely to German rule. At first, following their total defeat and occupation by a police state, the nations were stunned and quiescent. Then, from about 1942-43, resistance began to grow, ranging from sporadic acts by individuals to full-scale sabotage and overt military action by widespread underground organizations, sometimes acting independently and sometimes with the material aid, advice or direction of the Allies. The greater part of the populations remained inactive, or at best lent passive and fluctuating support to the resistance—more could not be expected of human nature and frailty. A good many organizations existed to promote their own highly questionable post-war objectives and to fight each other, and a few people were active traitors. But the actions of the minority who were not afraid to suffer and who were prepared to die for their cause were of very great value to the war effort of the free world. They distracted and tied down the Axis armed forces, hampered their communications and damaged their morale, carried out espionage for the Allies, committed sabotage, and did a good deal to preserve the morale of their own people. Faced with their own and their compatriots' human weaknesses and the efficiency of the German secret police, their failures and sacrifices were many, but the sum of their contribution to the winning of the war was incalculable.

· · · — The Symbol of Resistance

THE V sign is the symbol of the unconquerable will of the occupied territories, and a portent of the fate awaiting the Nazi tyranny. So long as the peoples of Europe continue to refuse all collaboration with the invader, it is sure that his cause will perish, and that Europe will be liberated.

Winston Churchill, 20 July 1941

The Invader

Our shops and farms wide open lie;
Still the invader feels a lack:
Disquiet whets his gluttony
For what he may not carry back.

He prowls about in search of wealth
But has no skill to recognize
Our things of worth: we need no stealth
To mask them from his pauper eyes.

He calls for worship and amaze;
We give him yes-men in a row,
Reverberating that self-praise
He wearied of a while ago.

He casts around for some new whim,
Something preposterously more:
"Love me," he bids. We offer him
The slack embraces of a whore.

And when he spitefully makes shift
To share with us his pauperdom,

By forcing on us as a gift
The shoddy wares he brought from home,

And watches that we sell and buy
Amongst us his degrading trash,
He gets no gain at all. Though sly
With what he knows, the guns and cash.

What he knows not he may not touch:
Those very spoils for which he came
Are still elusive to his clutch—
They swerve and scorch him like a flame.

Invader—outcast of all lands,
He lives condemned to gorge and crave,
To foul his feast with his own hands:
At once the oppressor and the slave.

Norman Cameron

NORWAY

An Agent is Dropped

It was the night of 19-20 April 1943; the time was
one forty-five. For the third time I was sitting at the edge
of the hole in the after-part of the Halifax. This was the
last night of the full moon, the last night before the
summer months, in which agents could not be dropped
into Norway. It was the last chance I really had of
carrying out the task I had undertaken.

The aircraft had a Polish crew. I sat staring hard at
the dispatcher, trying to guess his thoughts from the
movements of his features. Again we circled round, again
the plane was flung from side to side by a too-strong wind;
again I sat for seconds and minutes on the edge of the
open hole, undergoing the worst mental torture. The plane
began to climb again!

There must be some limits to what a man can endure.

This time it was not at a dispatcher's request that I took off my rubber helmet for a talk with the captain on the intercom. He gave three reasons for not letting me jump: (1) there was a good thirty-mile wind force, i.e. fifteen miles too much; (2) he could not find any stretch of open moss which should be there according to the map, only mountains and forests everywhere; (3) he dared not go too low because of the violent gusts of wind, and he could not reduce speed to less than 160 miles, against the normal 115-120 miles, because if he did he would lose steering way in the violent air currents.

I will not report the discussion that went on for a quarter of an hour, but will only state that in the hearing of witnesses—the rest of the crew by intercom—I took the whole responsibility on myself.

I was sitting on the edge of the hole again; the time was 2.7 a.m. This time the dispatcher had inherited my nervousness, and for me there was only one thing to do: to take the chance of things going right, and jump. The Halifax went lower—the contours of water, mountain and forest grew sharper—there was a terrible lot of snow—the plane swung—went straight for a few seconds—swung again—speed was reduced slightly, and the propellers set at high pitch—we went steadily lower—I was heaved to and fro—I stared at the dispatcher—green light, and "action stations" from the dispatcher, who had now raised his arm—I flung both my legs into the hole—fractions of seconds—red light . . . "Go!" I started and—was out. . . .

The wind howled in my face. I was slung round—struck my head against something, the rear wheel of the Halifax—I saw stars—many stars—a terrific jerk—more stars—a sharp pain in my back, my head—everywhere—the night was dark—I became unconscious.

The next thing I knew was that I was being jerked and flung about pretty violently; it was a little while before I really paid any attention to what was happening—and there—a few yards away, against the fearful wind, I saw the rear turret of the Halifax and the rest of the plane silhouetted against the sky. I was hanging from the plane!

If it was fear or pain which made me faint again, I cannot say, most probably both. I recovered consciousness, feeling that I was still hanging, that I was being flung up and down, to and fro at a furious pace—and I fainted again.

Before I finally recovered consciousness a miracle must have happened: I was on my way to the ground far below. I looked up instinctively: yes, the parachute was open, but only partly. It looked to me as if some of the many silk cords which went up to the parachute had got entangled in the material and divided the whole "umbrella" into several sections.

I looked down—far below in the darkness lay water, mountain tops and forest. I could only feel that I was falling a good deal faster than I had ever done before. But there was nothing I could do about it one way or the other. Yet there was something seriously wrong with my right foot or leg. It was hanging all wrong in relation to the left, almost at a right angle. I tried to lift my leg as I hung—but the only reaction was a stab of pain.

It was blowing hard: I was approaching a ridge just below me—dense wood—no, I was caught again by a violent gust, passed the top of the ridge and went at full speed down into the valley on the other side. I held my breath—now for it! A bunch of big fir-tops came rushing at me—the noise of branches breaking—something like a big besom hit me in the face—everything became still and strange—I had fainted again.

How long I was unconscious I do not know, but gradually and surely I came to myself again. A strange noise in my ears, a strange silence, and for a few seconds, minutes perhaps, I felt that I was dreaming—felt that I had come into quite a new world. At first I dared not move, but at last I tried. A burning pain in my back brought me back to reality, and I looked up, sideways and down.

I had landed in the top of a tree: I was hanging with my back against the trunk, and above me, a dark mass against the lighter sky, hung my pack. The fir-top itself was broken off and lay across a tree next to it and beyond, while the remains of the parachute were entangled in another. What a fantastic piece of luck! So fantastic that it could hardly be true.

It did not take me long to get hold of my commando knife and cut away the parachute straps: at the same time I twisted myself round to face the trunk, and slid down through the fir-boughs as carefully as possible. I now understood what was the matter with my right leg; the knee had been dislocated and the whole lower part of my leg, with the foot, had been twisted ninety degrees out to one side. I could only hope that nothing was broken; but that a knee out of joint could be so horribly painful I should never have believed.

I just collapsed at the foot of the fir-tree like a pile of wet rags and lay there with closed eyes. I stretched out my hand, caught hold of a piece of reindeer moss, and inhaled its scent. Never, never, would anyone make me do another parachute jump; indeed, I never wanted to see a plane again!

This was Norway: Norwegian fir and pine, Norwegian bilberry and reindeer moss. Despite the burning pain in my back and knee I could not help enjoying their familiar scent, taking long draughts of the night air.

Oluf Reed Olsen

Sabotage

The factory worked in shifts all round the clock. The Kjeller aircraft factories had been bombed a little while before by sixty American Flying Fortresses. The result was that everything had been moved down to Korsvoll. This was very unpopular with the people at Sagene, for the bombing of the factory would mean a catastrophe for all the dwelling-houses round about. It was typical of the Germans to protect their war industry by putting it in the midst of a dense civilian population. Naturally the Germans took all possible precautions: they posted guards at the most incredible places. After having studied the area and the Germans' security measures we came to a solution which really was quite simple.

The Germans had naturally posted sentries at all the entrances to the area, and they had placed searchlights and machine-guns in the yard. When the alarm went the searchlights were switched on, and we should be rather badly placed. We knew that there were seven guards at one end of the building alone, and that three Germans and one Norwegian watchman patrolled the sheds regularly, ready to sell bells ringing, and so on.

Nevertheless, when we decided to make an attempt, it was not because our own plan was so clever as that the Germans' defence system was very absurd despite all those security measures. There was one very weak point in the system, a hole in the wall of the fortress which gave us our great chance; part of the buildings were still at the disposal of Oslo Tramways. We reckoned that we could, with a bit of luck, reach without being seen a door which led to Oslo Tramways' office. We could wait for the watchman in the office, overpower him when he came, and use his keys to lock ourselves into the actual tram shed. Thence we could go down into a cellar which ran from the Norwegian part right over to the German. The Germans had tried to show foresight and had set up three thick wire fences right up to the roof to keep saboteurs away. Ridiculous things! With the cutters we had it would be like cutting soft butter. We would lay our charges down in the basement and try to blow up the whole roof, which was identical with the floor of the factory building. We learnt that the floor was three feet thick and of reinforced concrete.

Roy and I had at first thought of taking on the job alone, but when we realized how exacting it was we decided not to take any chances. We asked whether the boys of the Oslo gang would not join us. It was decided that 24, Rolf, Egil, Hermann, Roy and I should participate. We also took with us one of Hermann's men to guard the car and act as a driver if necessary. His name was Erik, and he took part in many tough jobs later along with Hermann.

We pondered a good deal over the sort of charge we should use, and how large it should be. What we wanted was lifting, not cutting power, so the right thing would certainly have been to use amonal, i.e. explosive in powdered form. It burns comparatively slowly and has great lifting power. But we had no amonal, so we had to use plastic. I had got hold of some dynamite and we laid a charge consisting of two hundred and seventy pounds of plastic and seventy pounds of dynamite. We divided this among five suitcases with seventy pounds in each. We laid the charges in such a way that we could place all the suitcases on top of one another and couple together the fuses which stuck out of each suitcase. We calculated that we must do the job in twelve minutes and must therefore have everything ready beforehand in the smallest detail. The job must be done on Saturday night, the only night when there were not people working there. We did not want to risk blowing up good Norwegians along with the aircraft.

We met on Saturday in Fru Oeynebraaten's flat. She guessed with good reason that something was going to happen again. We had had some of the American plastic in the house, and it had the peculiar strong smell which some kinds of explosive have. She tried to conceal her nervousness, but that is not easy for a woman when she has, figuratively speaking, to wade in 250 lb. of explosive. It may be said that it was very imprudent of us to have it in the house at all, and that it would have been a bad business if we had blown up the whole of Frichsgate, but there was no other way of dealing with it at the moment, and Frichsgate, I am glad to say, came out of it almost intact. We had also a place up in Sagene which we called the office. We used to make our charges there, and there we had our main dump. So we were a menace to everyone at that time.

Fru Oeynebraaten took it as a man, or rather as a woman. Women in such cases were as a rule much less frightened than men. She made coffee for us and served home-made cakes, so we had something to stiffen ourselves up with.

We made the following plan for the evening: Roy and I were to drive the car containing the explosive up to the cross-street where we were to go into action. Here we were to meet the other boys at the tram terminus. At 1.45 a.m. everything would be ready. Two men would creep up to the door and hold up the guard when he came to open it. These were to be Roy and 24. When the door was opened, two other men would go into the factory with Roy and 24. They would start cutting the wire in the cellar at once. The two of us who remained were to act as cover till the signal was given. Then we would drive the car up, and each man would take a suitcase and bring it down to Rolf, who would tie the fuses together and light them.

To begin with everything went more or less according to plan. It was no light matter to drive through the town with the car full of arms and explosives, but we got through all right. Then we had to begin handing out Sten guns to the boys. Now the time had come, and we set to work.

Hermann and I took our places, likewise Rolf and Egil, Roy and 24 crept off, and we saw them gliding along the wall towards the door. We could hear the German guards talking as they walked to and fro behind the fence.

We waited and waited, but nothing happened. No one who has not been through it can imagine what a strange feeling one has when one is waiting for something to happen. Anything can happen on a job like that. And yet it is just when nothing happens that the strain is worst. The time grew long; people passed suspecting nothing; a young fellow stopped and asked if I had any spirits to sell.

Suddenly Roy and 24 returned. The job had miscarried. The watchman had not opened the door when they knocked. Presumably he had heard nothing. We agreed to meet on Monday at Fru Oeynebraaten's and lay our plans afresh.

We talked it over on Monday and came to the conclusion that the only thing to do was to break in, so that we should be independent of the guard. The door was fitted with a Yale lock and was comparatively easy to open. To open an ordinary Yale lock we used a celluloid plate of the thickness of a razor blade. This was pressed into the door-frame and the lock pushed back. (A certain degree of technical skill is required for this.)

Another week of tension passed, and then we tried again. Everything seemed to favour a successful operation. Even the moon was considerate and kept away.

Rolf was absent too; for one reason or another he had not turned up. This was not quite so good, but there were plenty of us and we decided to do the job without him. All went well. We got the door open, slipped in and waited for the watchman with the vital keys. Just before he was due to come, Egil suddenly burst into roars of laughter. It was not exactly the place for loud laughter, and we were all sure that Egil had gone mad. Such things had happened before in similar situations. "The fuse, the fuse!" Egil stammered. "Oh, hell!" we said, and what else could we say? It was Rolf who had the fuse which was to connect all the suitcases. So we cleared out again, and pretty quick too.

We could not help laughing when we were out in the street. But we were terribly anxious about Rolf and felt sure that he had been shot or at any rate arrested. But it turned out that he had gone to sleep in the flat where he was hiding; and his alarm had not sounded. A man must have very strong nerves to be able to sleep so undisturbed just before a job like ours.

Rolf was much upset about the whole business, but we consoled him with the thought that we should try again on Saturday. Certainly there would be a full moon then, but we were so tired and sick of the whole job that we wanted to be through with it.

On Saturday everyone was there in time. The moon was almost full, but slightly obscured by clouds.

Roy and 24 crept along in the shadow of the houses. In a little while we saw a light from the door, which showed that it was open. Then came the signal. Hermann and I took a look round and set off. We reached the door and went in. And now we six were standing in a small room, all armed to the teeth. Roy and 24 were nearest to the door which the watchman would pass. It was dead silent in the little room; not a word passed between us, but we all had our own thoughts. Some of us were thinking of our families, some of girls, and all of us of the Germans, who perhaps had already detected us and were surrounding the whole building. Then we heard the guards coming. We knew that the Germans would part from the Norwegian outside our door, and that he would come in to us in a moment. The steps came nearer. I moved a little in the direction of the door, where 24 and Roy stood ready for action. Then we heard the Germans go on, while the Norwegian watchman came towards us. A key was put into the lock, the door was opened, there was a gulp, and the man was dragged into the room. He looked bewildered as he stood there, one man against us six. We explained to him the cause of our visit, and promised him his life if he obeyed our instructions. This he did in every detail. He had all the keys of the cellar, so it looked promising. It was his first day as watchman, he said. He usually worked on a bus, but he had a bad heart, and he had now been appointed watchman. This was supposed to be the softest job of all!

Rolf and Egil set to work immediately to cut the wire fences down in the cellar. 24 attended to the women cleaners who were washing the buses without suspicion of trouble or danger: he courted them as vigorously as he could to remove the risk of any disturbance from that quarter. Hermann and I acted as cover, and Roy looked after the watchman. I went out into the little room which we had first entered, and set the door slightly ajar in order to listen. I heard the German guards going up and down talking, while Rolf and Egil were working their way forward underneath them. I wished that Gregers had been there; it was just the sort of job he would have liked.

Hermann came and said all the fences would have been removed in a moment. I went out into the street, where Erik was keeping the engine running, and we drove the valuable load in. Each man took a suitcase and carried it down into the cellar; Rolf tied the fuses together, while I went up to warn the old porter who lived over the office. I thundered and kicked at the door, but no one answered. It was an awkward situation. I did not want him to be killed, but on account of the Germans there were limits to the amount of noise one could make. Hermann came up with the watchman and said that the explosion would take place in two minutes. We tried to break the door down with our combined strength, but had to give it up. The watchman thought the porter was not at home, and we consoled ourselves with that thought. 24 told the cleaners that the building would go up in two minutes, and they cleared out in a hurry. One of them, however, would not go till she had fetched her tobacco which she had in the cloak-room. They can be cold-blooded, these women.

We took the watchman out into the street, and asked if he wished to be sent to Sweden. But he said no, on account of his family. We advised him to give an exact report of what had happened; he could go straight down to the first telephone box and ring up. Now the women cleaners and the watchmen were running down the street, and at last the Germans too began to realize that something was happening. They shouted and beckoned, but I had already stepped on the gas and was about to turn the first corner. We rushed past Rolf and 24, who were both bicycling. I drove like fury, and we were a good way off when the explosion came. We had used a four-minute fuse, to the best of my recollection, so we had come quickly.

We stopped down in Vogtsgate, where we dropped

Erik, Hermann and Egil, and then swept on, Roy and I, out to Egil's home on Nordstand. Vesla gave us a splendid meal, and we spent the rest of the night in the highest good-humour. We were equally delighted that Korsvoll had at last been dealt with.

The job had meant a great deal of work. It is not so easy to explain now in a few words all the difficulties we met with beforehand, and it is always easier to preserve the good recollections than the bad ones. But in any case we felt that we had worked very hard.

Max Manus

When it was discovered that the Germans were producing heavy water in Norway for the purpose of atomic research, repeated attacks were made on their installations near Hardanger Fjord, and production was seriously hampered. Early in 1944 they attempted to ferry their entire stock of heavy water to Germany.

Armed with Sten guns, pistols and hand-grenades, we crept past Mel station and down towards the ferry. The bitterly cold night set everything creaking and crackling; the ice on the road snapped sharply as we went over it. When we came out on the bridge by the ferry station, there was as much noise as if a whole company was on the march.

Rolf and the other Rjukan men were told to cover me while I went on board to reconnoitre. All were quiet there. Was it possible that the Germans had omitted to place a guard at the weakest point in the whole route of the transport?

Hearing voices in the crew's quarters, forward, I stole to the companion and listened. There must be a party going on down there, and a game of poker. The other two followed me on to the deck of the ferry. We went down to the third-class accommodation and found a hatchway leading to the bilges. But before we had got the hatch open we heard steps, and took cover behind the nearest table or chair. The ferry watchman was standing in the doorway. He must have left the game of poker on hearing that there were other people on board. The situation was awkward, but not dangerous. We hurriedly explained to the watchman that we had to hide and were looking for a suitable place. The watchman immediately showed us the hatchway in the deck, and told us that they had several times had illicit things with them on their trips.

The Rjukan man now proved invaluable. He talked and talked with the watchman, while Rolf and I flung our sacks down under the deck and began to work.

It was an anxious job, and it took time. The charge and the wire had to be connected; then the detonators had to be connected to the wire and the ignition mechanism. Everything had to be put together and properly laid. It was cramped and uncomfortable down there under the deck, and about a foot of water was standing in the bilge.

The charge was placed in the water and concealed. It consisted of nineteen pounds of high explosive laid in the form of a sausage. We laid it forward, so that the rudder and propeller would rise above the surface when water began to come in. There was also a possibility that the railway trucks would roll off the deck and go to the bottom first.

When the charge exploded, it would blow about eleven square feet out of the ship's side. As the Tinnsjö is narrow, the ferry must sink in less than five minutes, or else it would be possible to beach her. I had spent many hours sitting and calculating how large the hole must be for the ferry to sink quickly enough.

To be on the safe side we used two alarm clocks. The operation must not fail, for everything was at stake. The hammer of the clock would short-circuit the current when it began to strike. The alarm clocks were set up on a rib of the vessel, and a wire led from them down to the charge. We counted on the train being ten minutes late. The clock was set to strike at a quarter to eleven, when the ferry would be over the deepest part of the lake.

Making the last connections was a dangerous job; for

an alarm clock is an uncertain instrument, and contact between the hammer and the alarm was avoided by not more than a third of an inch. Thus there was one-third of an inch between us and disaster.

In the meantime the Rjukan man had had a long and well-thought-out talk with the watchman, and had explained to him that we must go back to Rjukan to fetch some things. We should be on board in the morning in good time before the ferry started.

When I left the watchman I was not clear in my mind as to what I ought to do. He had shown himself to be a good and useful Norwegian. It was very probable that he was just the person whom the Germans would interrogate after the ferry was sunk, and I should have liked to warn him and get him out of the danger zone. I was tempted, too, to take him with us and try to bring him into safety. I remembered the fate of the two Norwegian guards at Vemork, who had been sent to a German concentration camp after the attack there. I did not want to hand over a Norwegian to the Germans. But if the watchman disappeared, there was danger of the German's suspicions being aroused next morning.

I contented myself with shaking hands with the watchman and thanking him—which obviously puzzled him.

The car was waiting for us as arranged, and it turned out that we had been away for nearly two hours. Rolf was to take to the hills and keep Einar company while I was away. We said good-bye to him, and the journey to Sweden began.

At Jondalen the car had to turn and go home; for the driver was afraid of getting back to Rjukan too late. We reached Kongsberg railway station and took tickets for the first part of our journey. We booked from Kongsberg to Hokksund, then from Hokksund to Drammen; and at Drammen we took tickets for Oslo.

Halfway between Hokksund and Drammen I looked at my watch; it was a quarter to eleven. If everything had gone according to plan the ferry should just be sinking; the heavy water would be done for and the German's last chance of having it for their atomic experiments would have gone. It had cost us immense toil. We had been maintaining ourselves in the wilds of the Hardanger Vidda for nearly a year and a half. Snow and cold had been our constant companions, and we had carried danger with us wherever we went. Our best friends in Rauland and Vinje had not known what important work they were doing when they helped us. The certainty that a mistake on our part would bring death and destruction on many districts had been a heavy burden to us; for the Germans would have shown no mercy if they had found out who our helpers were.

What would happen now at Rjukan? How many Norwegian lives would be lost through this piece of devilry? The explosion on board the ferry must cost lives, and the reprisals at Rjukan certainly no fewer. Larsen and I did not talk much on the journey. I was thinking of the past.

The English had sacrificed thirty-four men with the gliders. Those men had known they would not be able to get away after they had done their work. The bombing had cost twenty-two lives. How many would it be this time? I was glad to know that one of those who were most in the danger zone at Rjukan would probably escape. The engineer Nielsen, who had been concerned with the transport, was, according to our plan, to be taken to hospital and operated on for appendicitis the next morning, before the ferry went down. The doctors would not ask if he were ill or not.

To be on the safe side, Rolf had given me a contact on Heröya, whence the heavy water was to be shipped to Germany. If anything had gone wrong I could take up the work again there. But I found that London too had been prepared for a hitch. Without my knowing it they had sent another sabotage party to Heröya to attack the transport there if we should fail. Submarines were lying in wait in the Skagerak. In Oslo we stayed with Trond as usual.

It was in the papers on Monday evening:

RAILWAY FERRY *HYDRO* SUNK IN THE TINNSJO

This was the headline on every front page. The ferry had sunk in a few minutes and was lying in deep water.

Fourteen Norwegians and four Germans had gone down with her.

Knut Haukelid

DENMARK

Gernant has reported to me about conditions in Denmark. From his report, prepared at the request of Best, I gather a situation has arisen which can only be called critical, because of the rather lax and feeble way in which the Danes were handled by the Reich's Plenipotentiary, Dr. Best. The Danes put a wrong interpretation on the generous treatment accorded them. Especially in Copenhagen events occurred that are more than shocking. German soldiers could hardly appear on the streets; German girls had swastikas branded on their bodies; acts of sabotage against Wehrmacht barracks and communication installations increased day by day; and the government was neither willing nor able to do anything about it. Best was ordered to the Führer's G.H.Q. and given a vigorous dressing-down. He thereupon had to transfer his powers to the military command. The Danes at first tried to oppose martial law by a few stupid tricks, but when German tanks appeared they quickly became subdued. Since then everything has been going its normal way.

Dr. Goebbels, 8 September 1943

FRANCE

The Beginning

There was really no one. And one could not gauge the price one might have to pay. The enthusiasts were prepared to take a chance on anyone, yet everyone was reluctant or afraid with the excuse of being realistic.

The beginners had lost their nerve at the first disaster early in December 1940, when Edouard, my second-in-command, had been arrested in Marseilles and placed in solitary confinement in Fort Saint-Nicolas. Though we had gone so far as to sabotage a locomotive on its way to Italy, it was musical comedy stuff: sunshine, women bathing, petrol from the growing black market, traffic in gold and jewels. . . . Terrified crowds of emasculated, cowardly Jews, repentant Left wingers, petrified deputies and dubious capitalists, whose protecting régime had collapsed, were prepared to deny it now in the hope that some arrangement was possible with the new bunch. They groused in secret but avoided trouble, or prepared for flight to more clement lands when their affairs had gone too far awry.

In the Midi, where people, saturated with the sun and the landscape, perpetuated the mirage of happier days, it was difficult, wherever one turned one's eyes, to discover a trace of decent feeling or find men who, unless they themselves or their possessions were in danger, were prepared to take a stand because what was being done was a disgrace, for the whole scene was pervaded with a stench of swindling, in a sort of comic opera set, representing the end of the world. To my eyes it appeared the first sign of the Apocalypse.

. . . . After three months I had found five disinterested people, who were prepared to act without counting the cost and take a deliberate chance rather than resign themselves to the ignominy of a profitable conformity—five people sincerely concerned with Utopia, fired with rational despair or irrational hope: a Professor

of Philosophy, a journalist who squinted, a manufacturer
of bedding, an Amazon with a history degree and a Métro
employee. . . . Add to them Bertrande and Jean—the
family, that part of the family who, in their youth, refused
to admit certain realities and rebelled against the
dishonesty of certain social forms and conventions—who
could travel without a ticket and stand for fifteen hours
at a stretch.

At three o'clock in the morning, Jean woke up with
a start because I was whistling to stop him snoring.

"What did you think when you met me in Vichy in
November 1940?"

"That you were mad . . . I didn't know what you were
up to when you spoke of the 'last column'."

"It was for *Libération,* the newspaper. The 'last
column'—one could not call it the sixth, seventh or
eighth."

Emmanuel d'Astier, Resistance leader

A Recruit

I went to see my friends the Saint-Denises and met
there a Dr. Meeus from Nantes, who offered his services
and became Rivière in our organization. Madame de
Hautecloque said to me:

"I'd like to introduce you to the son of a woman I
know very well. He is very eager to work for you. His
name is Paul Mauger."

Together, we went to see Madame Mauger. She lived
in a little house in the new part of town. Paul was quite
young, hardly eighteen. I was particularly struck by his
eyes. They were a blue I had never seen before, a blue
with a tinge of violet beneath great black lashes. His
hair was cut short.

"Sit down, Paul," I told him. "What gave you the idea
of working for me?"

He was shy and stammered a little.

"I felt I ought to do something, monsieur," he managed
to get out.

"What Paul hasn't told you," added Nicole de Hautecloque, "is that he has already tried to get through Spain to join up with General de Gaulle."

"Oh, yes?" I said. "Tell me about it."

Paul turned bewildered eyes towards his mother. She looked at him encouragingly.

"There were two of us," he went on at length, "a friend and myself. We had asked our parents' permission. . . ."

His mother smiled further encouragement.

"They told us we could. So we went off together and got over the frontier all right. We were arrested in the station at Madrid."

"And then?"

"They put us in prison, at the Puerta del Sol, in the cellars. There were two or three hundred of us there. My friend died. I was brought back by train to Cerbère, with a civil guard on either side of me. French gendarmes were waiting for me, and I was put in prison again after having had my hair clipped short. An officer told me that if I joined the *Armée de l'Armistice* they would let me out, otherwise I would have to stay in prison for the rest of my life. So I joined up. The first day that they let me out of barracks I deserted, crossed the Line,* and got home. I am stuck now because I don't know how to get to England to join the general."

I looked at the youth, almost a child, he seemed, who had given proof of real heroism, but could still keep such surprising simplicity. I read great anxiety in his eyes and in those of his mother. It was just as if his mother were introducing her boy to the manager of a business and was waiting to know whether her son would be taken on.

"I am in no position to get you to England, Paul," I told him. "But would you like to work for me?"

"Yes, please," he replied eagerly.

"You realize that I shall have to give you dangerous things to do."

"That doesn't matter."

---

* Dividing Vichy France from Occupied France (Ed.)

"You realize, too, that you will be travelling all the time, often very uncomfortably?"

"That doesn't matter."

"If they ever discover the papers you are carrying, you will be shot."

"That doesn't matter."

"Of course they will torture you first to make you talk. In no case must you ever say anything."

The tears came to his eyes. I had already seen much the same look of reproach in Lhermite's eyes.

"I know all that," was his answer.

"I shall be very exacting, very severe."

"Yes," he said.

"Right you are then, Paul. I'll take you on."

I can still see the smile on Paul's lips as I agreed to let him work for me. He took to heart what I told him that day.

"From to-day on I shall give you another name. Among us you will be known as Pierre."

He was as pleased as if I had given him a medal.

I rose. His mother shook hands with me warmly.

"I am very grateful to you," she said. "When can he begin?"

"This evening," I replied. "We shall leave together for Brest."

Colonel Rémy

Crossing the Line

After he had left me near the Pont Mirabeau on that sunny afternoon of 30 May 1942, Maurice Rossi (Maurice we called him), had quickly put his more urgent affairs in order. On 1 June, he heard that the day before the Gestapo had turned up at the Traktir, the restaurant Prunier in the Avenue Victor Hugo, in order to arrest him. No one at the Traktir, save the manager, Monsieur Barnagaud, knew his address at the Place Saint-André-des-Arts; he thought, therefore, that he could leave his wife and small boy there without exposing them to any great risk, whilst he crossed over to the Unoccupied Zone. They could join him later when he had found them a safe place.

On 2 June he took the train at the Gare de Lyon, meaning to cross the Line secretly at Montchanin, but the station there was closely watched by the Germans, and they were getting into the carriages of the trains to examine the travellers' papers. Maurice had not had time to get himself fixed up with a false identity card; and it was probable that his real name had been telegraphed to all frontier stations. He thought it more prudent, therefore, to get out on the wrong side of the compartment and jump into a train that was just leaving in the opposite direction for Creusot. There was a woman in the compartment. Maurice took his place opposite her and proceeded quietly but painstakingly to tear his identity card into small pieces which he scattered through the open window.

At Montceau-les-Mines a German appeared and demanded his papers.

"I haven't got them," replied Maurice. "They were asked for at Montchanin and your people kept them. Didn't they, Madame?"

The unknown woman took her cue. "Why, yes," she replied.

But the *Feldgendarm* was by no means convinced.

"You must stay here until your papers arrive from Montchanin; we'll have them sent up. Open that bag."

The only luggage that Maurice had taken with him was a leather satchel. This the German searched methodically. He found nothing but underwear, an ordinary razor, toilet articles, a few unimportant papers, a bottle of Alsatian sloe gin and twenty packets of cigarettes.

"How about letting me have some cigarettes?" asked the German.

Maurice, usually so quiet and smiling, foolishly lost his temper.

"If you want cigarettes," he told the German, "all you've got to do is to ask your Führer for them!"

So direct a snub was hardly calculated to please the German. He made Maurice leave the train and shut him up in the lamp room of the station under the guard of an armed sentry. In the corner was a young man who had also been arrested for having no papers.

Maurice considered him in silence for a while.

"Were you trying to get across the Line?" he asked him finally.

"Yes."

"Shall we work this together?"

"I'm willing."

"All right, then; but let me deal with the sentry."

Maurice tapped on the door; the sentry opened it.

"I want to go to the lavatory."

"*Was?*" enquired the sentry, who understood nothing.

"Lavatory, W.C., *cabinets*," explained Maurice.

"Oh, *ja, gut*."

The lavatory was next door. As he came back to the lamp room Maurice said to the sentry:

"You're a good chap. Like a drink?"

"*Was?*"

"Drink," insisted Maurice, explaining at the same time in dumb-show. The sentry accepted immediately and followed him in. Maurice took the sloe gin from his satchel, uncorked it and gave the German a full glass; he swallowed it at one gulp.

"*Gut, gut,*" he gasped.

As a consequence the sentry saw no valid reason why Maurice should not be allowed to go to the lavatory several times, since each time he returned he was overwhelming with his thanks for the favour and did not fail to offer another glass of sloe gin which was always accepted with alacrity. In this way the German drank three-quarters of the bottle. Having tossed off a final glassful he slipped slowly to the ground, a vacant smile on his face, and, his back to the partition, fell asleep at once.

Maurice, in the course of his different peregrinations, had had ample opportunity to spy out the lie of the land.

It was dark outside now. The moment for action had come.

"I'm not too happy about that bloke," he said to his companion with a nod in the direction of the sentry. "Suppose he opens an eye, just as we are slipping out, and starts shouting at the top of his lungs. We'd be in a worse mess than when we started."

"What shall we do?" enquired the other.

"I see nothing for it but to kill him. Anyhow, it'll make one German less in the world."

"What with? His rifle?"

"My word, no. Think what the noise would be like. Haven't you got anything in your bag?"

"Only tools."

"Let's have a look."

The other opened his bag. He must have been a mechanic; there was nothing but files, screw-drivers, spanners. Maurice pouted. The young man offered him a hammer, but Maurice shook his head.

"No good. We might miss, and then he'd only make a row," he explained.

"That's all I have," said the young man.

"I've got something better. A razor. We'll cut his throat."

"We did it together," Maurice told me afterwards. "The mechanic chap held his head and I used the razor. When we'd finished the job, we slipped out. The German never opened his eyes."

Fifty yards from the frontier line Maurice told his companion:

"You don't know my name, and I've not asked yours. You go your way, and I'll go mine. Good-bye."

They separated, and Maurice crossed over the Line during the night without difficulty.

Colonel Rémy

Resistance Leaders in London

. . . . It is here in London that I feel lonely.

Everyone with whom I have talked seems to be making war at a distance, a distance in life and space. Eggs and bacon, hot baths and the morning taxi are transformed into a thought, a report, which will bear fruit to-morrow in Athens or Bordeaux, via the high seas, factories, ship and how much else, perhaps!

I have had a harassing day. The men I see have nothing to say to me as yet: perhaps they think that's what newspapers are for. But they have a great deal to ask me.

The Security people made me recount my whole life for two hours on end: they seem to know it better than I do myself and are trying to discover whether I am an imposter. Their tireless courtesy, therefore, changes to anxiety when I confess that I do not know my mother-in-law's maiden name, nor what I was doing in 1927.

After the Security people, the Intelligence people endeavoured to sum me up, in order to classify me: desire for money, patriotism, ambition, political objectives. . . . I am left with the impression that if they examined me with the X-rays of their universe, they would class me as an adventurer. But above all they're conscientious: I am a tool, either good or mediocre. Why leave it to others: de Gaulle, the *Deuxième Bureau* or Utopia. . . . It is with grains of sand that mountains are made.

At midday, I saw my first Frenchman: Colonel Bourse,* fair-haired—what remained of it—his eyes pale and red-rimmed, something rather porcine in the texture of his skin and hair, a high voice: immediate antipathy.

"What have you come to do here?"

I did not reply, I thought I had simply come to ask that we should be taken seriously. . . . Also, perhaps, that I had come to seek hope and confirmation of a plan which was both desperate and unreasonable. But since,

---

* Colonel Passy.

in spite of his growing power, Bourse is still only an agent, he sent me to Symbole.**

"You'll dine with him to-night at nine o'clock."

I went there at nine.

It was the Connaught Hotel, the most exquisitely old-fashioned of hotels in London. A porter, as padded as the carpets and the life, led me to an empty drawing-room where a table was laid for two.

I stood waiting. Symbole came in.

He's even taller than one expects.

His movements are slow and heavy like his nose. His small head and waxen face are carried on a body of indeterminate structure. His most habitual gesture is to raise his forearms while keeping his elbows to his side. At these moments, his inert, very white, rather feminine hands, their palms turned downwards and attached to his arms by too-slender wrists, seem to be raising a whole world of abstract burdens.

He asked me no questions. We dined.

He does not love his fellow men: he loves their history, above all the history of France, in which he is acting a chapter that he seems to be writing concurrently in his head, like an impassioned Michelet.

As for me, traveller and seeker that I am, I said things which were either much too precise or much too confused, in which were mingled concrete details and Utopian sentiments. He gathered up only odds and ends here and there and put them in his history.

As with the others this morning, I had so great an impression of insurmountable incredulity—that incredulity in which I have been living in France for the last eighteen months as if in a cloud of cotton-wool—that I pleaded both his cause and our own. But why should he be incredulous? Suspicious, yes, because he despises men too much and too many things in the universe. Incredulous, no, because I am a French ant bringing him a fragment of straw, a piece of material for his history

** General de Gaulle.

about which revolves a world of supernumerary friends
and enemies, as Henri, Charles, Isabeau and Calixte
revolve about Jeanne in a phrase-book.

I came out with my head in a whirl.

I had been in a theatre of history, I wanted to go out
into life, my life.

Down below, the night porter reduced everything to
scale again: insomnia of the cloakroom attendant, the
mixture of keys to heart and mind, food, sleep, childhood
and old age, women and their scent atoning for war and
its uniforms. I went to the telephone: a familiar voice
replied . . . remote, sunk in time. But it re-awakened a
past life, stifled by the clamour of brotherhood and the
passions of one race among races.

                                        Emmanuel d'Astier

Supplies for the Maquis

Although she was vastly useful, the countess could only
get comparatively small things, personal things, or
presents for my friends and helpers. For the bulk needs
of our headquarters or the Maquis we fell back on
Paincheau.

The first thing I desired to end was the tobacco
situation. And Paincheau ended it for us. He sent some
men and trucks to Besançon and, working with a gang
he ran in the town, they went to the place where French
tobacco for the use of the German military garrison was
stored. Breaking into the warehouse, these men coolly
loaded their trucks with hundreds of cases of cigarettes.
Germans passing in the street never imagined that
anything illegal was going on. One night's work in the
grand manner had provided enough cigarettes for all our
Maquis for months. Paincheau had killed the *"bureau de
tabac"* menace.

Next we asked him for boots, and these he supplied
in the same grand manner. The Frisé also captured a
truck-load of boots. All the Maquisards, including the
officers, now appeared in brand-new lemon or banana-

coloured boots. This became such a menace to security that we had to issue an order that all boots were to be dirtied or stained dark before worn. It was said that when a customer entered a shoe-shop in Besançon to ask for a pair of boots, the salesman said:

"But why not join the '*Equipes Boulaya*,' monsieur? There you get boots without disbursement and without coupons."

The next thing was petrol. Paincheau already had fairly large stocks of this which he had requisitioned. But he decided that these must be increased. With his Besançon gang he devised the following plan. The main German petrol supply in Besançon was kept in tanks which were in a guarded building. One night Paincheau's men drew up in a large tanker truck beside one wall of the building which was not guarded. One of the men was a mason. Scientifically and silently he cut a hole in the brick wall. His comrades ran a pipe through the hole and into a tank in the interior. All night they pumped petrol out of the German store into their truck. As the first light of dawn came over the hills surrounding the city they stopped pumping and the mason re-built the wall. The tanker returned to Rougemont to empty its precious load. The following night the operation was repeated successfully. But now the level of the petrol in the tanks had sunk so drastically that the Germans discovered the loss. Since there were always guards on the door of the building, the Gestapo arrested all German soldiers who had been on this guard in the past seven days. Paincheau decided that we would get no more petrol. So that night four of his men volunteered to go back into the store building, to put two hundred pounds of sugar into the remaining stocks. They entered the building by the same route. The same mason closed the hole after them. The operation was an entire success.

Once Boulaya was short of money. All our Maquisards were paid like soldiers regularly by the week on a fixed scale according to the number of their dependents. Their pay was small, but it was important

that it should not be interrupted. Paincheau could get
anything from a bottle of absinthe to a funeral cortège
with a black-and-silver hearse, lilies, and black Belgian
horses. He met us in a wood between Devecey and
Bonnay and unstrapped from the back of his *"pétrolette"*
an enormous sack.

"What have you there?" Boulaya asked.

"Eight million francs," he replied calmly.

It was Gestapo money deposited in banks in Besançon.
Paincheau explained that four men had succeeded in
getting this money by several visits to banks with an
accomplice, a woman who worked for the Gestapo. But
the story was so complicated that I could not follow it.
Perhaps it was because he spoke so softly. At any rate,
the men who did the coup had only, we understood, kept
two million of the German money for themselves, and
the rest they presented to the Resistance. They were real
patriots. Boulaya and I were greatly touched by the
patriotism of the experts. We laughed a lot.

Jacques Paincheau was a magician. With his help we
were able to organize the food situation. Where lesser
beings thought in kilos, he thought in terms of truck-loads,
barge-loads, warehouses. He could produce sugar, rice,
gruyère, yes, even tyres for vehicles and chocolate by
the ton. And all taken from the enemy. Although, like
a skilful prestidigitator, he produced all those valuable
things without apparent effort, his coups were all the result
of faultless planning and execution. He worked everything
out to the minutest detail, and he was prepared to lead his
men into anything that he planned. He and I became close
friends. We were not able to meet very frequently because
we were both too busy. But each time that I met him I
found that his mind was packed with ideas for work, and
each time they were new ideas.

George Millar, British agent

The Patriot

In November 1941, Espadon had given me in Paris

a blade of metal, about the size of two postage stamps.

"Send it off to London," he requested, "it's the sample they asked for by wireless."

I turned the little blade over in my hand. The metal of which it was made seemed extraordinarily light and very hard. It was of a bluish-grey colour. It was not aluminium.

"I reported to London," Espadon informed me, "that the S.N.C.A.S.O. factory [*Société Nationale de Constructions Aeronautiques du Sud-Ouest*] at Bordeaux was making this metal in great secrecy on behalf of the Luftwaffe."

"Yes," I told him, "I read your report. You said there that the Germans were taking extraordinary precautions against any leakage of the material through the workpeople; that they were obliged to take off their clothes and put on special overalls which had the hems unsewn; that they were very carefully searched when they left the factory, and that they were obliged to wash their hands and brush their nails in case they took away even the tiniest particle or filing in that way."

"That's right."

"How did you manage to get hold of this bit, then?"

"Do you remember," he recounted, "that on 11 November, five minutes of silence was observed everywhere, together with a general stoppage or slowing down of work, according to the request General de Gaulle made over the radio? In the S.N.C.A.S.O. factory all the workpeople downed tools, except one who went on working as if there was nothing unusual on. When the five minutes were up, all his neighbours turned on him, and knocked him down. The Germans intervened, and the man, who had fainted, was carried home. The next day I had the piece of metal."

"So it was he . . ." I concluded his story for him.

"Yes, he was one of our men. I had asked him for the sample. He had heard the General's order and had said to himself that the attention of the Germans would be entirely occupied with those who stopped working. He was wearing clogs, underneath which were fixed strips of rubber cut from old motor tyres. Many of them do that. On the morning of 11 November, he managed to cut off a piece of metal the right size. When the others downed tools, he went on working and let this piece fall to the ground, without the Germans noticing. By pushing his foot against the bench he managed to slip the piece of metal between two bits of rubber on one of his clogs."

"What a marvellous man!" I exclaimed.

"There's better than that," Espadon went on. "I went to see him and told him that it was absolutely essential that the Germans should not know that we had a piece of the metal. He went on with his work at the factory and never told a soul. None of his companions would speak to him now after that business on 11 November; they treated him as a pariah and avoided him like the plague. They looked on him as a traitor."

Colonel Rémy

The Mountain of Miserey

One day after lunch Philippe asked if he might take some of the others out and do a job on the Vesoul railway. We had just heard a train pass below us in the valley, and this was such an unusual sound that it roused us to action. Boulaya refused permission, but I persuaded him to let Philippe take out the Pointu and two new lads, Communists whom Maurice and Philippe together had rescued from imprisonment in the German hospital in Besançon, where they had been convalescing from German-inflicted wounds. The four of them departed happily on foot, carrying an arsenal of miscellaneous weapons and the heavy tools we used for unscrewing the railway lines. They promised to work as far afield as Miserey. Things appeared to go badly. That afternoon we heard the sound of firing, and the story came back to us that while they were derailing a train near Misery a German truck full of soldiers passed on the road and opened fire. The Maquisards replied and then withdrew.

One by one that evening the young men dribbled back into the camp, bringing with them all their weapons and the tools. The story of the Germans was true, but Philippe had turned their arrival to our profit, for while the little battle was going on he had walked into Miserey station, found another train there and obliged the railwaymen to start it at full speed. This, crashing into the derailed train in cutting, broke up the battle and allowed the other three Maquisards to withdraw in good order. On the way home Philippe and the Pointu seized a third train near Devecey, made all the occupants descend, and hurled this train on to the wreckage near Miserey. This was a wonderful day's work. I cycled out to see it, and I knew that if the enemy still had a crane he would need it for this, and it would be a long job. The cutting was deep, and the wreckage was well wedged in.

But our Philippe was irresistible. Boulaya gave him a holiday in Besançon to celebrate this important victory. He spruced himself up and left on a new bicycle. (We had just taken eight new ones from the police in Besançon, and Boulaya and I each bought one on the black market, so we were now astoundingly well off for bicycles.) Bronzed and bleached by the sun now, Philippe looked more cherubic than ever.

Unable to avoid the scene of his crime, he cycled past the still smoking remains where the Gestapo were examining tracks and questioning civilians and railwaymen. He saw another locomotive in Miserey station. Unarmed as he was, he cursed and swore at the railwaymen until they sent their engine rushing down the track. It hit the wreckage while the Gestapo were still there, and jumping, said onlookers, thirty feet into the air it landed upside down on the other side of the heap of twisted metal. Its wheels continued to revolve for some time. Already crowds were gathering for this fantastic sight. Cycling excursions were setting out from all the

villages. Many of them were to have their money's worth.
Philippe, tranquilly continuing on his way to Besançon,
found another train and again, with only his gruff and
determined voice to help him, succeeded in getting it
launched at full speed on the right rails. In front of a large
audience this train added itself to the heap in the cutting.

Sightseers were still visiting the place six weeks later.
And it was known locally as "the mountain of Miserey".
This closed the Vesoul line until (and, alas, after) the
Allied armies arrived.

George Millar

HOLLAND

As everybody knows, the Dutch are the most insolent
and obstreperous people in the entire West.

Dr. Goebbels, 10 September 1943

Jews in Hiding

Saturday, 20 June 1942

My father was thirty-six when he married my mother,
who was then twenty-five. My sister Margot was born
in 1926 in Frankfort-on-Main. I followed on 12 June
1929, and, as we are Jewish, we emigrated to Holland
in 1933, where my father was appointed Managing
Director of Travies N.V. This firm is in close relationship
with the firm of "Kolen & Co." in the same building, of
which my father is a partner.

The rest of our family, however, felt the full impact
of Hitler's anti-Jewish laws, so life was filled with anxiety.
In 1938 after the pogroms, my two uncles (my mother's
brothers) escaped to the U.S.A. My old grandmother
came to us; she was then seventy-three. After May, 1940,
good times rapidly fled: first the war, then the capitulation, followed by the arrival of the Germans. That
is when the sufferings of us Jews really began. Anti-Jewish
decrees followed each other in quick succession. Jews

must wear a yellow star, Jews must hand in their bicycles, Jews are banned from trams and are forbidden to drive. Jews are only allowed to do their shopping between three and five o'clock and then only in shops which bear the placard "Jewish shop". Jews must be indoors by eight o'clock and cannot even sit in their own gardens after that hour. Jews are forbidden to visit theatres, cinemas, and other places of entertainment. Jews may not take part in public sports. Swimming baths, tennis courts, hockey fields, and other sports grounds are all prohibited to them. Jews may not visit Christians. Jews must go to Jewish schools, and many more restrictions of a similar kind.

Thursday, 19 November 1942

Apart from that, all goes well. Dussel has told us a lot about the outside world, which we have missed for so long now. He had very sad news. Countless friends and acquaintances have gone to a terrible fate. Evening after evening the green and grey army lorries trundle past. The Germans ring at every front door to enquire if there are any Jews living in the house. If there are, then the whole family has to go at once. If they don't find any, they go on to the next house. No one has a chance of evading them unless one goes into hiding. Often they go round with lists, and only ring when they know they can get a good haul. Sometimes they let them off for cash—so much per head. It seems like the slave hunts of olden times. But it's certainly no joke; it's much too tragic for that. In the evenings, when it's dark, I often see rows of good, innocent people accompanied by crying children, walking on and on, in charge of a couple of these chaps, bullied and knocked about until they almost drop. No one is spared—old people, babies, expectant mothers, the sick—each and all join in the march of death.

How fortunate we are here, so well cared for and undisturbed. We wouldn't have to worry about all this misery were it not that we are so anxious about all those dear to us whom we can no longer help.

I feel wicked sleeping in a warm bed, while my dearest friends have been knocked down or have fallen into a gutter somewhere out in the cold night. I get frightened when I think of close friends who have now been delivered into the hands of the cruellest brutes that walk the earth. And all because they are Jews!

Wednesday, 13 January 1943

Everything has upset me again this morning, so I wasn't able to finish a single thing properly.

It is terrible outside. Day and night more of those poor miserable people are being dragged off, with nothing but a rucksack and a little money. On the way they are deprived even of these possessions. Familes are torn apart, the men, women and children all being separated. Children coming home from school find that their parents have disappeared. Women return from shopping to find their homes shut up and their families gone.

Wednesday, 29 March 1944

People have to queue for vegetables and all kinds of other things; doctors are unable to visit the sick, because if they turn their backs on their cars for a moment they are stolen; burglaries and thefts abound, so much so that you wonder what has taken hold of the Dutch for them suddenly to have become such thieves. Little children of eight and eleven years break the windows of people's homes and steal whatever they can lay their hands on. No one dares to leave his house unoccupied for five minutes, because if you go, your things go too. Every day there are announcements in the newspapers offering rewards for the return of lost property, typewriters, Persian rugs, electric clocks, cloth, etc. Electric clocks in the streets are dismantled, public telephones are pulled to pieces—down to the last thread. Morale amongst the population can't be good, the weekly rations are not enough to last for two days except the coffee substitute. The invasion is a long time coming, and the men have to go to Germany. The children are ill or undernourished, everyone is wearing old clothes and old shoes. A new sole costs 7.50 florins in the black market; moreover, hardly any of the shoemakers will accept shoe repairs, or if they do, you have to wait four months, during which time the shoes often disappear.

There's one good thing in the midst of it all, which is that as the food gets worse and the measures against the people more severe, so sabotage against the authorities steadily increases. The people in the food offices, the police, officials, they all either work with their fellow-citizens and help them or they tell tales on them and have them sent to prison. Fortunately, only a small percentage of Dutch people are on the wrong side.

Tuesday, 11 April 1944

We have been pointedly reminded that we are in hiding, that we are Jews in chains, chained to one spot, without any rights, but with a thousand duties. We Jews mustn't show our feelings, must be brave and strong, must accept all inconveniences and not grumble, must do what is within our power and trust in God. Some time this terrible war will be over. Surely the time will come when we are people again, and not just Jews.

Who has inflicted this upon us? Who has made us Jews different to all other people? Who has allowed us to suffer so terribly up till now? It is God that has made us as we are, but it will be God, too, who will raise us up again. If we bear all this suffering and if there are still Jews left, when it is over, then Jews, instead of being doomed, will be held up as an example. Who knows, it might even be our religion, from which the world and all peoples learn good, and for that reason and that reason only do we have to suffer now. We can never become just Netherlanders, or just English, or representatives of any country for that matter, we will always remain Jews, but we want to, too.

Be brave! Let us remain aware of our task and not grumble, a solution will come; God has never deserted our people. Right through the ages there have been Jews, through all the ages they have had to suffer, but it has

made them strong too; the weak fall, but the strong will
remain and never go under!

            Anne Frank, died Belsen concentration camp, 1945

CRETE

The Fighters

I tried hard not to judge Papadakis from his appearance alone. His swept-back grey hair and iron-grey
clipped moustache were typical of any senior Greek Army
officer; but his hard black eyes glittered with peasant
cunning and his general expression could best be described
by the American term of "sour-puss". His voice oscillated
between arrogance and plaintiveness; at a moment's notice
he would switch it from the didactic tone he used when
exploiting his rank, of which he was exaggeratedly proud,
to the wheedling notes of a pauper begging for alms.

But I did my best to overlook these unattractive
qualities, remembering that he was the first man in the
island to have established contact with the Allies and to
have put himself at the disposal of our clandestine service.
He alone had maintained Stockbridge and the wireless
station ever since we started operations in Crete, and he
had thereby reduced his own standard of living, which
on his small pension would in any case not have been
high, to a bare subsistence level—at Vouvoure there was
nothing to eat but seed potatoes.

But his gestures of selfless patriotism, his quixotic plans
for the freedom of Crete, were largely prompted by a
personal ambition so vainglorious that he scarcely
bothered to conceal it. He had set himself up as the head
of a "Supreme Liberation Committee", unrecognized by
anyone except its four members, all of whom had been
elected by himself. This would have been an admirable
venture had it lived up to its rather grandiloquent
name—for in Crete bombast and bluster were not
necessarily divorced from courage and efficiency—but

from the first conversations I had with Papadakis it became increasingly clear that, like himself, his fellow members were less interested in organizing immediate resistance than in securing post-war political positions.

Even this ulterior activity could have been put to good purpose had the committee been prepared to co-operate with the other local leaders whose names I had been given in Cairo; but Papadakis was reluctant to enlist their assistance in case, I suppose, he should have to surrender to them a vestige of his self-arrogated authority or, worse still, in case they should recognize that authority for what it was: a purely notional attribute. So during the first week I spent in Vouvoure, while I vainly enquired after the potential strength of his organization, its dispositions and eventual requirements, Papadakis not very craftily avoided the issue by claiming that nothing could be done until he received official recognition from G.H.Q. Middle East. Since I was not prepared to commit myself on this point, nothing practical was done.

Xan Fielding

June had ended, and in July—it must have been about two months since the fall of the island—three boys from a neighbouring village (Kastelos in Apokoronas), called Levtheri Daskalakis and George and Andrea Vernadakis, went down to the flat country near Aspouliano where the plane which had made the forced landing still lay. A German guard post had been set up to watch over it. But the boys went at midday when the men of the guard were inside eating, and, creeping up to the plane unobserved, they set fire to one of the petrol tanks. It went up in a flash, the whole plane catching in a moment and blazing like a firework. The Germans rushed out, but they did not see who had set fire to it, and (as we learnt later), fearing punishment by their superiors—for their only duty had been the guarding of this plane—they told the owners of the vegetable plots round about (if the military authorities should question them) to say that they had seen nobody: that the plane, in fact, had caught fire by itself. The gardeners said they would back them up in their report. Unfortunately, a "bad Greek"* called Evangelos Stagakis of Dramia went to the local German command-post at Episkopi and asked to be taken to the Kommandant. When the interpreter learnt that he wanted to reveal the truth about the burning of the plane, he turned him out. But Stagakis started threatening the interpreter, and went on until he managed to appear before the Kommandant, to whom he betrayed the whole business. The men at the guard post were arrested at once and (we learnt) put in the lock-up where the Germans beat them up. To the devil with them. But what happened to the neighbourhood? A large German force immediately surrounded the villages of Dramia, Kastelos and Kourna and rounded up the male inhabitants. But the boys, forewarned, had left their villages. The Germans announced that unless the people who had burnt the aeroplane were given up the villagers would all be shot. But how could the villagers have found them, even if they had wished to give them up? In the end, after all the denials of the villagers (who constantly repeated: "We don't know anything. How could we find them?"), it was decided that the blame rested only with the boys' fellow-villagers, the Kastelians; so the Germans began to threaten the Kastelians and especially the relations of the three boys. But they were determined to die rather than hand their children over to be killed. The matter was very serious. If they did as the Germans demanded, the killing of their children would weigh heavy on their hearts for the rest of their lives. They would never be able to still their consciences. So they decided to warn them not to come near the village, but to flee far away and take care never to be caught by the Germans, even if everybody else were killed. And then they waited, resigned to the firing squad. Meanwhile the boys (who had gone into hiding near our village), learning that all their own people would be killed for shielding them, began to be tormented in their minds as to what they ought to do. Finally they decided to

* i.e. A traitor.

give themselves up. They lingered in the neighbourhood to
observe the actions of the Germans, in order that, the moment they saw the Germans about to execute their relations, they might surrender and take the road to Golgotha.
But here, too, bad Greeks were in evidence. The then
Mayor of their village, Stavros Romanias, learning that the
boys were in hiding nearby, sent a man to verify the fact,
and, when he had made quite certain, took a large number
of Germans who set out in ones and twos for Asi Gonia.
Fortunately we saw them before they reached the village,
and had time to lead the English farther off and then to
escape ourselves. Unfortunately some villagers were mad
enough not to escape, so the Germans arrested about a
dozen of them and led them away to Archontiki. They gave
them a certain time limit in which to betray the boys;
otherwise they were to be shot.

The luckless boys, learning all this, and seeing that
the Germans were in no joking mood, took the path of
death with heavy hearts. Only Andrea, the youngest, was
unwilling to give himself up, so he hid at the place called
Koumara,* where some Psychoundakis cousins of mine,
who pastured their flocks thereabouts, looked after him.
As bad luck would have it, some fellow-villagers, relations
of the people who were being held in Archontiki, losing
patience and not knowing what the Germans were going
to do with their kinsmen, set off one day to Andrea's
hiding-place to persuade or compel him to give himself
up. But the moment he saw them he took to his heels.
They set off after him in pursuit, and he ran tirelessly
for many hours. Some of the ones in front fired shots
at him to make him stop, but it was all in vain. At last,
when he had shaken them off, he fell into the hands of
some others, who caught him, half-dead with exhaustion.
They took him to Argyroupolis and handed him over to
the Germans. He showed no signs of fear but laughed at
them as though it were all a game of hide and seek.

The Germans took him to Canea along with the other

* The arbutus-berries.

two, where they were tried. Andrea, being under age, was only sentenced to six months' hard labour but the other two, who were nearing twenty if they had not actually reached it, were condemned to death. So, after a few days, in a street in Archontiki and under the eyes of all the inhabitants, these two martyrs to freedom and death-deriders stood before the firing squad—naked, hungry, barefoot and in chains. Their bonds were removed and their executioners, with rifles levelled at their bare breasts, were waiting for the word "Fire!" The leader of the German party read out the sentence and asked if they had any last words to say. Daskalakis asked for a glass of water which they gave him, and the question was repeated to Vernadakis, who said, "A glass of wine and permission to sing a *mantinada*."** Saying which, naked, barefoot and utterly exhausted as he was from thirst and hunger (for, during their confinement in Ayia jail they had been given neither food nor water), he mustered all the strength of his soul—and what greater strength is there?—and took to his heels. Straight away the firing squad began shooting after him as he ran. But neither the rifle bullets nor the bursts from the sub-machine-guns could touch him. He ran like lightning from lane to lane until he was out of the village. Then, as it was difficult to run farther without being seen, he climbed up into an olive tree and stayed there until night fell. When it was quite dark he climbed gently down and, slipping through the sentries, fled far away. Later he escaped to the Middle East where he volunteered for the Air Force.

While they were chasing Vernadakis through the village, Daskalakis remained motionless in his place

---

** A Cretan fifteen-syllable rhyming couplet, usually with a sting in it. Sung in solo to one of a half dozen ritual tunes, the last half of each line being repeated, after the words 'Ela! Ela! Ela!', by the rest of the company. They are sung and improvised by all Cretans, especially in the mountains.

although he too had a chance of taking to his heels and escaping. "Run for it!" several onlookers shouted, but he refused, saying the Germans would avenge themselves on his kinsmen. It would be better for him to die, he said. In a few moments the Germans were back again, and they opened fire on Daskalakis with fury. He fell at once, quite transformed and unrecognizable from the bursts of the German machine-guns.

George Psychoundakis

The Kidnapping of General Kreipe

I find it impossible to go to sleep because of the benzedrine which I took last night, so I shall try to put on paper all that I can remember of the events of the past twelve hours.

It was eight o'clock when we reached the T-junction. We had met a few pedestrians on the way, none of whom seemed perturbed at seeing our German uniforms, and we had exchanged greetings with them with appropriately Teutonic gruffness. When we reached the road we went straight to our respective posts and took cover. It was now just a question of lying low until we saw the warning torch-flash from Mitso, the buzzer-man. We were distressed to notice that the incline in the road was much steeper than we had been led to believe, for this meant that if the chauffeur used the foot-brake instead of the handbrake when we stopped him there would be a chance of the car's running over the edge of the embankment as soon as he had been disposed of. However, it was too late at this stage to make any changes in our plan, so we just waited and hoped for the best.

There were five false alarms during the first hour of our watch. Two *Volkswagen,* two lorries, and one motor-cycle combination trundled past at various times, and in each of them, seated primly upright like tailors' dummies, the steel-helmeted figures of German soldiers were silhouetted against the night sky. It was a strange feeling

to be crouching so close to them—almost within arm's
reach of them—while they drove past with no idea that
nine pairs of eyes were so fixedly watching them. It felt
like going on patrol in action, when you find yourself very
close to the enemy trenches, and can hear the sentries talking or quietly whistling, and can see them lighting cigarettes in their cupped hands.

It was already one hour past the General's routine time
for making his return journey when we began to wonder
if he could possibly have gone home in one of the vehicles
which had already passed by. It was cold, and the canvas
of our German garb did not serve to keep out the wind.

I remember Paddy asking me the time. I looked at
my watch and saw that the hands were pointing close
to half-past nine. And at that moment Mitso's torch
blinked.

"Here we go."

We scrambled out of the ditch on to the road. Paddy
switched on his red lamp and I held up a traffic signal,
and together we stood in the centre of the junction.

In a moment—far sooner than we had expected—the
powerful headlamps of the General's car swept round the
bend and we found ourselves floodlit. The chauffeur, on
approaching the corner, slowed down.

Paddy shouted, "*Halt!*"

The car stopped. We walked forward rather slowly,
and as we passed the beams of the headlamps we drew
our ready-cocked pistols from behind our backs and let
fall the life-preservers from our wrists.

As we came level with the doors of the car Paddy
asked, "*Ist dies des Generals Wagen?*"

There came a muffled "*Ja, ja*" from inside.

Then everything happened very quickly. There was a
rush from all sides. We tore open our respective doors,
and our torches illuminated the interior of the car—the
bewildered face of the General, the chauffeur's terrified
eyes, the rear seats empty. With his right hand the
chauffeur was reaching for his automatic, so I hit him

across the head with my cosh. He fell forward, and George, who had come up behind me, heaved him out of the driving-seat and dumped him on the road. I jumped in behind the steering wheel, and at the same moment saw Paddy and Manoli dragging the General out of the opposite door. The old man was struggling with fury, lashing out with his arms and legs. He obviously thought that he was going to be killed, and started shouting every curse under the sun at the top of his voice.

The engine of the car was still ticking over, the hand-brake was on, everything was perfect. To one side, in a pool of torchlight in the centre of the road, Paddy and Manoli were trying to quieten the General, who was still cursing and struggling. On the other side George and Andoni were trying to pull the chauffeur to his feet, but the man's head was pouring with blood, and I think he must have been unconscious, because every time they lifted him up he simply collapsed to the ground again.

This was the critical moment, for if any other traffic had come along the road we should have been caught sadly unawares. But now Paddy, Manoli, Nikko and Stratis were carrying the General towards the car and bundling him into the back seat. After him clambered George, Manoli and Stratis—one of the three holding a knife to the General's throat to stop him shouting, the other two with their Marlin guns poking out of either window. It must have been quite a squash.

Paddy jumped into the front seat beside me.

The General kept imploring, "Where is my hat? Where is my hat?"

The hat, of course, was on Paddy's head.

We were now ready to move. Suddenly everyone started kissing and congratulating everybody else; and Micky, having first embraced Paddy and me, started screaming at the General with all the pent-up hatred he held for the Germans. We had to push him away and tell him to shut up. Andoni, Grigori, Nikko and Wallace Beery were standing at the roadside, propping up the chauffeur between them, and now they waved us good-bye and turned away and started off on their long trek to the rendezvous on Mount Ida.

We started.

The car was a beauty, a brand-new Opel, and we were delighted to see that the petrol-gauge showed the tanks to be full.

We had been travelling for less than a minute when we saw a succession of lights coming along the road towards us; and a moment later we found ourselves driving past a motor convoy, and thanked our stars that it had not come this way a couple of minutes sooner. Most of the lorries were troop transports, all filled with soldiery, and this sight had the immediate effect of quietening George, Manoli and Stratis, who had hitherto been shouting at one another and taking no notice of our attempts to keep them quiet.

When the convoy had passed Paddy told the General that the two of us were British officers and that we would treat him as an honourable prisoner of war. He seemed mightily relieved to hear this and immediately started to ask a series of questions, often not even waiting for a reply. But for some reason his chief concern still appeared to be the whereabouts of his hat—first it was the hat, then his medal. Paddy told him that he would soon be given it back, and to this the General said, *"Danke, danke."*

It was not long before we saw a red lamp flashing in the road before us, and we realized that we were approaching the first of the traffic-control posts through which we should have to pass. We were, of course, prepared for this eventuality, and our plan had contained alternative actions which we had hoped would suit any situation, because we knew that our route led us through the centre of Heraklion, and that in the course of our journey we should probably have to pass through about twenty control posts.

Until now everything had happened so quickly that we had felt no emotion other than elation at the primary success of our venture; but as we drew nearer and nearer

to the swinging red lamp we experienced our first tense
moment.

A German sentry was standing in the middle of the
road. As we approached him, slowing down the while,
he moved to one side, presumably thinking that we were
going to stop. However, as soon as we drew level with
him—still going very slowly, so as to give him an
opportunity of seeing the General's pennants on the wings
of the car—I began to accelerate again, and on we went.
For several seconds after we had passed the sentry we
were all apprehension, fully expecting to hear a rifle-shot
in our wake; but a moment later we had rounded a bend
in the road and knew that the danger was temporarily
past. Our chief concern now was whether or not the guard
at the post behind us would telephone ahead to the next
one, and it was with our fingers crossed that we approached the red lamp of the second control post a
few minutes later. But we need not have had any fears,
for the sentry behaved in exactly the same manner as the
first had done, and we drove on feeling rather pleased
with ourselves.

Presently we found ourselves approaching the Villa
Ariadne. The sentries, having recognized the car from a
distance, were already opening the heavily-barbed gates in
anticipation of our driving inside. I hooted the horn and
did not slow down. We drove swiftly past them, and it
was with considerable delight that we watched them
treating us to hurried salutes.

We were now approaching Heraklion, and coming
towards us we saw a large number of lorries. We
remembered that Micky had told us that there was to
be a garrison cinema-show in the town that evening, so
we presumed that these lorries were transporting the
audience back to various billets. We did not pass a single
vehicle which was travelling in the same direction as
ourselves.

Soon we had to slow down to about twenty-five k.p.h.,
because the road was chock-full of German soldiers. They
were quick to respond to the hooting of our horn, how-

ever, and when they saw whose car it was they dispersed
to the sides of the road and acknowledged us in passing.
It was truly unfortunate that we should have arrived in
the town at this moment; but once again luck was with
us, and, apart from a near-miss on a cyclist, who swerved
out of our way only just in time, we drove down the main
street without let or hindrance. By the time we reached
the market square in the centre of the town we had
already left the cinema crowd behind us, and we found
the large, open space, which by daylight is usually so
crowded, now almost completely deserted. At this point
we had to take a sharp turning to the left, for our route
led us westward through the old West Gate to the Retimo
road.

The West Gate is a relic of the old days when Heraklion
was completely surrounded by a massive wall, and even
to-day it remains a formidable structure. The gate itself,
at the best of times not very wide, has been further
narrowed by concrete anti-tank blocks; and a German
guard is on duty there for twenty-four hours a day.

I remember saying "Woops" as I saw the sentry
signalling us to stop. I had proposed to slow down, as
on the previous occasions, and then to accelerate upon
drawing level with the sentry; but this time this was
impossible, for the man did not move an inch, and in
the light of the headlamps we saw several more Germans
standing behind him. I was obliged to take the car forward
at a snail's pace. We had previously decided that in the
event of our being asked any questions our reply would
be simply, *"Generals Wagen"*, coupled with our hopes
for the best. If any further conversation were called for
Paddy was to do the talking.

George, Manoli and Stratis held their weapons at the
ready and kept as low as they could in the back seat. The
General was on the floor beneath them. Paddy and I
cocked our pistols and held them on our laps.

The sentry approached Paddy's side of the car.

Before he had come too near Paddy called out that
this was the General's car—which, after all, was true

enough—and without awaiting the sentry's next word I accelerated and we drove on, calling out *"Gute Nacht!"* as we went. Everyone saluted.

We drove fast along the next stretch of road.

The General, coming to the surface, said he felt sorry for all the sentries at the control posts, because they would surely get into terrible trouble on the morrow.

W. Stanley Moss

JUGOSLAVIA

Tito Changes Headquarters

A few days after Vivian reached partisan headquarters an incident had occurred which aroused his suspicion. One morning a single German aircraft made its appearance over the valley, and, instead of dropping bombs or machine-gunning, as these aerial visitors usually did, had spent half an hour or more flying slowly up and down at a height of about two thousand feet. Each time it passed directly over the little house on the rising ground outside the village where he and the others were living. Standing outside in the orchard, in the warm spring sunshine, looking up at it, they discussed what it could be doing and came to the conclusion that it was making a photographic reconnaissance.

Now the Germans would not do this without a reason, and Vivian's guess was that the visit of the little aeroplane would be the forerunner of a heavy air attack that would put anything else we had experienced into the shade. Accordingly he sought out Tito in his cave and told him what he thought was going to happen, adding that in the circumstances he proposed to move a little farther out. That afternoon he and the others transferred themselves with wireless sets and escort to a little house in the hills a mile or two away from the village.

Two days passed; and nothing happened. Then a third day. Vivian began to wonder if he had not perhaps been rather over-cautious. That night he dined with Tito, and after a good meal walked home to bed through the orchards.

Next morning he was awakened, just as it was getting light, by the familiar shout of *"Avioni!"* from the partisans on guard outside. The shout was repeated, so he went out to see what was happening.

A number of small aircraft, considerably more than usual, were bombing the village, circling round and then, when they had dropped their bombs, pulling away to make room for others that were coming in from every direction. Then just as those who were watching were reflecting what short work a couple of Spitfires would make of the intruders, a deeper note fell on the ears of the watchers, and out of the sun came six great JU 52s, flying in formation down the valley. The Germans were doing things in style.

They waited for the whistle and crash of the bombs. The planes reached the village and circled it. Then, as they watched, something fell from the leading plane, and, falling, billowed out into a great canopy with a man dangling from it. Then more and more, from one plane after another. The air seemed full of them. More planes followed, and gliders, bringing guns and reinforcements to the parachutists, who by now were shooting their way into the village. A glider seemed to be landing almost on top of the little house which the Mission had left three days before.

For a few moments Vivian and the others stood and looked. Then, taking the wireless sets and anything else they could carry, they moved off along the hillside to establish contact with the partisan corps headquarters situated farther up the valley.

Meanwhile, in Drvar itself, the partisans had driven back the Germans from the village. But they were firmly established on the slopes outside it. A glider which had come down on the flat ground immediately below Tito's cave had crashed and the crew had been killed. But now some other Germans had succeeded in gaining a position from which they commanded the mouth of the cave, and this was now under heavy fire. Tito's position was precarious, for to use the ordinary way down would have meant almost certain death. But, with the help of a rope he hoisted himself up a cleft in the rock to the high ground above his cave. From there he was able to join the main body of partisans.

Now came the news that, on top of the airborne attack, strong forces of the enemy were converging on Drvar from all sides. The partisans had already suffered heavy losses. They could not hope to hold Drvar in the face of such overwhelming odds. The order was given to withdraw into the hills.

After a ten hours' march Vivian and the others reached the little group of huts deep in the forest which we had left some months before, to find Tito and his staff already there. Soon the wireless was working and a message on its way to Bari saying what had happened and asking urgently for air support.

Meanwhile, the enemy had taken Drvar. They had inflicted severe casualties on the partisans, but at heavy cost to themselves, and they had failed to capture Tito or the Allied Missions. For this failure, they revenged themselves on the defenceless civilian population, known to be loyal to the partisans. When the village was re-captured some months later it was found that most of the inhabitants had been massacred. One of our officers who went back with the partisans tried to find some of the peasants who had lived near us. At last he found one who had somehow survived. He said that during the fighting the Germans had forced the civilians to carry ammunition for them at the point of the rifle, making them go on even after they had been wounded and could barely crawl: old men, women and even children. After the fighting was over and they no longer had any use for them, they had shot them. And the child Ginger? Ginger had been shot, too.

Having missed Tito at Drvar, the enemy began to close in on him in the woods. Soon they reached the edge of the forest. Firing could be heard coming nearer. Tito decided to break out.

The break-out took place at night. Fierce fighting was in progress. Flashes could be seen on the ridge above them. The sound of firing came ever closer. From time to time a Verey star shot up into the sky.

Then Vivian saw something that amazed him. There, on a siding in the woods, was drawn up the Partisan Express, with steam up and smoke and sparks belching from the funnel. Solemnly, Tito, his entourage and the dog Tigger entrained; the whistle blew; and, with much puffing and creaking, they started off down the five miles of track through the woods, with the enemy's bullets whining through the trees all round them.

During the days that followed, Tito and his staff, with the Allied Missions and a force of a few hundred partisans, were almost constantly on the move: dodging through the woods, lying up in the daytime, moving at night. Again and again they had narrow escapes from the enemy. German patrols, aircraft and light tanks seemed to be everywhere. Food and ammunition were getting desperately short, but once they managed to stop long enough to receive a supply dropped from British planes based in Italy. At the same time other British aircraft were giving much-needed air support, wherever they could. During the week that followed the attack on Drvar our planes flew over a thousand sorties in support of the partisans, thereby doing much to relieve the pressure on them.

All this time Vivian kept in close touch with Tito. He was, he told me afterwards, impressed throughout by the way in which Tito dominated the situation, remaining calm and collected under the severest strain, personally directing the operations of the small body of troops which accompanied him as well as those of the other partisan formations in the neighborhood, quietly giving orders to the partisans round him. This from Vivian, an experienced soldier and a severe judge in such matters, was high praise.

Then one day, as they were resting after a long march, Tito sent for him. Vivian found the Marshal looking tired and depressed. He had, he said, reluctantly reached the conclusion that it was impossible for him to direct the operations of his forces throughout Jugoslavia while being chased through the woods and kept constantly on the move. The complexity of this task now made it essential for him to have a relatively firm base for his headquarters. Already he had lost touch with nearly all the formations under his command. He must ask Vivian to arrange for the evacuation of himself and his staff by air to Italy until such time as the situation permitted his return to Jugoslavia.

At first Vivian was surprised. Tito was connected in his mind with the hills and forests and it was hard to imagine him leaving them. But he soon realized that the decision which he had taken was the right one.

A signal was dispatched to Bari and the answer came back almost immediately. The R.A.F. would do everything in their power to pick them up from a nearby stretch of flat ground, now held by the partisans. That afternoon they set out for the landing-strip.

They reached it after dark. It was raining and there was low cloud. Not much hope, it seemed, of getting out. Then the moon came through the clouds and they cheered up a little. Anxiously they waited. At last came the sound they were waiting for: the faint hum of an aircraft engine in the distance. Bonfires were lighted and soon the Dakota was circling the field, ready to land. It touched down; they climbed in. Tito, his dog Tigger, half a dozen of his staff, Vivian and the Russian Mission. Almost immediately they were airborne.

As Vivian got into the plane, he saw that it was manned by Russians. It was a Dakota, supplied under Lease-Lend, which the Russians were operating from Bari under British operational control. The Soviet officer concerned had shown considerable astuteness in securing this particular assignment for his plane. Afterwards the Russians were to make great capital out of the claim that it was they who had rescued Tito in this emergency.

An hour or two later they reached Bari.

The next thing to be decided was where Tito and his headquarters staff were to establish themselves. I went and called on him at the suburban villa on the outskirts of Bari in which he had been temporarily installed and found him in favour of moving over to the island of Vis until such time as the military situation made it feasible to return to the interior. This, indeed, seemed the obvious solution. Vis was Jugoslav territory; at the same time, thanks to its now substantial garrison and ever-present British naval and air support, it offered a degree of security and stability which was not to be found on the mainland of Jugoslavia.

The task of conveying the Marshal to his new abode was entrusted to the Royal Navy and H.M.S. *Blackmore,* a Hunt Class destroyer, under the command of Lieutenant Carson, R.N., was allotted to us for the purpose, with another destroyer for the rest of the party.

Carson and the officers and crew of the *Blackmore* immediately entered into the spirit of the thing as only the Navy can. In order to avoid any risk of enemy interference, the crossing was made at night. At about six in the evening Tito, followed by Tigger, was piped on board in fine style, and at once taken below and plied with gin. His original Marshal's uniform had fallen into the hands of the Germans during the attack on Drvar and been taken away to grace a museum somewhere in Germany, but a substitute had been found, and he once more looked and, I think, felt the part.

By the time we weighed anchor any initial shyness had completely worn off and I could see that we were in for a convivial evening. We sat down to dinner in the wardroom to find ourselves confronted with a menu magnificently illuminated by one of the crew and written in Serb as well as English. I noticed at once that the wine list was a formidable one: sherry followed the gin, then red wine, then white, then port, then liqueurs. The Marshal drank some of everything, only hesitating momentarily when a large bottle was produced mysteriously draped in a napkin. For an instant he wavered.

"*Cheri-beri?*" he enquired cryptically.

"No, champagne," said the Captain proudly.

"Ah, champagne!" said Tito and drained a tumbler of it.

It was not till later that we discovered that by *cheri-beri* he meant cherry brandy, though when, in due course, that stimulating beverage made its appearance, any distrust which he might have felt for it earlier in the evening had evidently vanished.

By this stage of dinner the Marshal, to my surprise, was speaking quite fluent English and rounded off the proceedings by giving a spirited recital of *The Owl and the Pussy-Cat.*

> The Owl and the Pussy-Cat went to sea
> In a beautiful pea-green boat.
> They dined on mince and slices of quince,
> Which they ate with a runcible spoon;
> And hand in hand, on the edge of the sand,
> They danced by the light of the moon. . . .

After that, we went up on deck.

By now the sky was starting to get lighter, and, outlined against it, we could already see the jagged outline of the Dalmatian mountains. Tito sat in an armchair on deck, contemplatively smoking a cigar. Soon we could make out the dark shape of Vis, rising from the sea, and twenty minutes later Carson, on the bridge, was bringing us skilfully alongside in the little harbour of Komisa.

Fitzroy Maclean

WARSAW

> . . . Brief landing in Warsaw. But I take no notice of
> the city; I would only get angry anyway.
>
> Dr. Goebbels

The Rising: August-October 1944

General Bor . . . commanded an underground force
of three hundred thousand men, the Polish Home Army,
whose anti-German efforts, including much of the actual
liberating of Lvov and Vilna, had been lauded by Russian
propaganda which at the same time continually demanded
greater efforts. He had been instructed unequivocally by
his government in London, having himself asked for
directives when the Red Army penetrated Eastern Poland,
that Russian commanders were to be accepted as hosts,
that they should be helped to the utmost, and that Polish
units were to be at their disposal. The Polish Home Army
had then fought the Germans all over Poland in support
of the 1944 spring-summer offensive of the Red Army;
and when the Russians reached the River Bug, five days'
march from Warsaw, General Bor summoned to his
Warsaw headquarters the leaders of all the Polish political
groups, including the Communists (who had appealed
ceaselessly for a general rising) and put it for decision,
whether they should liberate the capital themselves or wait
for the Red Army. Decision was unanimous for a rising.

No elaborate preliminaries were entailed. Plans had
long since been worked out for a general rising all over
Poland, and it was only necessary to excerpt the Warsaw
section of the plans, in which all knew what they had
to do without special orders. On 31 July, conveyed by
messenger-girls from General Bor's H.Q. to all units in
Warsaw, went the secret order: "5 p.m. to-morrow
afternoon—X." X was the code-letter for the project,
5 p.m. the hour chosen because workers would be leaving
the factories and the city would be busy with casually
unsuspicious movement.

1 August

Soldiers of the Capital!

To-day I have issued the order so long awaited by all of you, the order for an open fight against the German invader. After nearly five years of unceasing underground struggle, to-day you are taking up arms openly to restore the freedom of our country and to punish the German criminals for the terror and bestialities they have committed within our frontiers.

Bor, Home Army C.-in-C.

X-evening in fact completely surprised the unexpecting Germans. With machine-guns, machine-pistols, and hand-grenades three-quarters of Warsaw were quickly seized. German strongpoints in big buildings, occupied mainly by S.S. who had heavily prepared them for defence against the Russians, were approached and breached more slowly with explosives carried through the sewers.

At the time of this auspicious opening the Russian armies under Marshal Rokossovsky had pressed their rapid advance to within ten miles of Warsaw, east of the Vistula. General Bor had food and ammunition for a week; it seemed certain that that would be enough and that the Russians would in good time enter a city whose own people had hastened and facilitated its liberation.

The Fight for Mokotow

Mokotow was a residential district in the south of Warsaw. It was nearly lost by the insurgents during the first night's fighting, as described in the anonymous eyewitness account that follows. Owing to the stubborn resistance of Colonel Daniel, it was enabled to hold out for fifty-seven days.

It looked as if things were not going too well for us, either. To find out more about the situation Daniel, accompanied by Kubus, went out to establish personal contact with the commanders of Battalions B and O, who had been given the hardest assignments. Before leaving he told me to see to Woronicz's School, which was still in German hands.

It was after 8 p.m. Connected by telephone cable to all the centres of fighting in Mokotow, I sat and listened to reports coming in from the local commanders. Most of them confirmed my uneasiness and my fears. Nothing certain was known about the most distant units, but from scraps of information it emerged that Battalion K in Sluzewiec had been lost, and that Brigand's hand-picked company had been bled white in its assault on Mokotow Fort. The nearest troops, Burza's and Reda's companies, reported that they were still fighting desperately but only for their own survival now.

It was getting dark, and with the coming of dusk the fighting was losing in intensity. Our storm troops, for the last few hours interlocked in mortal combat with the Germans, had been kept pinned down in the open by accurate fire, and only now, using the last of their ammunition, were they fighting back, disengaging and pulling out to more advantageous positions.

The darkness allowed us to carry the wounded to safer places, and, helped by nurses, they were making their way in groups to the Elzbietanek Hospital.

More people were out in the streets; many were putting up barricades. Detachments of sappers were advancing boldly into the street openings and digging anti-tank trenches. There were numerous volunteers and the work was progressing swiftly.

Only now the picture of the burning capital assumed some sharpness of definition. Towering, billowing smoke topped the city like an immense parachute, lit from below by long tongues of flame. The roar issuing from that volcano of fire and smoke told us that the battle was not yet over, and this cheered us somewhat, though all the attempts of our radio-telegraphists to establish contact were unsuccessful.

Meanwhile the telephones in the Mokotow's H.Q. were ringing incessantly. The whole time the local commanders had something to report, and each one wanted to talk to Daniel personally, so that I couldn't put the receiver down for more than a second. Daniel was still out and I was beginning to worry, as the situation was difficult and important decisions had to be taken. I breathed at last when he returned from his tour of inspection, in complete darkness, shortly after ten. Though tired and evidently depressed, he at once went over all the reports received in his absence: we began summing up the results of the fighting so far and tried to appraise the situation. What we arrived at was not very encouraging. The results achieved were infinitesimal and the losses very serious. The forces at our disposal had been considerably weakened without seriously incapacitating the Germans. But as long as the rest of the capital fought on we could not resign ourselves to the role of mere spectators.

Daniel came to a decision: we were to attack again, as we could not afford to give the Germans a breather. The attack would raise the morale of our own troops, too. Daniel answered all telephone enquiries with a curt and decided: "One more effort."

Before midnight I ran over to Garbaty's detachment near Woronicz's School. The platoons assembled there were silently moving up to base positions. The S.S. troops in the school opened up blindly from time to time with all their machine-guns hidden in concrete shelters. The fire did us no damage, but, at a distance of fifty paces, it caused an uneasiness which was increased by the darkness prevailing all around. We did not answer the fire and our lads kept very quiet. There were twenty minutes to go before the attack. Garbaty asked me to send up a few more pistols and more hand-grenades. I promised to do so, then checked the preparations and returned to H.Q.

The commanders at various points were reporting their readiness for renewed attack. I managed to send up the supplies to Garbaty, and, in a slightly better mood, waited for the attack to begin.

There was a loud explosion which rumbled on for some seconds, followed by the staccato of furious automatic fire. I was surprised and very pleased at the violence of our attack. Obviously the initiative was with our men and for the moment they had the upper hand. Storm units were reaching the entrance-halls and staircases of many buildings where the Germans were holding out. Those dull explosions meant that the doors and gates were being blown up by mining patrols and that the way was open for others to rush in through the breached defences. Lighter explosions of hand-grenades tossed in through the windows followed, and then another wave of dull and heavy rumbling. They had got through the barrier of automatic fire and were storming the inner pockets of resistance.

But our forces were expendable. The enemy fire showed no signs of abating, and our troops had to withdraw again without achieving tangible success; only the fighting round Woronicz's School lasted some time longer. The reports started coming in. Nowhere had we managed to overpower the Germans in their fortified positions; and again a wave of wounded men streamed towards the hospital. The fighting ceased. The darkness was no longer rent by tracer bullets, and only occasional German flares lit up the sky above the battle-ground below.

About 2 a.m. we had a complete picture of the situation. This time it was really bad. Out of twelve quite well-armed companies there were only four left in a condition to carry on the fight. Battalion K could be written off altogether, as, after some initial success at Sluzewiec, it had been forced to withdraw into the adjacent woods*; the company commanded by Zdzich had disintegrated, and only one platoon commanded by Bozydar made its way back to our lines. Zych's company suffered a similar fate. Other companies had shrunk enormously. The spirit of the men was flagging, the

* Some time later Battalion K returned to Mokotow.

reversals were having a sad effect on morale.

The situation was not made easier by the remnants of defeated units from the neighbouring sectors who came streaming into our lines. They did not want to join us, but were all making for the woods. All round anxious voices were asking what was going to happen in the morning if the Germans attacked in full strength. Between 2 and 3 a.m. hardly anybody in Mokotow believed in the possibility of resisting a German attack, as so much ammunition had been used up and so many men killed, and as, with every person left lying in no-man's-land, a valuable rifle or pistol had been lost.

In the east, the sky over Praga* was beginning to be tinged with silver. The glow of fires over Warsaw was dying down and the sounds of battle were more subdued. In our part the silence was broken only by the Germans, who emptied their magazines in the air frequently and for no apparent purpose; while the freedom with which they spent their ammunition preyed on our minds and led to unpleasant guesses as to their stocks of it.

In their phone calls to H.Q. the unit commanders were betraying an increasing nervousness. More and more verbal phone reports suggested pulling out of Mokotow: the idea of withdrawing into the nearby woods was spreading even among the staff. Everybody was waiting for the commander's decision.

At 3 a.m. Daniel decided that we would remain as we were. Warsaw was still fighting on, and, anyway, we were not going to abandon the civilian population, whom the Germans would undoubtedly decimate after our withdrawal. It was up to us to stay on and share the fate of the rest of Warsaw and of the civilians. We threw ourselves into preparations for the battle, which was to begin again with daylight. The dawn of 2 August found us, with our ranks closed, holding a diminished peri-meter between Goszczynskiego and Odynca Streets. The soldiers looked at each other and saw that not all had

* A suburb of Warsaw on the right bank of the Vistula.

been killed the day before. Concentrated in a small area, our forces not only seemed larger but allowed a better tactical use to be made of them. The morale was much better than during the night.

It was raining and the low clouds overhead presaged a murky day. The advanced outposts found it very difficult to overcome their sleeplessness and fatigue. It was quiet except for concentrated bursts of German fire lasting about a minute each and, no doubt, preparing the way for some attack, though we had no means of knowing when and where it would develop.

At 8 a.m. enemy activity was reported from a few sectors. A fresh attack was signalled from Woronicz's School, where the Germans had received reinforcements in two armoured troop-carriers.

The fire from the detachment of our Battalions B and O stopped the swarm of S.S. men pouring forth from the school. But only for a time. More and more Germans joined the attack. Their fire was definitely superior to ours and the struggle became more vicious. The Germans were attacking due north, and their advance continued in spite of our efforts. They got through fences, jumped over walls and sprinted across streets, and one by one put our centres of resistance out of action. We saw that we were up against very good troops: the German success became more and more pronounced every minute. In places our units were beginning to retreat in disorder, as the battle reached its climax. Shortly before noon the German attack had penetrated to within a short distance of our reserve detachments, and the tension among us had risen appreciably.

Only Daniel kept cool and followed the developments, waiting for the right moment to counter-attack. The companies from Burza's battalion had been ready for some time, and their commanders, Szwarc and Krzem, were only waiting for a sign from Daniel.

The Germans were level with Malczewskiego Street and small groups of them were infiltrating into the Elzbietanek Hospital. Not more than sixty yards separated us from the Germans. The line of steel helmets pressed forward with increasing audacity: they treated our weakening resistance with ever-diminishing respect. There were at least two full companies in the attack, and they were well aware of their strength.

The tension among our reserve detachments was rising to a climax. The time was ripe for a counter-attack. At a given sign the mass of men moved forward. The impetus and fury of this initial rush swept back the German line, while a second group cut them off from their starting base at the school. The back of the German attack was broken. Now it was their turn to pull out in disorder, and, leaving many wounded and dead behind, they retreated south, by-passing their stronghold in the school.

At 3 p.m. Woronicz's School had been completely cleared of the enemy, and our companies were fighting a long way farther south. This was our first major success, and it resulted in the capture of large quantities of arms and ammunition stored in the school.

But the moral success was even greater. The Mokotow garrison had come through its first crisis with flying colours, and, as a result of this valuable trial of strength, it held out through many more crises during the next eight weeks of the Rising, which for Mokotow came to an end on 27 September 1944.

Anon.

Kurt Heller's Diary*

1 August. Street fighting began this afternoon in Warsaw.

2 August. We're surrounded.

3 August. Ulrich has been killed. Still no help from outside. Hollweg has been seriously wounded.

5 August. Rudolf killed, as well as several others. We've reached the limit of endurance.

* Kurt Heller, a German from Stettin, was taken prisoner in the Warsaw Telephone Exchange.

6 August. Got a little sleep this morning. Dinner was coffee with sugar. Death everywhere, but I want to live. Three men have committed suicide.

7 August. Our own artillery fired at us this afternoon, but no one was killed. An attempt to break out failed —one man killed, four badly hurt. We buried fourteen of our men to-day at 8 a.m. in the yard. The air smells bad.

8 August. Our positions are three hundred metres away, but the bandits' resistance is still strong.

9 August. Food very short.

11 August. The police have taken what food we had, including our cigarettes. We're in no condition to resist longer.

12 August. Hungry. Some soup, six cigarettes. The police have seized everything, even what was left of the jam. When will this end?

13 August. Heavy tank fire against the Poles so that our Tower is being hit, but no casualties. A tank has brought in food supplies for five days. I can hardly stand. When will they get us out of here?

16 August. Hunger. The men are afraid at night. When I saw the first star I thought of my wife and the boy, lying in the earth in Stettin. Can't stop thinking of them; am in the same position myself.

17 August. The Poles are trying to smoke us out with petrol bottles. More men have lost their nerve and committed suicide. The dead smell horrible, lying in the streets.

18 August. Cut off entirely from the outer world.

19 August. No hope. The Poles are surrounding us.

Kurt Heller

The Betrayal

But suddenly during the first day of the rising the Russian front went dead. The sky that had been full of Russian aeroplanes was vacant. The streams of exhortation from Russian radio ceased all at once. For thirteen days this silence in the east continued. On the thirteenth day it was broken. The friendly, familiar voice of Russian radio sounded once again—but the words that General Bor heard were not quite so familiar. He heard himself described as a "war criminal" and he heard the Rising stigmatized as "irresponsible". Then immediately with fatal clarity he saw that the struggle must fail, and knew equally that he "could not now stop it". The one hope, he thought, was that the importance of Warsaw might yet oblige the Red Army to intervene. But meanwhile the initially surprised Germans, who at first had reacted only defensively outside the city, had brought up two Panzer divisions, an S.S. division, and a quantity of bombers. They did not actually recapture much of what they had lost; but they did not have to. Their bombing, incessant and unhindered, brought havoc to the half-million civilian population, now foodless, and increasingly buried in collapsing cellars from which many could not be rescued. British aeroplanes from Italy dropped supplies, but so many were lost on their homeward journey that they had to desist. An American promise of a hundred Fortresses was doomed by the refusal of Russia to allow her airfields for refuelling; and when finally Stalin, after several telegrams from London reminding him that such contravention of the Anglo-Russian Treaty might have "political consequences", professed to alter his decision, it was too late. Warsaw was in the last throes.

The Sewers

It was 26 September. For the last fortnight I and my radio group had been in Mokotow, where the situation was critical, not to say hopeless, just as it had been in the Old Town a month earlier. We were on a narrow strip of territory like an island, with the Germans all round.

I was given the decision of Colonel Karol, commanding the fighting in Mokotow, to retreat to the City Centre, as less than a month before we had retreated from the Old Town. As I radioed the message about the withdrawal—the last one from Mokotow—I felt an unspeakable sorrow. One more stage was coming to an end, and we had thought that each successive stage would bring us closer to freedom. What had been my pride—my transmitters—which had been carrying on conversations uninterruptedly with London and the High Command ever since my transfer to Mokotow on 11 September, now had to close down. Never again would they speak on the ether. A radio man's sending key is his faculty of speech, and I felt as if I had lost mine.

It was 11 p.m. when I set out with my group on the last stage of our retreat, the town drains. Through them we were to reach the City Centre. We forced ourselves into the ranks of this strange procession: all round us were gloomy faces, unwashed for many weeks, blood-stained rags hiding wounds, clothes in ribbons. The long file of people moved in silence. After the noise and uproar above, the silence was unbearable.

We waded into the stinking filth, moving terribly slowly. A few steps and then a long halt. A few more steps and again a halt. I began to lose count of the time; I was losing any power of judging the distance covered. I thought we should have come out long ago, while really it was only a few steps forward and then stop.

At one point I shook myself into consciousness. With some difficulty I began counting the number of stops. I added up the short distances between them, and came to the conclusion that we had covered a few hundred yards at best. I looked at my watch. It was nine, nine in the morning. So we'd been going all night and had only gone a few hundred yards. I felt myself sinking into a quiet dementia.

I was up to the waist in the stinking stuff. I was hot. There was a long row of people in front of me and another behind. All of us in a similar mood.

We moved forward again. At one point I came up against an obstacle blocking my passage. I felt that someone stood in front of me, though the column ahead was moving. I touched the motionless figure, trying to force it forward. But the man I was touching would never move again.

After that we came on more and more dead bodies. Sometimes on several at once. Each time it filled one with disgust, and worse, with very dark conjectures, for the dead men had also been soldiers and also full of youth and hope. I knew I mustn't think of it, not think of anything, or things might go ill for me. After all, it was only because I wanted to live again and hope again that I was pushing through the damned darkness.

My group was holding out well. But the sewer seemed endless. Suddenly from those in front came cries: "Gas!" True, it was only tear gas. The Germans had discovered that we were passing and had gassed sections of the sewers. I didn't like to think what was happening at the front of the column, but we in our group were not spared the catastrophe either. Ewa, my cipher clerk, was seized with a fit of madness. I divided my men in two groups. One, under Smialy, I sent on after Karol's column; the other, consisting of Lieutenant Oko, the radio-telegraphist, Geniek and myself, stayed behind to help Ewa. Another girl, Stefa, Ewa's friend, decided to stay with us.

We carried her in turns, stumbling over corpses, knapsacks and arms. It was horrible. Ewa's demented howling mingled with other unearthly screams. She was not the only one.

I felt my strength ebbing away. At one point I lost my footing and fell heavily. My companions, Oko and Geniek, helped to put me on my feet again.

We set Ewa down and covered her with overcoats; we had to rest. She sat, propped against the side wall of the sewer, no longer screaming, and with glassy eyes. A procession of ghastly phantoms kept filing past us, some of them howling as Ewa did only a short time ago. Those screams, multiplied by echoes, were about as much as one could stand.

Then a new party approached. I wanted to warn them that we were resting, but before I could do so one of them had fallen, and the others, no longer aware of what they were doing, went over him, trampling him down into the bottom of the sewer—automatically, quite unconscious of the fact that he was still alive. In the same way they would have walked over us.

When they had passed we got up. Ewa no longer gave any sign of life, nor did the man who had been trampled on. We walked on.

We passed a barricade put across the sewer by the Germans. After some time we caught up with the group which had passed us. Then we came to another barricade. This one was well built and was a real obstacle. There was no way through here. I turned back with my group, and some of the others followed. When we came to the first barricade, the one we had just passed, we met a party of people who told us feverishly that the sewer beyond the barricade in the direction of Mokotow was flooded. So we should never get to the top!

A despairing argument took place between the two groups, the one that had brought the news of the flooding and the one that had come up against the impenetrable barricade. By then people had lost their senses; they were shouting in their fury and anguish.

Some remnant of judgment indicated a return to Mokotow. It was not very likely to succeed, but it was the only way of keeping alive—no matter for how long; the only thing that mattered was not to die in the sewer.

The gas was affecting our eyes more and more the whole time. I felt just as if I had sand under my eyelids; my head, too, was rolling to one side in a queer way. The mass of people all round were still arguing how to save themselves. From time to time a hideous bubbling was heard, as one more person whose strength had gone slipped into the foul liquid. But even more unbearable would be the voice of some woman pulling him out: "Look, he's alive, he's smiling! My darling, you'll soon be on top again!" Oh God, not to see it, not to hear it!

I realized during my increasingly rarer spells of clarity that I was beginning to lose consciousness. I held on to one thought: to get back to the surface. I did not want someone else to hear the splash and the bubbling which my ears would not hear.

I shouted then, at the top of my poice:

"Make way, I'll lead you out!"

But the angry yells which met me on all sides were the worst thing yet.

"Who said that? Fifth columnist! Shoot him!"

This shouting, like a sharp lash, spurred me to an extra effort. I escaped. I had enough sense left to realize that at such a moment what they threatened could well happen. Edging sideways close to the wall, my group and I crossed the barricade unnoticed by the rest.

We were over on the other side. We were going back, come what might.

At once we were deep in it. After a few steps we could no longer feel the bottom, but with the help of planks, knapsacks and abandoned bundles, we managed to keep our head above the surface. After a short time we again felt the ground under our feet. The cold water and the absence of the blasted gas helped to clear our heads, and, holding each other's hands, we crawled slowly forward. Forward, that was what mattered. I knew that by following that sewer we were bound to come out in Dworkowa Street. We had to make it.

At 4 p.m., seventeen hours after we first went down into the sewers, we were pulled out of them by S.S. men in Dworkowa Street.

Anon.

The Last Day of September

By radio telegram General Bor informed Marshal Rokossovsky that he would have to end resistance if within seventy-two hours he received no support or promise of support. He received neither. He received no reply at all; and when seventy-two hours had passed he sent two of his officers to General von den Bach, who had many times requested a meeting, and who now suggested, pleasantly if long-windedly, that there was "nothing left to fight for" and that Warsaw might as well capitulate rather than be completely destroyed. On this report from his officers General Bor overnight drew up his "conditions" for capitulation. The battle for Warsaw, planned for a week, had lasted sixty-three days; and perhaps the most remarkable testimony to the Polish defence, to General Bor, and to the blows that the Germans had received, was the alacrity with which General von den Bach accepted the "conditions", in all their unpalatable clemency, that General Bor had laid down.*

Poland Lives

This is the stark truth. We were treated worse than Hitler's satellites, worse than Italy, Roumania, Finland. May God, Who is just, pass judgment on the terrible injustice suffered by the Polish nation, and may He punish accordingly all those who are guilty.

Your heroes are the soldiers whose only weapons against tanks, planes and guns were their revolvers and bottles filled with petrol. Your heroes are the women who tended the wounded and carried messages under fire, who cooked in bombed and ruined cellars to feed children and adults, and who soothed and comforted the dying. Your heroes are the children who went on quietly playing among the smouldering ruins. These are the people of Warsaw.

Immortal is the nation that can muster such universal

---

* Among the chief conditions agreed and signed were:
  (a) All Polish Home Army to have P.O.W. status as under Geneva Convention—a white-red armband sufficing as uniform.
  (b) This equally for women as for men.
  (c) All Communists to have the same combatant rights.
  (d) No civilian to be charged in respect of any earlier anti-German activity.

heroism. For those who have died have conquered, and those who live on will fight on, will conquer and again bear witness that Poland lives when the Poles live.

This was one of the last messages broadcast from Warsaw.

PARTISANS IN RUSSIA

Organizing a Unit

Knocking a partisan unit into shape is a complicated business. Eugene is being assisted at the Combine by his former fellow students at the Institute. For years they attended lectures together, passed examinations and went on practical work, dreamed, argued, quarrelled, made it up, danced at socials, and courted young women. They know each other so well that one would think men could not know each other better; but even then it was hellishly difficult to pick our future partisans so that each retained his individual qualities and yet merged with the rest to form a single, indivisible whole.

In the hills we shall need primarily good fighters, men skilled in the use of all the different arms: snipers, machine-gunners and artillerymen. Every one of these will be needed. Hence, the first question I put to every candidate is: "What weapon can you handle?"

The unit must not be too large. I think it would be unwise to have more than fifty or sixty men. At the same time our operations will be extremely varied. Therefore, the men must be proficient in various departments. Those who can handle only one weapon must learn to handle others, and German weapons at that, because our chief source of supplies in the hills will come from the enemy.

. . . . In the hills we shall live like Robinson Crusoes. We shall get no orders for supplies or repairs up there, no shops will be open for us, no postman will bring us the latest newspapers. But we don't want, like Robinson

Crusoe, to clothe ourselves in animals' skins and live in shacks. Hardships of that kind would certainly affect our operations. Hence, we need builders, surgeons, cooks, tailors, cobblers, hunters, truck-drivers, mechanics and radio operators. Each of our partisans must know several civilian trades. This raises new difficulties in selecting our men.

One thing is now clear, and that is that our unit will consist mainly of intellectuals. This has its good and bad sides.

Its good side is that culture is needed everywhere. Its bad side is that up to now we have all led urban lives, whereas the life of a partisan will demand the habits and knowledge of one accustomed to country life. Of what use will the partisan be if he is unable to harness oxen, cook a meal over a campfire and patch a pair of trousers? Far more useful for him to be able to mend a pair of boots than solve a problem in mathematics.

We have any numbers of builders and mechanics. Genya, I'm sure, will make quite a good truck-driver. My wife, of course, will be the surgeon. She did that sort of work even during the Civil War. Pavel Pavlovich Nadryag, an oil engineer, turns out to be a first-rate farrier and harness-maker. Nikolai Demyanovich Prichina is an ardent amateur radio operator. Yakov Ilyich Bibikov, the director of our margarine plant, seems to be quite a fair cobbler, and even Mikhail Denissovich, the director of the oil-extracting plant, is a skilful ox-driver.

P. K. Ignatov

Ambush

Genya and Pavlik were on outpost duty.

This was at night. The long hours passed very slowly.

At last the sun rose from behind the mountains, a dazzling bright orb. The mist dispersed. The birds twittered in the woods.

Suddenly a strange note was heard amidst the

twittering. It was barely audible. It was difficult to determine what it was. Perhaps the distant patter of horses' hoofs?

Genya strained his ears. No, it was the rumble of an engine, far, far away. It was impossible to say as yet whether it came from the sky over the hills or from the road to Novo-Dmitriyevskaya Stanitsa.

The rumble grew into a distinct, steady drone.

"Pavlik!" whispered Genya. "Run to Eugene and tell him that tanks are approaching the Afips."

Gripping their grenades tightly in their hands, the men waited motionless in the roadside bushes.

The clang of tank treads and the rattle of heavy machines were now distinctly heard.

Suddenly a machine-gun burst split the air. A gun barked. Evidently the Germans feared the presence of partisans and to make sure were sweeping the bushes.

As usual the first to dash past was a tank. Behind it, wrapped in a cloud of yellow dust, came a heavy truck loaded with tommy-gunners. Standing close-packed against each other, they fired senselessly and aimlessly at the bushes.

Then came other trucks loaded with ammunition, with convoys of tommy-gunners and with provisions. These proceeded calmly and confidently, as if they were at home.

How infinitely long the seconds seemed! Surely the tank must have passed the spot where the mines were placed the night before!

Unexpectedly, although they had been waiting for it every second, an explosion caused the earth to tremble. At last! The leading tank was blown up.

Fire-bottles were flying, grenades bursting, and the machine-gun rattled without interruption.

Heavy trucks dashed down the road, crushing the wounded under their wheels in a desperate effort to find a way out of this fiery circle. But there was no way out. Bursting grenades, columns of fire, and the well-aimed bullets from partisan carbines and tommy-guns met them at every turn. Suddenly a new sound was heard amidst the din of battle.

A fascist tank, riding in the rear of the column, dashed into the bushes, to the rear of the partisans. Gaining speed every moment, it crushed the young trees under its treads with the greatest ease. In another instant it would have broken through the alder grove and have crushed this handful of men. But Genya rushed out to meet the tank, into the open, at full height.

A fascist spotted him and fired a short machine-gun burst at him, but the bullets flew wide. The tank pushed its way through the wood, Genya dashed forward to meet it. A long machine-gun burst came from the tank.

Unhurriedly, as if at his exercises, Genya swung his arm, hurled an anti-tank grenade and swiftly dodged behind a tree.

The tank halted and abruptly stopped firing.

Genya emerged from behind the tree and waited.

Several seconds later the tank came to life again. The muzzles of its machine-guns turned in Genya's direction.

Pavlik sprang towards his chum like a cat and, pulling him down by the arm, fell flat with him to the ground. A stream of bullets flew over their heads.

A short, sharp whistle was heard in the wood, repeated in quick succession. It was Eugene's signal to retreat. A second fascist column had arrived and the Germans were trying to surround the partisans. But the covering party went into action. Grenades were heard bursting in the woods while our riflemen held up the German tommy-gunners. In the same instant the main attacking group leapt out of the fiery ring.

Again the partisans proceeded in single file along the wild boar tracks, forded rivers, climbed the mountains, descended into deep gorges and again crossed the winding, capricious mountain rivers and at last arrived at the camp.

P.K. Ignatov

TERROR WITHOUT END

A leaflet duplicated and distributed in Germany by a group of Munich students in 1942. The leader, Hans Scholl, and five associates, including Professor Kurt Huber, were executed for these activities early in 1943.

One cannot argue intelligently with National Socialism because it is by nature unintelligent. To speak of a National Socialist philosophy is a mistake, for if such a thing existed one would have to try to prove it or disprove it by intellectual arguments. But the reality is totally different: even when it was first germinating this movement depended on deceiving the public; even then it was rotten through and through and could only maintain itself by continual lies. Hitler himself writes in an earlier edition of "his" book (the worst-written book I have ever read, imposed as a bible on the "nation of poets and thinkers"): "You cannot believe how much you have to deceive a nation in order to govern it." If this cancer of the German people was not all too obvious at the beginning, it was because there were enough healthy energies at work to restrain it. But as it grew and grew and at last, by a final piece of knavery, came to power, the cancer burst and made foul the whole political body. Then the majority of those who had opposed it went into hiding, German intellectuals took refuge in cellars, where they gradually suffocated, mere nocturnal shadows, cut off from light and the sun. Now we are facing the end. What matters now is to find the way to each other again, to enlighten each other, to keep the thought constantly in mind and give oneself no peace till everyone is convinced of the inescapable necessity of fighting against this system. If such a wave of revolt goes through the land, if revolt is "in the air", if large numbers join us, then, by a last mighty effort, this system can be shaken off. An end with terror is better than terror without end.

It is not given to us to reach a final conclusion about the meaning of our history. But if out of this catastrophe good is to come, then only thus: by purification through suffering, by searching for the light while immersed in black darkness, by gathering one's powers and helping to shake off the yoke that oppresses the world.

We shall not deal in this leaflet with the Jewish question, nor write their justification—no, we only want to state this fact as a brief example: Since the conquest of Poland three hundred thousand Jews have been murdered in the most bestial fashion in this country. This is the most frightful crime ever committed against human dignity, a crime without parallel in all history. Jews, too, are men—whatever may be one's views on the Jewish question—and it was men on whom these crimes have been committed. Perhaps someone will say that the Jews deserved their fate—such a statement would be a piece of monstrous arrogance, but suppose someone made it—what would he say to the fact that all the youths and girls of the Polish nobility have been destroyed (though, pray God, some have escaped)? How, you ask, was this done? All males of noble family between the ages of fifteen and twenty were carried away to forced labour in concentration camps in Germany; all girls between the same ages were sent to the S.S. brothels in Norway.

Why do we tell you all this when you know it already? Or, if not this, other crimes equally terrible, committed by these horrifying sub-humans? Because it touches a question which deeply concerns us all and *must* make us all think. Why does the German people show such apathy towards all these frightful and inhuman crimes? Hardly anyone seems to trouble about them. They are accepted as facts and put aside, and the German people falls again into its dull obtuse sleep, giving these Fascist criminals the courage and the opportunity to continue their havoc—and they take it. Can this be a sign that the Germans have been blunted in their deepest human feelings, that no chord in them vibrates when they hear of such deeds, that they have sunk into a deadly sleep from which there can never, never, be an awakening? It seems so, and it certainly will be so unless the Germans awake at last from their stupor, unless they seize every opportunity to protest against this criminal gang, unless they suffer with the hundreds of thousands of victims. But it is not enough merely to sympathize. Much more is required. We must feel our share of the guilt. For it is the apathy of the Germans that enables these sinister men to act as they do; the Germans put up with this "government", which bears such an immeasurable load of guilt; yes, they are themselves to blame for allowing such a government to exist. Everyone wishes to acquit himself of this guilt and, having succeeded in doing so, sleeps calmly again with a clear conscience. But he cannot acquit himself; we are all *guilty, guilty, guilty!*

Yet it is not too late to exterminate this most perverse and monstrous of governments, and thus to avoid adding still further to our guilt. In the last few years our eyes have been opened wide, we know with whom we have to deal, and it is now high time to eradicate this brown horde. Up to the outbreak of war the greater part of the German people were blinded, the National Socialists had not yet shown themselves in their true colours, but now we see them for what they are, and it is our most urgent, our sole duty, the most sacred duty of every German, to extirpate these wild beasts.

7

THE BATTLE OF THE LIFELINES

Her occupation of the Atlantic coast of Europe from the Pyrenees to North Cape gave Germany the submarine, warship and long-range aircraft bases she needed to launch her major onslaught on the shipping which supplied Britain and later Russia with food and war materials. The coming of this attack in its full intensity was heralded in a speech by Hitler on 30 January 1941, in which he declared that, with the coming of spring, Britain would be starved into surrender. The most important and long-drawn-out battle of the war was about to be joined; a battle whose fortunes fluctuated as one side or the other adopted improved techniques, weapons, tactics and strategy, or augmented the numbers of its ships and aircraft. As the tide of war slowly turned, the Germans found themselves fighting to delay or stave off the great counter-attacks which were coming—the landing in North Africa, southern Europe and Normandy. By the autumn of 1943 the crisis was past: the U-boats had summoned up their greatest strength; in 1942 had almost succeeded in crippling the Allied war effort; had failed and been defeated. They had sunk over fourteen million tons of shipping by the end of the war, and had lost 781 of their numbers at sea and in their harbours.

U-BOAT ATTACK

"OBJECT ahead!" The Commander spotted it first. All our eyes light up with excitement. "What a stroke of luck! She's right ahead and four miles off."

By now it is exactly ten o'clock. It'll take nine hours to manoeuvre into the correct firing position, but at 5 a.m. it'll be steadily getting light, and before dawn the torpedoes must be out of their tubes. . . .

We can only make a guess at the position of the ship, for we dare not let her catch sight of us. But we can increase speed. Down goes the engineer to the engine-room—before long we're going all out, the white spray splashing over our conning-tower. Upon the bridge the watch are drenched to the skin, for nobody thinks of putting on oilskins at such times. All our blowers and compressors are screeching for all they're worth—we keep on blowing our diving tanks every five minutes, for we have to keep as high above the waterline as we can, since the higher we are the faster we go. True, the increase in our speed is only fractional, but it is an increase. We're all keyed up for the chase and the odd thing is that nobody has time to feel afraid, though we all know there'll probably be at least two guns mounted on the stern of the ship we're after, to say nothing of machine-guns and automatic weapons, for every ship that doesn't travel in convoy carries a whole armoury. One hit from any of those guns would cripple us when we came to dive, and that would mean the end. A hit on the diesel tank would be enough to finish us too, for it'd be sure to leave a long oilslick in our wake which would make us a sitting bird target for any U-boat chaser that came along.

It is 4 a.m. at last, and now instead of getting darker the opposite is happening—we can distinguish the sky from the water-line. At five sharp we must fire; it'll be our last chance.

Fifteen minutes to go, and everyone is at their post—two men are operating the range-finder—one in the conning-tower, one in the control-room. The torpedoman and petty-officer torpedoman are at the for'ard torpedo tubes and there is another torpedoman aft. All this time the Commander is leaning against the rail at one corner of the bridge, his binoculars glued to his eyes and his long fair hair and beard hiding his face. He is like a being possessed, caught in the grip of our frenzied manhunt.

"Tubes one to five—ready!" the torpedo-officer's shouting—the tubes are wet and their outer doors open. Meanwhile the engineer is reckoning the quantity of water we'll need to have in our tanks to correct the boat's trim after the torpedoes have been discharged. All five of them are ready in case we need them.

"Tubes one to four—ready for surface fire", comes through the speaking-tube from the fo'c's'le, and from aft: "Tube number five—ready for surface fire. Bridge control!" Torpedoes can be fired from several positions, from the fore and after compartments, the control-room, the conning-tower and the bridge. The order passes to the control-room and the switches are made. Dim white lamps in the conning-tower show the petty-officer at the range-finder that the order has been correctly carried out, and he reports to the torpedo-officer, who in his turn reports to the Commander.

We're still moving parallel with the enemy and slightly before his beam. The attack-sight is "on", with the target in the centre of the crosswires.

"Target Red 90, speed sixteen and a half knots, range seven thousand metres, torpedo speed thirty knots, running depth seven metres." Our torpedoes are set to run at a depth of seven metres below the surface, to pass about two metres beneath the target. A magnetic pistol fires the charge, which blows in the keel plates and causes the ship to break up.

During the first World War they had to aim with the whole boat, since after leaving the tubes the torpedoes continued on the same course as that of the U-boat, under the control of their gyroscopic automatic steering-gear.

Attacks were difficult under these conditions, particularly when destroyers and other convoy escorts had to be avoided. But in the second World War our new torpedoes could take up a course automatically up to ninety degrees away from the direction in which they were fired—the latest models even up to a hundred and eighty degrees. The chances of success were in this way considerably increased, since the boat was no longer committed to a fixed course during an attack.

The torpedo-officer at the attack-table reports "Lined-up", and the switch is made by which the attack-table is connected with the gyro-compass and the attack-sight. The mechanism churns round and two red lamps indicate that the process of calculating the information which has been fed into it is not yet completed. The lights go out after a few moments, and the petty-officer at the attack-table reports the resulting settings to the torpedo-officer. From this point onwards our own alterations of course are of little importance, being allowed for automatically. The target must simply be held in the cross-wires of the attack-sight in order that the apparatus can do its job. The torpedo-officer gives the order "Follow" to the attack-table. A lamp glows, and the attack-table is now controlling the binoculars on the bridge. Meanwhile the constantly changing firing-settings are being transmitted automatically to the torpedoes and set on their angling mechanism. With this system we can fire at any moment and on any course, provided that the ninety-degree limiting angle is not exceeded. The torpedoes will run to a pattern that spreads over roughly a ship's length by the time they reach the range of the target. We turn to our attacking course.

We can now see the enemy clearly—a British tanker of eighteen thousand tons.

We are doing twelve knots and the range is now five thousand metres. The torpedo petty-officer at the attack-table reports the settings to the torpedo-officer whenever they alter, and the Commander is listening in.

Commander to torpedo-officer: "Fire at four thousand five hundred metres. Aim at her foremast." And then: "Rate of turn, red 3."

This is the speed at which the boat swings when the rudder is put hard-a-port. Our new torpedoes, combined with careful judgment of the moment to turn, which is helped by the attack-table, allow us to turn away before firing, which not only saves time but enables us to fire at shorter ranges.

Torpedo-officer to torpedo petty-officer: "Red 3. Stand by for surface fire."

Commander to helmsmen: "Hard-a-port."

Torpedo petty-officer to bow tubes: "Stand by for surface fire."

The acknowledgement comes back: "Tubes one, three and four ready."

Commander to torpedo-officer: "Fire when ready."

Torpedo-officer: "Ready."

Torpedo petty-officer: "On—on—on." By this he indicates that the change settings are being accurately transmitted to the torpedoes as the boat swings.

The torpedo-officer at the attack-sight is holding the ship's foremast in the crosswires. . . . "Fire!" and he presses the firing-push. "Fire!" repeats the torpedo petty-officer, and the torpedo-gunner's mate at the fore tubes hears the order through the loudspeaker system; he has a hand on two of the firing levers and a leg across the third, in case of a failure of the remote-controlled firing-gear. The boat shivers three times in succession and three short heavy hissing sounds are heard—the noise of the compressed air by which the torpedoes are discharged. Firing is "staggered" at 1 1/5-second intervals to prevent mutual interference between the discharges. At the order "Fire", the Chief floods to a prescribed amount in order to compensate for the weight of the three torpedoes—for the boat must be ready for an instantaneous crash-dive if necessary. The Commander looks at his wristwatch —fifteen seconds running time yet.

Boom! "Hurrah! hit!" The Commander at the periscope is the only man who can see anything. He switches his microphone in to the general loudspeaker system: "Hit aft; stern seems to be buckled!" The magnetic pistol has worked well, it appears.

Her wireless is still working, however. An S.O.S. goes out on the six hundred metre wavelength. *German submarine*—with our position.

"Very good," remarks the chief quartermaster, "it's friendly of the English to give us an exact position. No more need to worry to-day."

She's no longer moving through the water and is giving off steam. Rudder and steering apparatus seem to be damaged. We attack again. It's easy now, for we are just over a thousand metres away. They've spotted our periscope, though, and with all their machine-guns and quick-firers let fly at us, endangering the periscope glass. We attack from the other quarter and dive under the ship at ten fathoms. The hydrophone-operator reports:

"She's right overhead!"

In a submarine attack the Commander controls the ship, gives the target information and fires the torpedoes himself. The torpedo-officer only sees that the proper settings are put on the attack-table. This time we are going to fire the stern tube, which we don't often get the chance to use.

"Range four hundred metres . . . fire!"

The roar's terrific. We've fired from much closer this time; underwater the noise is frightful. The tanker has broken in two.

Everyone has a look through the periscope. The fine ship before us is sinking into the sea. Emotion overcomes us. The daemonic madness of destruction that becomes law the moment a war breaks out has us in its grip. Under its spell as we are, what else can we do? Lifeboats and rafts are meanwhile being lowered, those aboard saving themselves as best they may. We can't help without running into grave danger, and in any case we've no room aboard—U-boats are built to allow space for the ship's

company and no more. The enemy is well equipped with
life-saving gear and these men on the tanker will certainly
soon be picked up by a warship.

Heinz Schaeffer, U-boat officer

THE VICTIMS

Merchantman

At 11.30 p.m. that night the moon had just set. I was
on the lower bridge talking to a half-English, half-
Portuguese business man, Mr. D'Aguila, and his two
sisters. We were having a nightcap before they turned
in. I remarked that if we were attacked, and I thought
it highly likely we would be, they were to make straight
for the boat which was just below the bridge on the
starboard side.

A few minutes later the D'Aguilas had just left me
and were on their way down the ladder; I was about to
go to the upper bridge to see the master and officer-of-the-
watch. A violent tremor went through *Avoceta*. She
staggered like a stumbling horse and shuddered to a
lurching stop as a violent explosion came from the
direction of the engine-room aft. My ears were buzzing
from the crash of the exploding torpedo—I had no doubt
but that that was what it was. My left arm was numb
from being flung against the side of the bridge ladder.
The vicious scream of escaping steam smothered some
of the unearthly gargling sounds coming from the
drowning and the tearing squeals of those trapped in the
scalding agony of the engine-room. All those sounds
darted into my ears during the two or three seconds before
I picked myself up and stumbled across with Signalman
Erskine to fire the distress rockets as an indication that
we had been hit. As they whizzed up I glanced aft and
saw the stern was already under water and the dreadful
noises were ceasing from that part of the ship. The escape
of steam was easing now as *Avoceta* sat back on her

haunches and the bows rose to an ever more crazy angle into the air. No boats could be lowered. There was complete pandemonium; the thunderous bangs and crashes of furniture and cargo being hurled about below decks all mingled with the ghastly shrieks of the sleeping people waking to their deaths. As the bows went higher so did the shrieks. I clung to a stanchion feeling sick and helpless as I had to look on while the children were swept out into the darkness below by the torrent of water which roared through the smoking-room.

Instinctively I must have blown up my lifebelt and I thrust my false teeth into my jacket pocket—thinking, I suppose, of other commodores who had been sunk and not been compensated for the loss of their teeth.

By then I was standing on what was normally the vertical front of the bridge . . . then, scrabbling up the deck towards the forecastle, I caught on to a ring bolt at the edge of the hole, but the water overtook me and I found myself forced below the surface by the foremast and rigging. Everything became hazy. I suppose I was drowning. I felt curiously as if I was pleasantly drunk and enveloped in cotton wool. This was displaced by a sharp pain in my chest caused by the pressure of water from being forced so deep. The only way to stop this agony was, it seemed to me, to expel the remaining air in my lungs, swallow water and become unconscious and drown as soon as possible. I was about to do this when the pain suddenly eased. I looked up and saw the stars twinkling overhead. My lifebelt and an escaping bubble of air from the *Avoceta* had pushed me to the surface. During all this time I never saw a parade of my past life which is supposed to be traditional on these occasions. The whole affair from the time the torpedo struck until I found myself floating on the surface must have been less than four minutes.

The D'Aguilas, who had been with me on the lower bridge, I heard later from Miss D'Aguila, the only member of the family to survive, had reached the bottom of the ladder when they heard the explosion. They linked arms and tried to reach the boat I had pointed out. "But before we got there," she said, "a wall of water forced us apart and I never saw my brother and sister again."

Miraculously finding myself on the surface and alive I looked round and saw a raft about the size of a small sofa with a cluster of people on it. Dazed, sick and dopey, my eyes misting and with waves splashing over me I swam towards it. It can only have been around fifty yards away but it seemed ages before I got close.

Every so often I called out to the men on the raft; a faint noise reached me in reply.

As I came alongside I cried, "Any room for another?"

I could see by the man's face that he was saying something. But only a faint unintelligible sound came through. I realized I must be deaf. Then I was hauled half on to the raft where I lay sodden, gasping and conscious now of feeling bitterly cold and quivering with a sort of ague. Dimly I saw the others on the raft and we huddled together trying to raise some kind of warmth between us. The temperature of the water, I learned afterwards, was forty-two degrees.

In the sky there was a glare from the starshell fired by the escorts trying to seek out the U-boats and find survivors. I was aware of the crump of depth charges coming from some way off. But generally everything was very hazy.

In the immediate vicinity of the raft there was complete silence; it may have seemed more so because of my deafness, but it was an awe-inspiring contrast to the cries of distress and the fearful sounds of the foundering ship a short while ago.

The master of *Avoceta* and six other men were on the raft with me. Several, their throats clogged with fuel oil, were choking and coughing. Gradually their strength ebbed, they became insensible and slipped off unnoticed in the darkness. The rest of us clung on for nearly three hours. All that time the spray and water sloshed over us as the raft rocked on the deep swell.

Sprinkled about in the darkness around us we could

see little red lights bobbing up and down. These were the lamps attached to lifebelts and operated by a battery in a watertight container. Suddenly someone noticed that they were beginning to disappear; a ship must be picking up survivors, we thought.

It seemed a long time but when we were beginning to think we had been mistaken the shape of a corvette appeared close by. At last, she drew alongside and we were hauled on board by sailors holding on to scrambling nets draped over the side.

Admiral Sir K. Creighton, Convoy Commodore

Escort

Next morning we were still sweeping in line abreast. It was a lovely clear morning, with bright sun, but bitterly cold. After "Sunday Morning Rounds" I spent an hour practising radar control of the guns, and painting the arcs of fire of each gun on the gyro-repeater compass on the upper bridge. If we were to tackle E-boats we must shift our main interest in life from asdics to guns. At midday I sent for the Engineer Officer and the First Lieutenant to protest about the state of the strokers' messdeck at "rounds" that morning. I also sent a message to the asdic officer of my own ship and to Commander Heath to say that I was not satisfied with the asdic, and would they please do something about it. As all these officers had gathered in the wardroom before lunch I unwittingly saved their lives when I brought them forward. Then the anti-submarine officer telephoned from the asdic compartment to say that he would like to shut down the set for half an hour and I agreed. I then turned to the First Lieutenant and the Engineer Officer to discuss the messdeck problem.

The sky suddenly turned to flame and the ship gave a violent shudder. Then the flame had gone, and as far as I could see everything was strangely the same. Looking ahead, I could see something floating and turning over in the water like a giant metallic whale. As I looked it rolled over farther still and I could make out our own pennant numbers painted on it. I was dumb-founded. it seemed beyond reason. I ran to the after-side of the bridge and looked over. The ship ended just aft of the engine-room—everything abaft that had gone. What I had seen ahead of us *had really been the ship's own stern*. There were small fires all over the upper deck. The First Lieutenant was down there organizing the fire parties. He saw me and called, "Will you abandon ship, sir?"

"Not bloody likely, Number One. Get those fires out, and then all the lifesaving equipment over the side and secured by boat-ropes. We'll not get out till we have to."

I went back to the compass platform.

"Signalman."

"Sir?"

"Make to *Scimitar*—'I think I've been torpedoed.' Then get down to the main deck. Yeoman, you go too—but first take all your books down to the wireless cabinet. Collect all the charts you can lay your hands on, and push them in there as well, and lock the door."

The officer of the watch was still standing by the compass. I wondered how much longer he was going to stand there.

"Must have been hit in the magazine—the stern's been blown clean off," I told him.

He leant forward to the wheelhouse voicepipe and called down: "Stop both."

"Both wizzers have been blown to glory." I could not help laughing. "Better get down to the main deck and give Number One a hand."

When he had gone I was all alone on the bridge. It was strangely quiet. I took off my sea boots and tried to blow up my inflatable lifejacket. It would not fill with air. I put my hand behind my back and found that both the rubber tube and my jacket had been cut, I supposed by some flying fragment. I had often complained that lifejackets were lying about the wheelhouse, so perhaps there would be one there now. I went down to see. But no, my recent words had taken effect. I seized a "sorbo" cushion, and tucked it into the jacket of my battle dress.

It gave me a feminine silhouette, but it could be a help if the worst was to happen. I went on to the wheelhouse deck. The ship was upright and apparently floating well. The carley-floats were by then all over the side, and secured by boat-ropes. The First Lieutenant had all the small fires out. We might save her yet.

I could hear a high windy sort of noise that I could not place. The deck began to take on an angle —suddenly—so suddenly. She was almost on her side. I was slithering, grasping all sorts of unlikely things. My world had turned through ninety degrees. I just caught sight of Harries, the navigator, going over the high side of the main deck. He had a polished wooden box in either hand, the chronometer and the sextant. I wished that I had someone to laugh with over that one. I jumped for the galley funnel which was now parallel with the water and about two feet clear, and flat-footed it to the end. I could see water pouring into the main funnel. It made a gurgling sound, like an enormous bath drain. The sea around me was covered with bobbing heads. I paused at the end of my small funnel to look at the faces. They were laughing as if this were part of some gigantic fun fair. The men called to me.

"Come on, sir. The water's lovely."

"I'm waiting for the *Skylark*," I shouted back. But the galley funnel dipped, and I was swimming too—madly. The man beside me turned to look over his shoulder. "She's going!"

I turned to look. He was right. Her bow was pointed at the sky. "Swim like hell—suction," I shouted back. We swam like hell. I turned once more, but now there were very, very few bobbing heads behind me. I swam on. The destroyer of my old group was passing through us. I could see her men at action stations. They were attacking. They were attacking the wreck of the *Warwick*! I screamed at them in my frenzy. Wherever else the U-boat might have been it could not have been there. The depth-charges sailed up into the air. Funny how they wobbled from side to side, I'd never noticed that before.

When, I wondered, would they explode? It was like being punched in the chest, not as bad as I had expected. I swam on. Things were a bit hazy. I was not as interested in going places as I had been. I could only see waves and more waves, and I wished that they would stop coming. I did not really care any more. Then I felt hands grasp my shoulders and a voice say, "Christ, it's the skipper. Give me a hand to get the bastard in," and I was dragged into a carley-float which was more than crowded to capacity.

Commander D. A. Rayner

Rescue

From the higher vantage-point of the bridge, Ericson had watched everything; he had seen the ship hit, the shower of sparks where the bomb fell, and then, a moment afterwards, the huge explosion that blew her to pieces. In the shocked silence that followed, his voice giving a routine helm-order was cool and normal: no one could have guessed the sadness and the anger that filled him, to see a whole crew of men like himself wiped out at one stroke. There was nothing to be done: the aircraft was gone, with this frightful credit, and if there were any men left alive—which was hardly conceivable—*Sorrel,* the stern escort, would do her best for them. It was so quick, it was so brutal. . . . He might have thought more about it, he might have mourned a little longer, if a second stroke had not followed swiftly; but even as he raised his binoculars to look at the convoy again, the ship they were stationed on, a hundred yards away, rocked to a sudden explosion and then, on the instant, heeled over at a desperate angle.

This time, a torpedo. . . . Ericson heard it: and even as he jumped to the voice-pipe to increase their speed and start zig-zagging, he thought: if that one came from outside the convoy, it must have missed us by a few feet. Inside the asdic-hut Lockhart heard it, and started hunting on the danger-side, without further orders: that was a routine, and even at this moment of surprise and crisis, the routine still ruled them all. Morell, on the fo'c'sle, heard it, and closed up his gun's crew again and loaded with star-shell: down in the wheel-house Tallow heard it, and gripped the wheel tighter and called out to his quartermasters: "Watch that telegraph, now!" and waited for the swift orders that might follow. Right aft, by the depth-charges, Ferraby heard it, and shivered: he glanced downwards at the black water rushing past them, and then at the stricken ship which he could see quite clearly, and he longed for some action in which he could lose himself and his fear. Deep down in the engine-room, Chief E. R. A. Watts heard it best of all: it came like a hammer-blow, hitting the ship's side a great splitting crack, and when, a few seconds afterwards, the telegraph rang for an increase of speed, his hand was on the steam-valve already. He knew what had happened, he knew what might happen next. But it was better not to think of what was going on outside: down here, encased below the water-line, they must wait, and hope, and keep their nerve.

Ericson took *Compass Rose* in a wide half-circle to starboard, away from the convoy, hunting for the U-boat down what he presumed had been the track of the torpedo; but they found nothing that looked like a contact, and presently he circled back again, towards the ship that had been hit. She had fallen out of line, like one winged bird in a flight of duck, letting the rest of the convoy go by: she was sinking fast, and already her screws were out of water and she was poised for the long plunge. The cries of men in fear came from her, and a thick smell of oil: at one moment, when they had her outlined against the moon, they could see a mass of men packed high in the towering stern, waving and shouting as they felt the ship under them begin to slide down to her grave. Ericson, trying for a cool decision in this moment of pity, was faced with dilemma: if he stopped to pick up survivors he would become a sitting target himself, and he would also lose all chance of hunting for the U-boat: if he went on with the hunt, he would, with *Sorrel* busy elsewhere, be leaving these men to their death. He decided on a compromise, a not too dangerous compromise: they would drop a boat, and leave it to collect what survivors it could while *Compass Rose* took another cast away to starboard. But it must be done quickly.

Ferraby, summoned to the quarter-deck voice-pipe, put every effort he knew into controlling his voice.

"Ferraby, sir."

"We're going to drop a boat, sub. Who's your leading hand?"

"Leading-Seaman Tonbridge, sir."

"Tell him to pick a small crew—not more than four—and row over towards the ship. Tell him to keep well clear until she goes down. They may be able to get some boats away themselves, but if not, he'll have to do the best he can. We'll come back for him when we've had another look for the submarine."

"Right, sir."

"Quick as you can, sub. I don't want to stop too long." Ferraby threw himself into the job with an energy which was a drug for all other feeling: the boat was lowered so swiftly that when *Compass Rose* drew away from it and left it to its critical errand the torpedoed ship was still afloat. But she was only just afloat, balanced between sea and sky before her last dive; and as Tonbridge took the tiller and glanced in her direction to get his bearings, there was a rending sound which carried clearly over the water, and she started to go down. Tonbridge watched, in awe and fear: he had never seen anything like this, and never had a job of this sort before, and it was an effort to meet it properly. It had been bad enough to be lowered into the darkness from *Compass Rose,* and to watch her fade away and be left alone in a small boat under the stars, with the convoy also fading and a vast unfriendly sea all round them; but now, with the torpedoed ship disappearing before their eyes, and the men shouting and crying as they splashed about in the water, and the smell of oil coming across to them thick and choking, it was more like a nightmare than anything else. Tonbridge was twenty-three years of age, a product of the London slums, conditioned by seven years' naval training; faced by this ordeal, the fact that he did not run away from it, the fact that he remained effective, was beyond all normal credit.

They did what they could: rowing about in the darkness, guided by the shouting, appalled by the choking cries of men who drowned before they could be reached, they tried their utmost to rescue and to succour. They collected fourteen men: one was dead, one was dying, eight were wounded, and the rest were shocked and prostrated to a pitiful degree. It was very nearly fifteen men: Tonbridge actually had hold of the fifteenth, who was gasping in the last stages of terror and exhaustion, but the film of oil on his naked body made him impossible to grasp, and he slipped away and sank before a rope could be got round him. When there were no more shadows on the water, and no more cries to follow, they rested on their oars, and waited; alone on the enormous black waste of the Atlantic, alone with the settling wreckage and the reek of oil; and so, presently, *Compass Rose* found them.

Ferraby, standing in the waist of the ship as the boat was hooked on, wondered what he would see when the survivors came over the side: he was not prepared for the pity and horror of their appearance. First came the ones who could climb aboard themselves—half a dozen shivering, black-faced men, dressed in the filthy oil-soaked clothes which they had snatched up when the ship was struck: one of them with his scalp streaming with blood, another nursing an arm flayed from wrist to shoulder by scalding steam. They looked about them in wonder, dazed by the swiftness of disaster, by their rescue, by the solid deck beneath their feet. Then, while they were led to the warmth of the mess-deck, a sling was rigged for the seriously wounded, and they were lifted over the side on stretchers: some silent, some moaning, some coughing up the fuel oil which was burning and poisoning their

intestines: laid side by side in the waist, they made a
carpet of pain and distress so naked in suffering that it
seemed cruel to watch them. And then, with the boat
still bumping alongside in the eerie darkness, came
Tonbridge's voice: "Go easy—there's a dead man down
here." Ferraby had never seen a dead man before, and
he had to force himself to look at this pitiful relic of the
sea—stone-cold, stiffening already, its grey head jerking
as it was bundled over the side: an old sailor,
unseamanlike and disgusting in death. He wanted to run
away, he wanted to be sick: he watched with shocked
amazement the two ratings who were carrying the corpse:
how can you bear what you are doing, he thought, how
can you touch—it . . . ? Behind him he heard Lockhart's
voice saying: "Bring the whole lot into the fo'c'sle—I
can't see anything here," and then he turned away and
busied himself with the hoisting of the boat, not looking
behind him as the procession of wrecked and brutalized
men was borne off. When the boat was inboard, and
secure, he turned back again, glad to have escaped some
part of the horror. There was nothing left now but the
acrid smell of oil, and the patches of blood and water
on the deck: nothing, he saw with a gasp of fear and
revulsion, but the dead man lying lashed against the rail,
a yard from him, rolling as the ship rolled, waiting for
daylight and burial. He turned and ran towards the stern,
pursued by terror.

In the big seamen's mess-deck, under the shaded
lamps, Lockhart was doing things he had never imagined
possible. Now and again he recalled, with a spark of
pleasure, his previous doubts: there was plenty of blood
here to faint at, but that wasn't the way things were
working out. . . . He had stitched up a gash in a man's
head, from the nose to the line of the hair—as he took
the catgut from its envelope he had thought: I wish they'd
include some directions with this stuff. He had set a
broken leg, using part of a bench as a splint. He bound
up other cuts and gashes, he did what he could for the
man with the burnt arm, who was now insensible with

pain: he watched, doing nothing with a curious hurt detachment, as a man who had drenched his intestines and perhaps his lungs with fuel oil slowly died. Some of *Compass Rose*'s crew made a ring round him, looking at him, helping him when he asked for help: the two stewards brought tea for the cold and shocked survivors, other men offered dry clothing, and Tallow, after an hour or two, came down and gave him the largest tot of rum he had ever seen. It was not too large. . . . Once, from outside, there was the sound of an explosion, and he looked up: by chance, across the smoky fo'c'sle, the bandaged rows of wounded, the other men still shivering, the twisted corpse, the whole squalid confusion of the night, he met the eye of Leading-Seaman Phillips. Involuntarily, both of them smiled, to mark a thought which could only be smiled at: if a torpedo hit them now, there would be little chance for any of them, and all this bandaging would be wasted.

Then he bent down again, and went on probing a wound for the splinter of steel which must still be there, if the scream of pain which the movement produced was anything to go by. This was a moment to think only of the essentials, and they were all here with him, and in his care.

It was nearly daylight before he finished; and he went up to the bridge to report what he had done at a slow dragging walk, completely played out. He met Ericson at the top of the ladder: they had both been working throughout the night, and the two exhausted men looked at each other in silence, unable to put any expression into their stiff drawn faces, yet somehow acknowledging each other's competence. There was blood on Lockhart's hands, and on the sleeves of his dufflecoat: in the cold light it had a curious metallic sheen, and Ericson looked at it for some time before he realized what it was.

"You must have been busy, Number One," he said quietly. "What's the score down there?"

"Two dead, sir," answered Lockhart. His voice was very hoarse, and he cleared his throat. "One more to go,

I think—he's been swimming and walking about with a badly-burned arm, and the shock is too much. Eleven others. They ought to be all right."

"Fourteen. . . . The crew was thirty-six altogether."

Lockhart shrugged. There was no answer to that one, and if there had been he could not have found it, in his present mood: the past few hours, spent watching and touching pain, seemed to have deadened all normal feeling. He looked round at the ships on their beam, just emerging as the light grew.

"How about things up here?" he asked.

"We lost another ship, over the other side of the convoy. That made three."

"More than one submarine?"

"I shouldn't think so. She probably crossed over."

"Good night's work." Lockhart still could not express more than a formal regret. "Do you want to turn in, sir? I can finish this watch."

"No—you get some sleep. I'll wait for Ferraby and Baker."

"Tonbridge did well."

"Yes. . . . So did you, Number One."

Lockhart shook his head. "It was pretty rough, most of it. I must get a little book on wounds. It's going to come in handy, if this sort of things goes on."

"There's no reason why it shouldn't," said Ericson. "No reason at all, that I can see. Three ships in three hours: probably a hundred men all told. Easy."

"Yes," said Lockhart, nodding. "A very promising start. After the war, we must ask them how they do it."

                                        Nicholas Monsarrat

How is it with the Happy Dead?

The ship lay there on the bottom of the sea, as big as the whole world; quiet as a cathedral; gently breathing from the slanting ripple of light filtering down from above, through the grey North Sea water. She lay on her side, well down by the stern, the bow riding clear of the mud, a mile long in the water.

In the first mad rush of escaping steam, explosion and weaving lane of bubbles gouting from her sides, mixed with the cries of men, weak like babies at a baby show, everything buoyant had come away, to shoot to the surface, where later the gulls whirled, crazy screeching. Other objects followed the slow sinking of the ship.

The gear which broke surface was mixed and poor pickings for the birds, mops and brooms; the bosun's chair, odd cork jackets, an unused Carley float, oars, air-tight tins of duty-free tobacco, a cap, two cans; bottles and the ship model the Leading Seaman was making for his little boy.

Sinking to be lost forever in the soft mud was another array of gear; buckets, empty shell cases, tin hats, thrown away in the last scramble for the boat, the skipper's binoculars, a pair of boots that "Bunts" was always on the point of mending, depth charges, broken from their lashings; smoke floats; rowlocks and pieces of torn rail and bridge-house. All these came down first, the ship herself followed, stern first, jerking uncertainly, as tank after tank burst or caved in, or as bulkheads carried away. Fiercely belching a wavering column of bubbles and debris, her buoyancy leaving her, the ship fought against gravity to the end, before finally accepting fate and settling quietly on the bottom.

Occasionally, as she settled still further, or as lashings parted or rotted away, various objects detached themselves and floated up to the surface. On the very first evening the body of a stoker found its way through the gash in her starboard side and drifted away, upwards and to the east with the young flood tide. On the third day the engineman and the coxswain, sworn enemies while alive, owing to a disagreement over a tot of rum, broke surface within three minutes of each other. Floating obscenely, stern uppermost, their drift overcame the light wind and they set out on a long voyage together until, the lashings of their clothes mercifully bursting, they both sank once more; soon to be two heaps of bones, white like pebbles, clean picked by the sea.

It was not long before the ex-trawler—she was one of the Footballers—lost her freshness and began to take on the colour of her new surroundings. Crabs and then small shoals of fish began to make her their home. The crabs, lumbering and sliding on the metal plates, like miniature tanks, found much food. The fish, suspended in tiny clouds, fed in the shadow of the cocked up bow; then, at a flick, darted off to reappear somewhere else. Eels came also, twining in and out of the rusting frames, and small green jellied growths appeared; to grow and spread and trail in the current.

The white ensign still floated at the stern. It was badly burnt, pierced by splinters, torn and discoloured, but the east-going current stirred it gently, so that it flapped against the staff. A depth charge, ready lashed in the Y thrower, looked as if it would overbalance, as it sprouted from the deck. The mizzen mast and its boom had altogether disappeared.

The galley door hung open. Inside, ashes from the fire, trapped in the roof, formed a thick scum up against the cork-flecked paint. The cook, suspended by his rubber lifebelt, floated up there, face downwards. He had gone back from the boat to get a joint of beef and some tinned apples, then, coming out, he slipped on the potatoes, broken from their bin and rolling on the deck—a ludicrous mishap, like a comic film. The last explosion from the boiler lifted the red-hot galley stove on top of him and there he lay—jammed; watching his skin blister and break and wishing the ship would soon go down so as to put the fire out. However, it was not until she listed on the bottom that the stove rolled off him and his body was released to rise majestically to the jobble of scum, like a stage fairy suspended on a wire.

He had never planned on going out like this. He was Hostilities Only, and in peace-time he and his wife ran a little boarding-house at a coast resort. He was disappointed when he realized that he was going to die lying beneath his own galley stove. However, when the sea did froth in over the coaming, the pain of the salt was so great that he fainted and never regained consciousness.

Above the engine-room casing the davits hung empty; the falls trailing, the first of the many ropy growths that would later spread and weave in the current, clinging to the hull as the ship settled lower and lower and fell away into little piles of rust and scrap.

The remains of the smoke-stack hung at a giddy angle, the stays parted and nothing supporting it. The whistle, somehow adrift from its fastenings, stood upright on its steam pipe, the lanyard now only the remains of a seized eye-slice. Most of the bridge and the skipper's cabin had disappeared. The first bomb had done that, shearing the steel like butter with a knife. Now there were only the queerly shaped jags of stanchions, twisted frames and the black charred or white splintered edges of the deck planking.

The starboard bridge wing remained and the gunner hung suspended in his harness, feet clear of the sloping deck, both ankles broken from the upward heaving explosion. His hair, escaping from the cap and the navy-blue chinstrap, floated out in the water like a fern. The barrels of the twin Lewis pointed up, rainbow-coloured with grease. Small fish fed on the ropy clots which trailed from his finger-tips.

In the well deck, the false hatch had carried away when the engine-room bulkhead blew in; little pieces of cork lining, straw, and charred wood floated up, eddying as they met the cross-current at the hatchway.

Below all was chaos.

Caught in the airlock on the starboard side, five unlashed sea-chests chafed their corners. A kapok mattress slimy with scum and trailing a blanket as a winding sheet remained pressed hard up against the pipe cot of an upper berth. His head jammed in a locker, a seaman knelt as if in prayer, his wide trousers gently

weaving with the current. One foot was bare, the other
covered in a soiled rubber gym shoe. He had gone back
to look for the bottle of rum he had saved up, and when
the boiler exploded it broke his neck.

Farther forward, the dart-board in the wardroom
showed a double twenty and a nine, the steel points
already corroding and the feathers spiked with the wet.
In the corner a pile of broken glasses glinted in the grey-
green light, not yet entirely silted over. On the settee,
under a cushion, lay the body of a ship's cat. She had
gone there when the alarm gong had sounded and a
chance splinter, ricochetting off the companion way,
entered her head—an unlucky chance.

On deck, the mainmast had gone by the board, the
steel shrouds and rigging screws trailing, an unbelievable
tangle of wire, over the port bow.

Forward, over the "whale-back", the "bandstand",
shorn of its rails and iron ladder, remained intact. The
gun, half-torn from its mounting, leaning at a giddy angle.
Only one of the gun's crew remained. The second bomb,
bursting just forward of the bow, had torn the remainder
into queer and unanatomical shapes as they struggled to
get elevation on a weapon not designed to beat off the
attacks of aircraft.

The remaining gunner was the layer. The blast had
removed most of his clothing and some of his flesh, the
rest was stained a bluey-purple. The lifted gun mounting
trapped the lower part of his body, pressing him down
against the gun platform.

When they went for the boats they had thought he was
along with the rest, but he awoke in time to feel her go
down. Through a red curtain of mist he felt himself lifted
up, like a swing at a fair, while the stern settled, then
he watched the seethe of the advancing water. "I'll never
see the Argyle Bar again," he thought. "No more Saturday
nights, no more wallop either."

He was lying on his stomach, with no feeling at all
below his thighs. His arms, stretched straight out to left
and right, were pinned that way by the shoulder pad of

the gun which lay across his back. He could, however, move his head from side to side, scraping his chin over the criss-cross pattern of the steel gun platform. He could move each arm from the elbow too, but because he was unable to raise his neck easily he could not see clearly outside the ship—everything was concentrated into a little circle close to his eyes. On the left hand third finger was the ring she had given him, and between the first finger and the thumb was the L-shaped white scar from a broken bottle gained in a scrap when he and Pincher Martin had beaten up the Thistle Bar and got thirty days No. 11 apiece. This scar hardly showed now, through the black grease which the handling of the gun had polished to a dull black-lead finish.

He turned his head painfully to look at his right hand.

The first joint of the little finger was missing—that was Bear Island, when he was deckie on the *Floral Queen*, trawling. The thumb-nail was blackened at the base from the crack he had caught it at target practice. Practice that wasn't at all like the rush and tumble of the real action, which had been over almost before it had started. A whining roar, the alarm gong, two bombs—one a direct, the other a near miss and that was all.

Tattooed on the back of his hand, blue and red against the scorched hair, was a swallow design with "Mother" written on the scroll. On his forearm, three inches above the wrist, was a heart and arrow design and on the scroll was "G" and "M"—George and Maggie. He wouldn't see her again—or the kids either. He felt very sleepy—he would sleep and he would see no one ever again. Yet he wasn't afraid, why worry? Trawling all your life and then the war—always so near to death—seeing your mates lost overboard or smashed—always so near to death. Afraid? Why worry about a thing you've known of for so long. Still, perhaps it was a pity. No more beer, no more nights out with the boys—nothing ever any more. He felt so sleepy that it wasn't very difficult when the water did reach him.

The ship kicked hard under him, fighting. Then the

bows shot up and he felt giddy with lying head down and
the rush of her as she settled. The boiling waves rushed
at him, brown with scum. He wondered how cold the
water would be, how deep beneath him, how long——

It reached him, snapping at his face, jumping, exultant.
As he went down, the water darkening, he gave one frothy
gulp and saw the spreading purple cloud go spiralling
up to the surface above him.

Eric Joysmith

BATTLE OFF THE BEACHES

*The U-boats scored some of their greatest successes in
the six months after the United States entered the war,
descending on the American seaboard and slaughtering
shipping which was for some time unprotected by convoys or by adequate escorts.*

December 1941

Should enemy submarines operate off this coast, this
command has no forces available to take adequate action
against them, either offensive or defensive.

Admiral Andrews, commanding
U.S. Eastern Seaboard Defences

We have issued a special communiqué to the effect that
German submarines have succeeded in sinking 125,000
tons of enemy shipping off the American Atlantic coast.
This is an exceedingly good piece of news for the German
people. It bears testimony to the tremendous activity of
our submarines and their widely extended radius of action,
as well as to the fact that German heroism conquers even
the widest oceans. At last a special bulletin! We certainly
needed it, and it acts like rain on parched land. Everybody
regards the communiqué as a very effective answer to
the warmonger Roosevelt, whom the whole German

people curse. Many people are in a quandary whether
to hate him or Churchill more.

Dr. Goebbels, 25 January 1942

On 6 February the cumbersome title North Atlantic
Naval Coastal Frontier was officially established as the
Eastern Sea Frontier, and the command itself was
lengthened southward to Jacksonville, Florida, where it
hooked into the newly made Gulf Sea Frontier. Andrews
was now known as C.E.S.F.—Commander, Eastern Sea
Frontier.

But change of name and additional areas to defend
brought no appreciable new permanent forces to use
against Doenitz, although Britain was sending over
twenty-four anti-sub trawlers. A full two months after
war had begun, Nazi U-boats could roam and strike at
will.

Andrews' letter of 7 February to C.N.O. was
indicative: "The Eastern Sea Frontier has no long-range
planes available for offshore work. Newport (Rhode
Island) has one single-engined plane capable of carrying
one bomb; the Fourth Naval District (Philadelphia
headquarters) has no planes capable of attacking a sub.
New York has a single squadron available for inshore
patrol."

March: The Score Mounts

It was no longer two or two and a half ships a day for
the Nazis. U-boats were driving their average up to three
every twenty-four hours. The Eastern Sea Frontier had
the dubious international Allied distinction of being "the
most dangerous sea area in the world".

The Climax

All the German boats operating in the Atlantic,
Caribbean and Gulf of Mexico had impressive records

for June. Forty-eight ships were lost in the Caribbean and its approaches; twenty-one ships in the Gulf; thirteen in the Eastern Sea Frontier; fourteen in the Bermuda area; and another fourteen along North Atlantic convoy routes.

Sinkings were heavy in all areas, but Doenitz seemed most pleased with his boats in the western seas. At a press conference late in the month, he said with obvious pride, "Our submarines are operating close inshore along the coast of the United States, so that bathers and sometimes entire coastal cities are witnesses of that drama of war whose visual climaxes are constituted by the red glorioles of blazing tankers."

There was fire on the beaches. The German submarine admiral was at the height of his career.

AID FOR RUSSIA: THE ARCTIC CONVOYS

P.Q. 16: Summer 1942

Whit Monday, 25 May

I don't know when exactly the little bastard joined us, but he's been circling round and round the convoy all day. He is keeping well outside the range of the guns on the destroyers, and sometimes he disappears, but before long he, or his relay, turns up again. He's a Focke-Wulf, and the crew, who are irritated by his presence, refer to him as "George". At five this morning the first alarm went, and I dressed in under three minutes, but nothing happened. Then, at dinnertime, the alarm bell rang again, and the destroyer fired several rounds at our German "escort", but he was out of range, and for the rest of the afternoon he gave us no more trouble, except by being *there*. The crew looked longingly at the catapult Hurricane on the *Empire Lawrence,* but apparently it was decided not to waste the Hurricane on chasing George, especially as there was much cloud, and he would probably have escaped had the Hurricane been sent after him. At half-past six the alarm went again—and this time it was the real stuff.

They appeared in the distance, on the starboard side, low above the water: three—four—five, then three more, then four or five after that, farther to the right. We were all on deck—the R.A.F. boys, with their tin hats, and the deckhands, the cabin boys—and we counted and watched. Eleven, twelve, thirteen. . . . Something was already happening ahead of us. The gunners had rushed up to the gun-turrets. The two cruisers which had suddenly joined us earlier in the day, and the destroyers on the edge of the convoy were firing like mad. It was a beautiful bright day, the sea calm and blue like the Mediterranean, and the sky was now dotted with specks of smoke from the flak shells. They went in a half-circle round the front of the convoy, then, after a few seconds of suspense, they came right out in the sun. They swooped over us, two or three in succession, and from their yellow bellies the yellow eggs dropped, slowly, obscenely. They were after the cruisers, in the middle of the convoy. The tracer-bullets from our Oerlikons were rushing at the yellow belly of the Junkers as he swooped over us. A loud squeal, growing louder and louder, and then the explosion, as a stick of bombs landed between us and the destroyer, on the port side. Three pillars of water went high up in the air, and the ship shook. As he dived, almost to the water-level, our tracer-bullets followed him, but he got out of their way, and on the bridge Captain Dykes, wearing a wide navy-blue beret, was waving and shouting frantically: "Don't fire so low! You're hitting the next ship!" Then after a few minutes they came again, out of the sun—three of them. This time they seemed to make a dead set at the cruisers. On the upper deck, on the fo'c'sle, the Flight Lieutenant was looking on, his long hair waving in the wind. He had his life-jacket on, with a drawing of naked "Loulou". The R.A.F. boys and I, and ginger-haired Harry with the blackheads, stood amidships, watching the battle. Suddenly something happened. The cruiser, which had put out a very impressive barrage, had got one. He began to reel and swoop down, on our port side, then he staggered over us. It was like a football match. Harry and the R.A.F. boys were shouting: "He's on fire! He's on fire! That's it! He's down!" Harry jumped about with joy, frantically. He *was* down. Something brown and large and soft detached itself from the plane, and the plane itself slid into the water without much of a splash. The barrage was still going full blast, but a destroyer sailed up to the brown parachute or whatever it was, and proceeded to pick them up. Meantime the catapult Hurricane on the *Empire Lawrence* had leaped swiftly into the air, in pursuit of the dive-bombers. Swiftly it went in a wide circle round the convoy, ready to pounce on one of them; but here something unfortunate happened; one of the American cargoes, no doubt mistaking the Hurricane for a German plane, fired what gun or machine-gun it had at him, and the next thing we saw was the pilot bailing out by parachute, with nothing to show for his exploit, and with the Hurricane nothing to show for its £5,000.

Wednesday, 27 May

I am not likely ever to forget this day, and yet its exact sequence is hard to restore to one's mind, and what I remember, above all, is moments. I had had a good sleep; we had not been disturbed by anything all night, and one of the moments I remember is sitting on deck after breakfast, reading *Our Mutual Friend,* and feeling wonderfully contented. Life on the *Empire Baffin* seemed to have returned to normal. Pushkov was again giving his Russian lesson to the R.A.F. boys in the smoke-room, and, after yesterday's feeble attempts, the Luftwaffe was clearly not as terrifying as people were apt to imagine. But then, at half-past ten the alarm bell went. From the gun-turret somebody shouted: "Here they come!" Again people rushed on deck—counting: three—three more, that's six—ten—twelve—fifteen. Now they came from all directions. Gun flashes and clouds of smoke came from the destroyers; then the barrage of the flak ship and the

convoy ships went up; like a vulture pouncing on its prey, a dive-bomber swept down on to the submarine, right down to the water-level, but she crash-dived and the three pillars of water went high up in the air. For forty long minutes they attacked, usually in twos and threes, usually coming straight out of the sun, some diving low, others dropping their bombs from two hundred feet. From their yellow shark-like bellies, one could see the obscene yellow eggs dropping, and after a moment of suspense, one saw with relief the pillars of water leaping up. They were concentrating in that first attack on the forward part of the convoy, and we were, apparently, reserved for later. And then we saw the first casualty. The pale-blue and pale-green destroyer was smoking furiously, and signalling, signalling, signalling. What were those flashes saying? Was it the destroyer that had picked up those Huns on Monday? Somebody on board said, "They are all right. They are not going to abandon her." That didn't seem so bad. She was still smoking, but they seemed to have got the fire under control. Soon they put it out. The planes disappeared; the attack was over. That wasn't so bad, people said; and then we realized that it *was* bad. Not very far away from us was a Russian ship—I had realized for the first time that we had two or three Russian ships in the convoy—and her foredeck was enveloped in clouds of smoke, and flames were bursting out of the hold. "They're going to abandon her," somebody said. Were they? Yes, they were lowering their lifeboats. But no. She was still keeping up steam, still keeping up with the other boats, but the clouds of smoke rising from her were growing larger and larger, her whole fo'c'sle was in a cloud of black smoke—but still she went on, and through the cloud of smoke one saw dim shapes of people running and doing something. I saw Alfred Adolphus rushing past me; he was streaming with sweat, and there was a look of panic in his yellowish eyes. "Hullo, Alfred Adolphus!" I said. "I think I'll go mad! I think I'll go mad!" he cried.

So the destroyer had been hit, and the Russian ship had been hit, and were fighting with the flames. And somebody said two more ships had been hit.

They came again in less than an hour. This was a short, sharp attack. They concentrated on the other end of the convoy. They dropped their bombs and disappeared. As we sailed on I saw a ship that had stayed behind, with a corvette by her side, blazing furiously. We were already a mile or two from her. And somebody said that another ship had received a direct hit, and had blown up.

Then there was a lull. Dinner was served punctually at noon; Cook wasn't a minute late. Everybody was there, as usual, the lanky first mate, and the young second mate, and the long skinny engineer's mate, with the fuzzy hair and the Hapsburg jaw, and our Flight Lieutenant and the R.A.F. boys. Everybody gulped tea, but appetites were at a low level and few words were exchanged. In their frames, the King and Queen were very calm. Like most of them I drank a lot of tea, but the food seemed to stick to my palate. Pushkov, with a wan smile, said the lesson could, he hoped, be resumed to-morrow. I went out on deck. The Russian ship was still enveloped in smoke though perhaps a little less than before. They had not abandoned ship. I saw Alfred Adolphus sauntering along the deck, now wearing his bright-blue suit with the red stripes and a new light-grey felt hat. "I'm through with it," he said defiantly. "I have refused to go down to the engine-room." "Why did you dress up like this?" "I want to save my clothes if we are torpedoed," he said. He was much calmer than in the morning. "It wouldn't matter," he suddenly cried, "but it's the *cargo*, the *cargo*!" With this remark, he slunk away. So that's what it is, I said to myself—T.N.T.? I had already heard somebody refer to it, but had taken no notice. The burning ship in the distance had now disappeared. Then the alarm bell went again. I forget what exactly happened at the beginning of that third attack, but this time they concentrated on our end of the convoy. The obscene yellow bellies were over us, and they dropped their eggs all round us. The

bearded bank clerk with the Oxford accent was on one of
the Oerlikons, and the man with the beret and the Soviet
badge on another, and Steward was working a machine-
gun, and the Flight Lieutenant, his hair waving in the wind,
was, I think, on an Oerlikon, and aft, the little R.A.F.
sergeant was on one of the two Lewis guns. And then
something happened which I shall never forget. I was
standing amidships with the R.A.F. boys and Pushkov
and several others, and we realized that something had
happened to our sister ship, the *Empire Lawrence,* now
without her Hurricane on board. She was no longer
steering a straight course. Her bows were pointing towards
us—was she moving at all? She was showing a slight list.
. . . And we realized that she was being abandoned.
Already two of her lifeboats were bobbing on the water,
and beside her was a little corvette, taking more men off.
As we watched her, we heard all our guns fire like mad.
Then one of the yellow-bellies swept over us with roaring
engines, almost touching our topmast, and . . . they made
a dead set at the helpless, dying ship. And suddenly from
the yellow belly the five bombs detached themselves and
went right into her. I don't think there was even a moment
of suspense; there was an explosion that did not sound
very loud, and a flash which, in the sun, was not very
bright, and like a vomiting volcano a huge pillar of smoke
and wreckage shot two hundred feet into the air—and
then, slowly, terribly slowly, it went down to the sea. The
Empire Lawrence was gone.

Alexander Werth

When daylight came on the fourth day there was, for
the first time, no escorting aircraft. It made the men in
the ships feel lonely not to see the familiar shape of the
Catalina flying-boat that had been with them on the
previous day. It was as though that last link with home
had been cut, and they were alone on the dark and dreary
Arctic Ocean. The cold was hardening now, closing on
them with steely fingers, feeling for the blood in their
veins; it took the wind for an ally and came shrieking

down from the North Pole, from the regions of eternal ice. Snow came with it too, and the ships became pale ghosts, moving on under the iron dome of the sky into a world of death and darkness, moving on towards the rim of the ice.

Daylight came late, a weak shadow of its southern self, and stayed only an hour or two. The sun, barely peeping above the grey horizon, rolled for a brief while upon the lip of the ocean and then sank to rest. It had no power to warm the men on watch, and they could observe it with undazzled eyes, observe it appear and disappear, like a new penny thrust up through the slot of a moneybox, only to be withdrawn again.

At night the Aurora Borealis flickered across the sky, its streamers twisting like cold flames, changing colour, growing and fading, casting an eerie glow over the vessels of the convoy and holding all who watched them spellbound by their wonder. It was as though a great luminous hand had been thrust up over the northern horizon, its fingers groping across the heavens; at any moment it seemed those fingers might fall upon the convoy and force it down into the bottomless depths of the sea.

Then came the moon, hanging like a child's plaything amid the drifting stars, and washing the ships with silver.

Vernon, for the first time in his life, was wearing long woollen underpants; the gunners called them John L. Sullivans. He was glad to wear them, glad to wear a thick vest, a flannel shirt, two pullovers, battle-blouse, lambswool jerkin, army greatcoat, and dufflecoat; glad to wear two woollen Balaclava helmets under the hood of his coat, two pairs of trousers, and thick sea-boot stockings and leather sea-boots. Even so, dressed like a walking clothes-store, even so, the wind came through; even so, the cold crept up from the feet, up and up as the dead hours of the night watches dragged slowly past.

And still it grew colder.

On the fifth day the enemy found them. A Dornier 24 flying-boat came up over the southern horizon and, keeping just beyond gunfire range, proceeded to circle the convoy. Round and round, hour after hour, it flew; and the gunners, standing at action stations, watched it with angry eyes and cursed their impotence.

"If only we had a carrier!" moaned Padgett. "Even a Woolworth would do. If only we had a carrier!"

But there was no aircraft carrier with the convoy, not even one of those converted merchant ships known irreverently as "Woolworths". There was nothing—nothing but the outranged guns—and they were powerless to touch the German plane, flying so leisurely in wide circles and signalling to its submarine allies, signalling all the time.

When night fell they lost the Dornier, and in the night they altered course, trying to throw their pursuers off the scent. But when day came the Dornier found them again, and an hour later it was joined by six friends. Heinkel torpedo bombers. Then the alarm was really on; then the ships really awoke; then the air suddenly became full of glowing tracer and bursting steel, and the crackle, bark, and boom of the guns flung noise towards the sky as though to burst open that great steel door and drive on to the freedom of eternity.

Vernon sat on one side of the Bofors gun, watching through his sight a Heinkel coming in low across the line of ships. Andrews was in the other seat, and Miller was on the platform, loading. Vernon could see the Heinkel crawling along the wire on his gun-sight, and he waited for Sergeant Willis to give the order to fire. It was a sitter: it was not doing more than a hundred knots. Surely it was in range? Why did not Willis give the order? What was he waiting for? Was he waiting to see the colour of the pilot's eyes? Now, now, now!

"Fire!" yelled Willis in Vernon's ear.

Vernon pressed his foot on the firing pedal, and the gun began to rock on its pedestal, flinging out shells at the rate of two a second. It was a harsh, staccato song that the gun sang, but it was sweet music to the men on the platform.

Vernon could see the tracers curving away towards the

Heinkel, and he could see that they were missing;
Andrews was giving too much aim-off; you did not want
so much with a plane coming in at that angle.

"Left, you idiot! Left!" he yelled; but he knew that he
was wasting his breath, for the voice of the gun beat his
voice aside and no one heard him. But Andrews was
bringing the gun over, bringing it on to the correct line;
the tracers were creeping nearer to their target.

Now, thought Vernon, now we've got the bastard.

And then the gun jammed, and Willis was swearing
at Miller. "You bloody, misbegotten fool! Don't you know
how to load yet?"

Miller was struggling to free the shells in the auto-
loader, but Willis thrust him aside.

"Gimme the unloading mask," he yelled. "You there,
Payne! Don't stand gaping; gimme that mask. Hell! You'd
think there was all day!"

But the action was over. Two Heinkels were in the
sea, and the others were away, heading for base. And
one ship lay crippled on the water, with a black column
of smoke joining it to the grey ceiling of cloud.

James Pattinson

U-BOAT ATTACKED

It was a fine spring day without a cloud in the sky,
and we could clearly see the Rock, that British fortress
commanding the Mediterranean. So here were the pillars
of Hercules, the Jebel Tarik, fresh from playing one more
fateful role in history. Under its protection the invasion
fleet had mustered and the African landings been carried
out—since when the African campaign was drawing to
its end and they were preparing to invade Italy.

Finally, the culmination of our monotonous waiting,
we sighted great plumes of smoke and innumerable
mastheads. But almost immediately planes appeared and
we were obliged to dive. Had they spotted us? If so,
warships would be on our trail within an hour. It was

a fine day, but not too good for us, for the sea was glassily calm, perfect for their asdic. A report came from the hydrophone operator:

"Propellers at high speed. Probably destroyers. Trying to pick us up on their asdics."

"Dive to seventy-five fathoms. Silent speed."

We were all ready, with our felt shoes on and all but the most essential lighting shut off to save current, as we had no idea how long the hunt would last. The enemy were in triangular formation, with us in the middle, and I must say they worked superbly. We had never known the first charges to fall with such uncomfortable accuracy as these did, invariably six at a time. All the glass panels on our controls were shattered and the deck was strewn with splinters. Valve after valve loosened, and before long the water came trickling through. The attack went on unremittingly for three hours without a break, the charges falling thicker and thicker around us, cruising as we were now at a depth of a hundred fathoms. With the need to save current we were working the hydroplane and steering-gear by hand, and meanwhile the hydrophone was picking up more destroyers, though only the men within earshot knew it. What was the point of upsetting the others?

Faces are pale, and every forehead's sweating. We all know what the other man's thinking. There are six destroyers now, three of them heading for Gibraltar, but fresh ones always coming up in relay. Like this they'll never run out of depth-charges—our position's truly desperate, the fine weather dead against us. Why doesn't a storm blow up, as it always did when we were on our way here?

By the time we have had sixteen hours of it we have long given up counting the depth-charges. During this time no one's had any sleep, and we've all dark rings under our eyes. Plenty of bulbs have broken, but we don't change them—with the emergency lighting we can only guess the position of the various installations. The darkness makes it all the more frightening.

There've been tricky moments before, but this time it's just hell. At times we have to dive to 125 fathoms. The steel bulkhead supports are buckling and may give at any moment. But perhaps just because of this we're calm.

"Well, it's not everyone who gets such an expensive coffin," a dry voice remarks. "Four million marks it cost."

Yes, when it happens it'll be quick enough.

If only we could defend ourselves, see something to shoot at—the sense of being trapped into inactivity is unbearable. The current is down to danger level, the compressed air cylinders almost empty and the air itself tastes leaden. Our oxygen is scarce, our carbon monoxide content continually increasing, so that we're breathing with difficulty like so many marathon runners in the last mile; at this rate we can last out twenty hours longer and then we'll just have to surface. We know what will happen then, we've read the dispatches: as soon as the U-boat surfaces all the warships open fire, and the bombardment goes on even though the crew have begun to jump overboard—they must be made to lose their nerve and forget to sink their boat. It was one of the enemy's dearest wishes to capture a U-boat, as that would have made it so much easier to devise means of countering the German underwater threat.

"Stand by for depth-charge attack!" They are falling right alongside now. A roar and a crash in the control-room enough to crack our eardrums—fragments of iron fly around—valves smash to bits. In spite of oneself one can't help stretching a hand out towards one's escape-gear. The petty officer in the control-room has his hand on the flood valve to let in compressed air for surfacing, but he's still awaiting the Commander's orders, and all the time they are still thundering at us. The helmsman shouts that the compass has been blown out of its frame—with its ten thousand revolutions a minute the gyro-wheel goes spinning round the boat, but luckily none of us is hit.

In a council of war with the officers, the Commander admitted the situation was pretty hopeless; it might even be that we should have to surface and sink the boat. On the other hand the moon would not rise until two in the morning and it would be dark till then—if we surfaced in the dark, there was still just a hundred-to-one chance we might break out of the trap that way. Meanwhile everything was ready to blow up the boat. Time fuses were laid against the torpedo warheads and in other vulnerable places all over the ship, so that if one didn't explode there was every chance that another would. In no circumstances must we fall into enemy hands and as a result be responsible for the deaths of many fellow U-boat men. Next we distributed escape-gear and lifeboats—a one-man collapsible rubber dinghy per head. The Commander and bridge-watch put on red glasses to accustom their eyes to the dark so that they should be able to see the moment that we surfaced—I couldn't help thinking this superfluous, for inside the boat it was as good as pitch dark anyway. Next the asdic decoys were thrown out, and we began to fill balloons with metal strips attached which were to be released when we surfaced to float low over the water and fox the enemy radar.

As we prepared to surface at fifty fathoms we caught the sound of asdics even more distinctly. Damn it, they'd still got us! As we shot up to twenty-five fathoms we could hear loud explosions. The hydrophone operator announced.

"Destroyers at close quarters. Six different propellers turning."

Swearing, the Commander gave the order to surface. By now we couldn't make full speed as the batteries weren't up to it. We brought up ammunition for the A.A. guns, large magazines with fifty rounds in each. Five torpedo-tubes could fire simultaneously, and so could four machine-guns. The belts of these latter did not give out as they do on machine-guns ashore, but, stretching right down the conning-tower into the control-room, were constantly replenished so as to fire between them six thousand four hundred rounds a minute. We could turn them on like hoses. Up to two thousand metres we could menace a destroyer and outside two thousand metres the destroyer couldn't spot us. Yet we knew that if it did come to an engagement we would certainly get the worst of it. We just hoped that we would not have to open fire and might get away unnoticed.

We drove to the surface as depth-charges were still dropping around us. The asdic decoys were obviously fulfilling their purpose. All of a sudden the conning-tower hatch burst open and we almost shot out of it. The pressure was terrific. The Commander looked out to port and I to starboard. Thank heaven it was a dark night and the sky was overcast. We made out three destroyers, one five hundred metres away at most, still dropping depth-charges. We started up both diesel engines and rang down full speed at once—no time to let them warm up. The generators were going too, as we had to recharge our batteries, besides the two compressors recharging the compressed-air cylinders. The fans began to drive fresh air through the boat. The fresh air tore into our lungs; we could hardly stand up and were practically fainting. Guns and machine-guns were loaded and trained on the nearest destroyer, but we all hoped it wouldn't sight us for both our sakes. We had a new type of torpedo that could zig-zag or make circular tracks, but we weren't starting anything. Had we done so we couldn't have got away unmolested, since we lacked a good supply of two essentials: current and compressed air. The range started to increase and the ten gas-filled balloons we had released went up and drifted with the wind. The enemy radar would be amazed to pick up so many U-boats all at once. He presumably suspected the presence of still more where the asdic decoys were in action. . . .

At last we lost sight of the destroyer. The enemy radar was confused by all the echoes, and even if the destroyers did pick us out in the dark they could not go all out after us for fear of ramming other British ships.

After an hour we had taken in fresh air enough to cruise underwater for sixteen hours, and in two hours we were all fit for duty again, though terribly exhausted.

We dived to fifty fathoms and left Gibraltar as far away and as fast as we could. I thought of the proverb, "When an ass steps on thin ice he generally falls through." Our ice had certainly been thin enough.

Heinz Schaeffer

COASTAL COMMAND

Ballad of Jack Overdue

1941

Come back, come back, Jolly Jack Straw,
  There's ice in the killer sea.
Weather at base closes down for the night:
  And the ash-blonde Waaf is waiting tea.

How many long Atlantic hours
  Has he hunted there alone:
Has he trimly weaved on the silent air
  The dullest patrol that's ever flown?

How can they know he found at last
  That he made a hunter's strike:
And swooped on a sly swift shark as it dived:
  Saw gouting oil mount carpet-like?

Jolly Jack Straw is beating it back,
  But his wireless set is blown.
He cannot report his long-sought luck,
  Or the ice-dark blinding the eye and bone.

Come back, come back, Jolly Jack Straw,
  For the ash-blonde Waaf drinks tea;
And the tea leaves tell her fortune as well.
  Come back, come back from the killer sea.

John Pudney

KEY TO THE SOURCES OF EXTRACTS

For an explanation of how to use this Key and the following section entitled *Sources*, see page xvi.

SOURCES

The Editors wish to express their gratitude to all the publishers, authors, literary agents and others who so kindly granted permission for the reproduction of the extracts in this anthology.

1. *American Treasury, 1455-1955, The,* by Clifton Fadiman. Harper, 1955.
2. *And Some Fell by the Wayside,* by A. R. Tainsh. Longmans, Green, 1948.
3. *Ball of Fire: The Fifth Indian Division in the Second World War,* by Antony Brett-James. Gale & Polden, 1951.
4. *Before the Dawn,* by Brigadier Sir John Smyth. Cassell, 1957.
5. *Black Watch and the King's Enemies, The,* by Bernard Fergusson. Collins; Crowell, 1950.
6. *Bomber Offensive,* by Marshal of the Royal Air Force Sir Arthur Harris. Collins: Macmillan, 1947.
7. *Collected Poems,* by Norman Cameron, Hogarth Press, 1957.
8. *Convoy Commodore,* by Admiral Sir K. Creighton. Kimber, 1956.
9. *Courage and Fear,* by Remy. Arthur Barker, 1950.
10. *Cretan Runner, The,* by George Psychoundakis. Murray; Transatalantic, 1955.
11. *Crisis in the Desert, May-July, 1942,* by J.A.I. Agar-Hamilton and L.C.F. Turner. Oxford, 1952.
12. *Cruel Sea, The,* by Nicholas Monsarrat. Cassel; Knopf, 1951.
13. *Defeat in the West,* by Milton Schulman. Secker & Warburg, 1947; Dutton, 1948.
14. *Defeat Into Victory,* by Field-Marshal Sir William Slim. Cassell, 1957.
15. *Diary of a Young Girl, The,* by Anne Frank. Vallentine, Mitchell; Doubleday, 1952.

16. *Eastern Approaches (Escape to Adventure)*, by Fitzroy MacLean. Cape, 1949; Little, Brown, 1950.
17. *Escort*, by Commander D. A. Rayner. Kimber, 1955.
18. *Fatal Decisions, The*, by Werner Kreipe and others, edited by Seymour Freidein and William Richardson. Joseph; Sloane, 1956.
19. *Fire on the Beaches*, by Theodore Taylor. Norton, copyright 1958 by Theodore Taylor.
20. *Galleghan's Greyhounds*, by A. W. Penfold, W. C. Bayliss, and K. E. Crispin, 2/30 Battalion Australian Imperial Forces Association, 1949.
21. *Goebbels Diaries, The*, by Louis P. Lochner, Doublèday, 1948.
22. *Happy Hunted, The*, by Brigadier George Clifton. Cassell, 1952.
23. *Hausfrau at War*, by Else Wendel. Odhams, 1957.
24. *Heavens Are Not Too High, The*, by Charles MacLean. Kimber, 1957.
25. *Hide and Seek*, by Xan Fielding. Secker & Warburg, 1954.
26. *History of the Northumberland Hussars Yeomanry, 1924-1949*, by Joan Bright. Mawson, Swan & Morgan, 1949.
27. *How Is It with the Happy Dead?*, by Eric Joysmith. *English Story*, 4th Series, edited by Woodrow Wyatt. Collins, 1943.
28. *Hundred Years of Army Nursing, A*, by Ian Hay. Cassell, 1953. Acknowledgments to Queen Alexandra's Royal Nursing Corps.
29. *Ill Met by Moonlight*, by W. Stanley Moss. Harrap; Macmillan, 1950.
30. *Infantry Brigadier*, by Major-General Sir Howard Kippenberger. Oxford, 1949.
31. *In Their Shallow Graves (Road to Stalingrad)*, by Benno Zieser. Elek, 1956; Ballantine, 1955.
32. *Invisible Flag, The*, by Peter Bamm. Faber; John Day, 1956.
33. *I Saw the Fall of the Philippines*, by Colonel Carlos P. Romulo. Doubleday, 1942; Harrap, 1943.

34. *Last Days of Sevastopol, The,* by Boris Voyetekhov. Cassell; Knopf, 1943.

35. *Last Flight From Singapore,* by Arthur G. Donahue. Macmillan, 1943.

36. *Leningrad in the Days of the Blockade,* by A. Fadeyev. Hutchinson, 1946.

37. *Lost Victories,* by Field-Marshal Erich von Manstein. Metheun; Regnery, 1958.

38. *MacArthur, 1941-1951: Victory in the Pacific,* by Major-General Charles A. Willoughby and John Chamberlain. McGraw, 1954; Heinemann, 1956.

39. *Malayan Postscript,* by Ian Morrison. Faber, 1942.

40. *Maquis (Waiting in the Night),* by George Millar. Heinemann, 1945; Doubleday, 1946.

41. *Memoirs of Cordell Hull, The,* Vol. 2. Hodder & Stoughton; Macmillan, 1948.

42. *Modern Anabasis, A,* by General Baron Leo Geyr von Schweppenburg; *An Cosantoir: The Irish Defence Journal,* 1950.

43. *Moscow Tram Stop,* by Heinrich Haape, Collins, 1957.

44. *Operation Victory,* by Major-General Sir Francis de Guingand. Hodder; Scribner, 1947.

45. *Other Side of the Hill, The (The German Generals Talk),* by Captain B. H. Liddell Hart. Cassell; Morrow, 1948.

46. *Panzer Battles, 1939-1945,* by F. W. von Mellenthin. Cassell, 1955; U. of Okla. Press, 1956.

47. *Panzer Leader,* by Heinz Guderian. Joseph; Dutton, 1952.

48. *Partisans of the Kuban,* by P. K. Ignatov, Hutchinson, 1945.

49. *Privileged Nightmare, The,* by Giles Romilly and Michael Alexander. Weidenfeld, 1954.

50. *Retreat, Hell!,* by William Martin Camp. Appleton-Century, 1943; Constable, 1944.

51. *Retreat in the East (Action in the East)*, by O. D. Gallagher, Harrap; Doubleday, 1942.

52. *Retreat With Stilwell*, by Jack Belden. Knopf, 1943.

53. *Return to the Sea*, by A. H. Rasmussen. Constable, 1956.

54. *Rifle Brigade in the Second World War, 1939-1945, The*, by Major R.H.W.S. Hastings and others. Gale & Polden, 1950.

55. *Rommel*, by Desmond Young. Collins, 1950; Harper, 1951.

56. *Rommel Papers, The*, edited by B. H. Liddell Hart. Collins; Harcourt, 1953.

57. *Royal Artillery Commemoration Book, 1939-1945, The*, Bell, 1950.

58. *Russia at War (Tempering of Russia)*, by Ilya Ehrenburg. Hamilton, 1943; Knopf, 1944.

59. *Schellenberg Memoirs, The (The Labyrinth)*, edited by Louis Hagen. Deutsch, 1956; Harper, 1957.

60. *Second World War, The*, by Winston Churchill, Vol. 3. Houghton, 1950.

61. *Second World War, The*, by Winston Churchill, Vol. 4. Houghton, 1950.

62. *Second World War, The*, by Winston Churchill, Vol. 6. Houghton, 1953.

63. *Seven Times Seven Days*, by Emmanuel d'Astier. MacGibbon & Kee, 1958.

64. *Seventy Days* by Waclaw Zagorski. Muller, 1957.

65. *Silent Company, The*, by Remy. Barker; McGraw, 1948.

66. *Singapore Is Silent*, by George Weller. Harcourt, 1943.

67. *Six Against Tyranny*, by Inger Scholl. Murray; Transatlantic, 1955; Verlag der Frankfurter Hefte, G.M.B.H. (Frankfurt am Main).

68. *Skis Against the Atom*, by Knut Haukelid. Kimber, 1954.

69. *Soldier, The*, by Karlludwig Opitz. Muller, 1954.

70. *Soviet Staff Officer*, by Ivan Krylov. Falcon Press; Philosophical Lib., 1951.

71. *Spirit in the Cage, The,* by Peter Churchill. Hodder & Stoughton, 1954; Putnam, 1955.
72. *Stalingrad,* by Heinz Schroter. Joseph; Dutton, 1958.
73. *Suez to Singapore,* by Cecil Brown. Random, 1942.
74. *Sun Goes Down, The,* edited by Jean Larteguy. Kimber, 1956.
75. *Sunk,* by Mochitsura Hashimoto. Cassell; Holt, 1954.
76. *Take These Men,* by Cyril Joly. Constable, 1955.
77. *Ten Summers: Poems,* by John Pudney. Bodley Head, 1944 (also in *Collected Poems,* Putnam, 1957; *Flight above Cloud,* Harper, 1944).
78. *This is Pearl!,* by Walter Millis. Morrow, copyright 1947 by Walter Millis.
79. *Tobruk 1941,* by Chester Wilmot. Angus & Robertson, 1945.
80. *Tokyo Record,* by Otto D. Tolischus. Hamilton, 1943; Harcourt, 1943.
81. *Trial of German Major War Criminals, The: Proceedings of the International Military Tribunal at Nuremburg, 1946.* H.M.S.O.
82. *Turn of the Tide, The,* by Sir Arthur Bryant. Collins; Doubleday, 1957.
83. *Twenty Thousand Thieves, The,* by Eric Lambert, Muller, 1952.
84. *Two Eggs on My Plate,* by Oluf Reed Olsen. Allen & Unwin; Rand McNally, 1952.
85. *U-Boat 977,* by Heinz Schaeffer. Kimber, 1952; Norton, 1953.
86. *Underwater Saboteur,* by Max Manus. Kimber, 1953.
87. *Unseen and Silent, The,* anon. Sheed & Ward, 1954.
88. *Voices From Britain,* edited by Henning Krabbe. Allen & Unwin, 1947; Macmillan, 1948.
89. *War Speeches of the Rt. Hon. Winston S. Churchill, The,* Definitive Edition, Vol. I. Cassell, 1951; Houghton, 1953.

90. *War Speeches of the Rt. Hon. Winston S. Churchill, The,* Definitive Edition, Vol. II. Cassell, 1952; Houghton, 1953.

91. *With Rommel in the Desert,* by Heinz Werner Schmidt. Harrap; British Book Centre, 1951.

92. *Year of Stalingrad, The,* by Alexander Werth. Hamilton, 1946; Knopf, 1947.

MAPS

THE GERMAN ATTACK ON RUSSIA

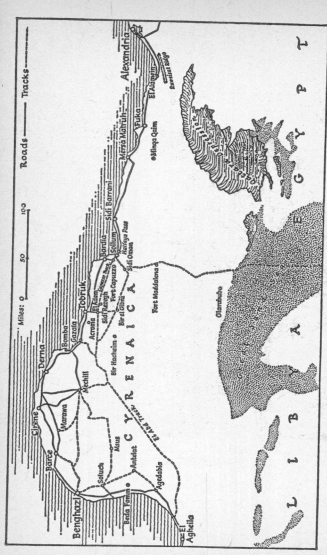

NORTH AFRICA – The Swaying Battle, 1940–42

THE CONQUESTS OF JAPAN

THE FRONT IN RUSSIA, APRIL 1942–MARCH 1943

INDEX

INDEX

THE TASTE OF COURAGE, THE WAR, 1939-1945
edited by Desmond Flower and James Reeves

A MAJOR FIVE-VOLUME SERIES ON WORLD WAR II FROM BERKLEY

The drama, the humor, the horror, amd sometimes the tenderness of men and women confronting their greatest ordeal speak through this absorbing narrative of World War II, told in eyewitness accounts by soldiers, housewives and journalists in the many countries involved.

VOLUME I: *THE BLITZKRIEG*

carries the story from the invasion of Poland through Dunkirk and the Battle of Britain to the end of the Italian Empire in North Africa and the intervention of Germany in Greece and the Middle East. (Z1814-$1.25)

VOLUME III: *THE TIDE TURNS*

is the story of the first Allied victories of the war, victories which followed endless defeats. In Russia, the Wehrmacht suffered its first major setback when the German 6th Army, commanded by von Paulus, was first held, then smashed, at Stalingrad. In North Africa, Montgomery and the British 8th Army defeated the hitherto invincible Afrika Korps at El Alamein. At sea, the victorious Japanese Navy was stopped at Midway. The Allied Air Forces were carrying the bombing war to Germany. For the time, it seemed that the Allies had a real chance of victory. (Z1991-$1.25)

(Please turn page)

VOLUME IV: *THE ALLIES ADVANCE*

describes the slogging advance of the Allied armies through
Italy, and the Italian surrender; the painful island-hopping
by the Americans as they beat the Japanese in the Pacific;
and the slow attrition of the Japanese armies in Burma
under the British onslaught.   (Z2008-$1.25)

VOLUME V: *VICTORY AND DEFEAT*

carries the story to its dramatic conclusion, in the collapse
of Germany under the twin pressures of the sweeping
Russian victories in the East, and the relentless advance of
the British and American armies in the West; and the final
surrender of the Japanese, demoralized by the atomic
holocausts of Hiroshima and Nagasaki.   (Z2018-$1.25)

Send for a free list of all our books in print
